CCNA Portable Command Guide
Second Edition

Scott Empson

Cisco Press

800 East 96th Street
Indianapolis, Indiana 46240 USA

CCNA Portable Command Guide, Second Edition

Scott Empson

Copyright© 2008 Cisco Systems, Inc.

Published by:
Cisco Press
800 East 96th Street
Indianapolis, IN 46240 USA

Printed in the United States of America

Third Printing   August 2008

Library of Congress Cataloging-in-Publication Data

Empson, Scott.

  Portable command reference / Scott Empson. -- 2nd ed.

    p. cm.

  ISBN 978-1-58720-193-6 (pbk.)

  1. Computer networks--Examinations--Study guides. 2. Internetworking (Telecommunication)--Examinations--Study guides. 3. Electronic data processing personnel--Certification. I. Title.

  TK5105.5.E4352 2007

  004.6--dc22

  2007023863

ISBN-13: 978-1-5872-0193-6
ISBN-10: 1-58720-193-3

Warning and Disclaimer

This book is designed to provide information about the Certified Cisco Networking Associate (CCNA) exam and the commands needed at this level of network administration. Every effort has been made to make this book as complete and as accurate as possible, but no warranty or fitness is implied.

The information is provided on an "as is" basis. The author, Cisco Press, and Cisco Systems, Inc. shall have neither liability nor responsibility to any person or entity with respect to any loss or damages arising from the information contained in this book or from the use of the discs or programs that may accompany it.

The opinions expressed in this book belong to the author and are not necessarily those of Cisco Systems, Inc.

Trademark Acknowledgments

All terms mentioned in this book that are known to be trademarks or service marks have been appropriately capitalized. Cisco Press or Cisco Systems, Inc., cannot attest to the accuracy of this information. Use of a term in this book should not be regarded as affecting the validity of any trademark or service mark.

Corporate and Government Sales

The publisher offers excellent discounts on this book when ordered in quantity for bulk purchases or special sales, which may include electronic versions and/or custom covers and content particular to your business, training goals, marketing focus, and branding interests. For more information, please contact: **U.S. Corporate and Government Sales** 1-800-382-3419 corpsales@pearsontechgroup.com

For sales outside the United States please contact: **International Sales** international@pearsoned.com

Feedback Information

At Cisco Press, our goal is to create in-depth technical books of the highest quality and value. Each book is crafted with care and precision, undergoing rigorous development that involves the unique expertise of members from the professional technical community.

Readers' feedback is a natural continuation of this process. If you have any comments regarding how we could improve the quality of this book, or otherwise alter it to better suit your needs, you can contact us through e-mail at feedback@ciscopress.com. Please make sure to include the book title and ISBN in your message.

We greatly appreciate your assistance.

Publisher	Paul Boger
Associate Publisher	Dave Dusthimer
Cisco Representative	Anthony Wolfenden
Cisco Press Program Manager	Jeff Brady
Executive Editor	Mary Beth Ray
Managing Editor	Patrick Kanouse
Senior Development Editor	Christopher Cleveland
Project Editor	Meg Shaw
Copy Editor	Keith Cline
Technical Editors	Robert Elling, Philip Vancil
Editorial Assistant	Vanessa Evans
Cover Designer	Louisa Adair
Composition	ICC Macmillan Inc.
Proofreader	Karen A. Gill

ıı|ıı,ı|ı,
CISCO.

Americas Headquarters	Asia Pacific Headquarters	Europe Headquarters
Cisco Systems, Inc.	Cisco Systems, Inc.	Cisco Systems International BV
170 West Tasman Drive	168 Robinson Road	Haarlerbergpark
San Jose, CA 95134-1706	#28-01 Capital Tower	Haarlerbergweg 13-19
USA	Singapore 068912	1101 CH Amsterdam
www.cisco.com	www.cisco.com	The Netherlands
Tel: 408 526-4000	Tel: +65 6317 7777	www-europe.cisco.com
800 553-NETS (6387)	Fax: +65 6317 7799	Tel: +31 0 800 020 0791
Fax: 408 527-0883		Fax: +31 0 20 357 1100

Cisco has more than 200 offices worldwide. Addresses, phone numbers, and fax numbers are listed on the Cisco Website at **www.cisco.com/go/offices.**

©2007 Cisco Systems, Inc. All rights reserved. CCVP, the Cisco logo, and the Cisco Square Bridge logo are trademarks of Cisco Systems, Inc.; Changing the Way We Work, Live, Play, and Learn is a service mark of Cisco Systems, Inc.; and Access Registrar, Aironet, BPX, Catalyst, CCDA, CCDP, CCIE, CCIP, CCNA, CCNP, CCSP, Cisco, the Cisco Certified Internetwork Expert logo, Cisco IOS, Cisco Press, Cisco Systems, Cisco Systems Capital, the Cisco Systems logo, Cisco Unity, Enterprise/Solver, EtherChannel, EtherFast, EtherSwitch, Fast Step, Follow Me Browsing, FormShare, GigaDrive, GigaStack, HomeLink, Internet Quotient, IOS, iPhone, IP/TV, iQ Expertise, the iQ logo, iQ Net Readiness Scorecard, iQuick Study, LightStream, Linksys, MeetingPlace, MGX, Networking Academy, Network Registrar, Packet, PIX, ProConnect, RateMUX, ScriptShare, SlideCast, SMARTnet, StackWise, The Fastest Way to Increase Your Internet Quotient, and TransPath are registered trademarks of Cisco Systems, Inc. and/or its affiliates in the United States and certain other countries.

All other trademarks mentioned in this document or Website are the property of their respective owners. The use of the word partner does not imply a partnership relationship between Cisco and any other company. (0701R)

About the Author

Scott Empson is the associate chair of the Bachelor of Applied Information Systems Technology degree program at the Northern Alberta Institute of Technology in Edmonton, Alberta, Canada, where he teaches Cisco routing, switching, and network design courses in a variety of different programs (certificate, diploma, and applied degree) at the post-secondary level. Scott is also the program coordinator of the Cisco Networking Academy Program at NAIT, a Regional Academy covering Central and Northern Alberta. He has earned three undergraduate degrees: a Bachelor of Arts, with a major in English; a Bachelor of Education, again with a major in English/Language Arts; and a Bachelor of Applied Information Systems Technology, with a major in Network Management. He currently holds several industry certifications, including CCNP, CCDA, CCAI, and Network+. Before instructing at NAIT, he was a junior/senior high school English/Language Arts/ Computer Science teacher at different schools throughout Northern Alberta. Scott lives in Edmonton, Alberta, with his wife, Trina, and two children, Zachariah and Shaelyn, where he enjoys reading, performing music on the weekend with his classic/80s rock band "Miss Understood," and studying the martial art of Taekwon-Do.

About the Technical Reviewers

Robert Elling is a content consultant in the Learning@cisco group in Florida. He works in the Data Center/Foundation group supporting the CCNA, CCNP, and CCIP curriculum. Before coming to Cisco, he worked for Bell Atlantic as a senior network analyst in the Networking Operation Center in Harrisburg, Pennsylvania. He holds numerous certifications, including CNE, ECNE, MCSE, CCNA, CCNP, and CCIP.

Philip Vancil is a technical education consultant with Cisco and has been in the communication industry for more than 20 years. Phil has extensive experience in both LAN and WAN environments. He has performed at the technical level as a national support engineer, at the managerial level running a TAC, and at the instructor level as an instructor for a major LAN/WAN product manufacturer. Phil has earned CCIP and CCNP certifications and is a CCSI for Customer Contact BU products. He has been developing courseware and certifications (including CCIP, CCSP, and CCNP) for Cisco for six years.

Dedications

This book is dedicated to Trina, Zach, and Shae, without whom I couldn't have made it through those long nights of writing and editing.

Acknowledgments

Anyone who has ever had anything to do with the publishing industry knows that it takes many, many people to create a book. It may be my name on the cover, but there is no way that I can take credit for all that occurred to get this book from idea to publication. Therefore, I must thank:

The team at Cisco Press—Once again, you amaze me with your professionalism and the ability to make me look good. Mary Beth, Chris, Patrick, Meg, Seth—thank you for your continued support and belief in my little engineering journal.

To my technical reviewers, Robert and Phil—thanks for keeping me on track and making sure that what I wrote was correct and relevant.

To the staff of the Cisco office here in Edmonton, especially Cesar Barrero—thanks for putting up with me and my continued requests to borrow equipment for development and validation of the concepts in this book. But, can I keep the equipment for just a little bit longer? Please?

This Book Is Safari Enabled

The Safari® Enabled icon on the cover of your favorite technology book means the book is available through Safari Bookshelf. When you buy this book, you get free access to the online edition for 45 days.

Safari Bookshelf is an electronic reference library that lets you easily search thousands of technical books, find code samples, download chapters, and access technical information whenever and wherever you need it.

To gain 45-day Safari Enabled access to this book:

- Go to http://www.ciscopress.com/safarienabled
- Complete the brief registration form
- Enter the coupon code 5BC2-RSEE-CZ7G-36EV-KAGK

If you have difficulty registering on Safari Bookshelf or accessing the online edition, please e-mail customer-service@safaribooksonline.com.

Contents at a Glance

Introduction   xxi

Part I   TCP/IP Version 4   1

Chapter 1   How to Subnet   3

Chapter 2   VLSM   21

Chapter 3   Route Summarization   29

Part II   Introduction to Cisco Devices   35

Chapter 4   Cables and Connections   37

Chapter 5   The Command-Line Interface   45

Part III   Configuring a Router   51

Chapter 6   Configuring a Single Cisco Router   53

Part IV   Routing   67

Chapter 7   Static Routing   69

Chapter 8   RIP   75

Chapter 9   EIGRP   81

Chapter 10   Single Area OSPF   91

Part V   Switching   103

Chapter 11   Configuring a Switch   105

Chapter 12   VLANs   117

Chapter 13   VLAN Trunking Protocol and Inter-VLAN Routing   125

Chapter 14   STP and EtherChannel   139

Part VI   Extending the LAN   159

Chapter 15   Implementing a Wireless LAN   161

Part VII   Network Administration and Troubleshooting   183

Chapter 16   Backing Up and Restoring Cisco IOS Software and Configurations   185

Chapter 17   Password-Recovery Procedures and the Configuration Register   193

Chapter 18   Cisco Discovery Protocol (CDP)   201

Chapter 19   Telnet and SSH   203

Chapter 20   The ping and traceroute Commands   207

Chapter 21   SNMP and Syslog   211

Chapter 22   Basic Troubleshooting   213

Part VIII   Managing IP Services   219

Chapter 23   Network Address Translation   221

Chapter 24   DHCP   231

Chapter 25   IPv6   237

Part IX   WANs   249

Chapter 26   HDLC and PPP   251

Chapter 27   Frame Relay   257

Part X   Network Security   267

Chapter 28   IP Access Control List Security   269

Chapter 29   Security Device Manager   283

Part XI   Appendixes   315

Appendix A   Binary/Hex/Decimal Conversion Chart   317

Appendix B   Create Your Own Journal Here   329

Contents

Introduction   xxi

Part I   TCP/IP Version 4   1

Chapter 1   How to Subnet   3

Class A–E Addresses   3
Converting Between Decimal Numbers and Binary   4
Subnetting a Class C Network Using Binary   4
Subnetting a Class B Network Using Binary   8
Binary ANDing   12
So Why AND?   14
Shortcuts in Binary ANDing   15
The Enhanced Bob Maneuver for Subnetting   16

Chapter 2   VLSM   21

IP Subnet Zero   21
VLSM Example   22
Step 1 Determine How Many H Bits Will Be Needed to
Satisfy the Largest Network   22
Step 2 Pick a Subnet for the Largest Network to Use   23
Step 3 Pick the Next Largest Network to Work With   24
Step 4 Pick the Third Largest Network to Work With   26
Step 5 Determine Network Numbers for Serial Links   27

Chapter 3   Route Summarization   29

Example for Understanding Route Summarization   29
Step 1: Summarize Winnipeg's Routes   30
Step 2: Summarize Calgary's Routes   31
Step 3: Summarize Edmonton's Routes   31
Step 4: Summarize Vancouver's Routes   32
Route Summarization and Route Flapping   34
Requirements for Route Summarization   34

Part II   Introduction to Cisco Devices   35

Chapter 4   Cables and Connections   37

Connecting a Rollover Cable to Your Router or Switch   37
Terminal Settings   37
LAN Connections   38
Serial Cable Types   39
Which Cable to Use?   41
568A Versus 568B Cables   42

Chapter 5 The Command-Line Interface 45

Shortcuts for Entering Commands 45
Using the (Tab⇄) Key to Complete Commands 45
Using the Question Mark for Help 46
enable Command 46
exit Command 47
disable Command 47
logout Command 47
Setup Mode 47
Keyboard Help 48
History Commands 49
show Commands 49

Part III **Configuring a Router** **51**

Chapter 6 Configuring a Single Cisco Router 53

Router Modes 53
Entering Global Configuration Mode 54
Configuring a Router Name 54
Configuring Passwords 54
Password Encryption 55
Interface Names 56
Moving Between Interfaces 58
Configuring a Serial Interface 59
Configuring a Fast Ethernet Interface 59
Creating a Message-of-the-Day Banner 60
Creating a Login Banner 60
Setting the Clock Time Zone 60
Assigning a Local Host Name to an IP Address 61
The no ip domain-lookup Command 61
The logging synchronous Command 61
The exec-timeout Command 62
Saving Configurations 62
Erasing Configurations 62
show Commands 63
EXEC Commands in Configuration Mode: The do Command 64
Configuration Example: Basic Router Configuration 64

Part IV **Routing** **67**

Chapter 7 Static Routing 69

Configuring a Static Route on a Router 69
The permanent Keyword (Optional) 70

Static Routes and Administrative Distance (Optional)   70
Configuring a Default Route on a Router   71
Verifying Static Routes   72
Configuration Example: Static Routes   72

Chapter 8   **RIP**   **75**
The ip classless Command   75
RIP Routing: Mandatory Commands   75
RIP Routing: Optional Commands   76
Troubleshooting RIP Issues   77
Configuration Example: RIPv2 Routing   78

Chapter 9   **EIGRP**   **81**
Configuring Enhanced Interior Gateway Routing Protocol
   (EIGRP)   81
EIGRP Auto-Summarization   82
Load Balancing: variance   83
Bandwidth Use   84
Authentication   84
Verifying EIGRP   86
Troubleshooting EIGRP   86
Configuration Example: EIGRP   87

Chapter 10   **Single Area OSPF**   **91**
Configuring OSPF: Mandatory Commands   91
Using Wildcard Masks with OSPF Areas   92
Configuring OSPF: Optional Commands   93
   Loopback Interfaces   93
   Router ID   94
   DR/BDR Elections   94
   Modifying Cost Metrics   95
   Authentication: Simple   95
   Authentication: Using MD5 Encryption   96
   Timers   96
   Propagating a Default Route   96
Verifying OSPF Configuration   97
Troubleshooting OSPF   98
Configuration Example: Single Area OSPF   98

Part V   Switching   103

Chapter 11   **Configuring a Switch**   **105**
Help Commands   105
Command Modes   105

Verifying Commands   106
Resetting Switch Configuration   107
Setting Host Names   107
Setting Passwords   107
Setting IP Addresses and Default Gateways   108
Setting Interface Descriptions   108
Setting Duplex Operation   109
Setting Operation Speed   109
Managing the MAC Address Table   109
Configuring Static MAC Addresses   109
Switch Port Security   110
Verifying Switch Port Security   111
Sticky MAC Addresses   112
Configuration Example   113

Chapter 12   VLANs   117
Creating Static VLANs   117
    Using VLAN Configuration Mode   117
    Using VLAN Database Mode   118
Assigning Ports to VLANs   118
Using the range Command   119
Verifying VLAN Information   119
Saving VLAN Configurations   119
Erasing VLAN Configurations   120
Configuration Example: VLANs   121

Chapter 13   VLAN Trunking Protocol and Inter-VLAN Routing   125
Dynamic Trunking Protocol (DTP)   125
Setting the Encapsulation Type   126
VLAN Trunking Protocol (VTP)   127
    Using Global Configuration Mode   127
    Using VLAN Database Mode   128
Verifying VTP   130
Inter-VLAN Communication Using an External Router:
    Router-on-a-Stick   130
Inter-VLAN Communication Tips   131
Configuration Example: Inter-VLAN Communication   132

Chapter 14   STP and EtherChannel   139
Spanning Tree Protocol   139
    Enabling Spanning Tree Protocol   139
    Configuring the Root Switch   140

Configuring a Secondary Root Switch 141
Configuring Port Priority 141
Configuring the Path Cost 142
Configuring the Switch Priority of a VLAN 142
Configuring STP Timers 143
Verifying STP 143
Optional STP Configurations 144
Changing the Spanning-Tree Mode 145
Extended System ID 146
Enabling Rapid Spanning Tree 146
Troubleshooting Spanning Tree 147
Configuration Example: STP 147
EtherChannel 150
Interface Modes in EtherChannel 151
Guidelines for Configuring EtherChannel 151
Configuring Layer 2 EtherChannel 152
Verifying EtherChannel 152
Configuration Example: EtherChannel 153

Part VI   Extending the LAN   159

Chapter 15   Implementing a Wireless LAN   161
Wireless Access Point Configuration: Linksys 300N Access
    Point 161
Wireless Client Configuration: Linksys Wireless-N Notebook
    Adapter 174

Part VII   Network Administration and Troubleshooting   183

Chapter 16   Backing Up and Restoring Cisco IOS Software and
    Configurations   185
Boot System Commands 185
The Cisco IOS File System 186
Backing Up Configurations to a TFTP Server 186
Restoring Configurations from a TFTP Server 187
Backing Up the Cisco IOS Software to a TFTP Server 188
Restoring/Upgrading the Cisco IOS Software from a
    TFTP Server 188
Restoring the Cisco IOS Software from ROM Monitor Mode
    Using Xmodem 189
Restoring the Cisco IOS Software Using the ROM Monitor
    Environmental Variables and tftpdnld Command 192

Chapter 17 Password-Recovery Procedures and the Configuration
Register 193

The Configuration Register 193
A Visual Representation 193
What the Bits Mean 194
The Boot Field 194
Console Terminal Baud Rate Settings 195
Changing the Console Line Speed: CLI 195
Changing the Console Line Speed: ROM Monitor
Mode 195
Password-Recovery Procedures for Cisco Routers 196
Password Recovery for 2960 Series Switches 198

Chapter 18 Cisco Discovery Protocol (CDP) 201

Cisco Discovery Protocol 201

Chapter 19 Telnet and SSH 203

Using Telnet to Remotely Connect to Other Devices 203
Configuring the Secure Shell Protocol (SSH) 205

Chapter 20 The ping and traceroute Commands 207

ICMP Redirect Messages 207
The ping Command 207
Examples of Using the ping and the Extended ping
Commands 208
The traceroute Command 209

Chapter 21 SNMP and Syslog 211

Configuring SNMP 211
Configuring Syslog 211

Chapter 22 Basic Troubleshooting 213

Viewing the Routing Table 213
Determining the Gateway of Last Resort 214
Determining the Last Routing Update 214
OSI Layer 3 Testing 214
OSI Layer 7 Testing 215
Interpreting the show interface Command 215
Clearing Interface Counters 215
Using CDP to Troubleshoot 216
The traceroute Command 216
The show controllers Command 216
debug Commands 216
Using Time Stamps 217

Operating System IP Verification Commands   217
The ip http server Command   217
The netstat Command   218

Part VIII   Managing IP Services   219

Chapter 23   Network Address Translation   221
Private IP Addresses: RFC 1918   221
Configuring Dynamic NAT: One Private to
   One Public Address Translation   221
Configuring PAT: Many Private to One Public Address
   Translation   223
Configuring Static NAT: One Private to One Permanent
   Public Address Translation   226
Verifying NAT and PAT Configurations   227
Troubleshooting NAT and PAT Configurations   227
Configuration Example: PAT   228

Chapter 24   DHCP   231
Configuring DHCP   231
Verifying and Troubleshooting DHCP Configuration   232
Configuring a DHCP Helper Address   232
DHCP Client on a Cisco IOS Software Ethernet Interface   233
Configuration Example: DHCP   233

Chapter 25   IPv6   237
Assigning IPv6 Addresses to Interfaces   237
IPv6 and RIPng   238
Configuration Example: IPv6 RIP   239
IPv6 Tunnels: Manual Overlay Tunnel   241
Static Routes in IPv6   244
Floating Static Routes in IPv6   245
Verifying and Troubleshooting IPv6   245
IPv6 Ping   247

Part IX   WANs   249

Chapter 26   HDLC and PPP   251
Configuring HDLC Encapsulation on a Serial Line   251
Configuring PPP on a Serial Line (Mandatory Commands)   251
Configuring PPP on a Serial Line (Optional Commands):
   Compression   252
Configuring PPP on a Serial Line (Optional Commands):
   Link Quality   252

Configuring PPP on a Serial Line (Optional Commands):
   Multilink   252
Configuring PPP on a Serial Line (Optional Commands):
   Authentication   252
Verifying or Troubleshooting a Serial Link/PPP
   Encapsulation   253
Configuration Example: PPP   254

Chapter 27   Frame Relay   257

Configuring Frame Relay   257
   Setting the Frame Relay Encapsulation Type   257
   Setting the Frame Relay Encapsulation LMI Type   258
   Setting the Frame Relay DLCI Number   258
   Configuring a Frame Relay map Statement   258
   Configuring a Description of the Interface (Optional)   259
   Configuring Frame Relay Using Subinterfaces   259
Verifying Frame Relay   260
Troubleshooting Frame Relay   260
Configuration Examples: Frame Relay   260

Part X   Network Security   267

Chapter 28   IP Access Control List Security   269

Access List Numbers   269
Using Wildcard Masks   270
ACL Keywords   270
Creating Standard ACLs   271
Applying Standard ACLs to an Interface   272
Verifying ACLs   273
Removing ACLs   273
Creating Extended ACLs   273
Applying Extended ACLs to an Interface   275
The established Keyword (Optional)   275
Creating Named ACLs   276
Using Sequence Numbers in Named ACLs   276
Removing Specific Lines in Named ACLs Using Sequence
   Numbers   277
Sequence Number Tips   278
Including Comments About Entries in ACLs   278
Restricting Virtual Terminal Access   279
Configuration Examples: ACLs   279

Chapter 29   Security Device Manager   283

Security Device Manager: Connecting with CLI   283
Security Device Manager: Connecting with GUI   285
SDM Express Wizard with No CLI Preconfiguration   287
Resetting the Router to Factory Defaults Using SDM   297
SDM User Interfaces   298
    Configuring Interfaces Using SDM   298
    Configuring Routing Using SDM   302
SDM Monitor Mode   304
Using SDM to Configure a Router to Act as a DHCP Server   305
Using SDM to Configure an Interface as a DHCP Client   307
Using SDM to Configure NAT/PAT   312
What to Do If You Lose SDM Connectivity Because of an erase
    startup-config Command   314

Part XI   Appendixes   315

Appendix A   Binary/Hex/Decimal Conversion Chart   317

Appendix B   Create Your Own Journal Here   329

Icons Used in This Book

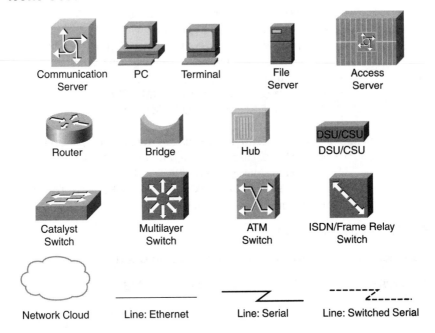

Command Syntax Conventions

The conventions used to present command syntax in this book are the same conventions used in the *Cisco IOS Command Reference*. The *Command Reference* describes these conventions as follows:

- **Boldface** indicates commands and keywords that are entered literally as shown. In actual configuration examples and output (not general command syntax), boldface indicates commands that are manually input by the user (such as a **show** command).
- *Italics* indicate arguments for which you supply actual values.
- Vertical bars (|) separate alternative, mutually exclusive elements.
- Square brackets [ ] indicate optional elements.
- Braces { } indicate a required choice.
- Braces within brackets [{ }] indicate a required choice within an optional element.

Introduction

Welcome to CCNA! Recently Cisco Press came to me and told me, albeit very quietly, that there was going to be some changes made to the CCNA certification exam, and asked whether I would be interested in updating my *CCNA Portable Command Guide* for release around the time of the announcement of the new exam. I was already working on the various command guides for the new CCNP certification exams, but I felt that a revision wouldn't take a lot of time, as hopefully there would still be a lot of concepts that hadn't changed.

I have long been a fan of what I call the "Engineering Journal"—a small notebook that can be carried around and that contains little nuggets of information—commands that you forget, the IP addressing scheme of some remote part of the network, little reminders about how to do something you only have to do once or twice a year (but is vital to the integrity and maintenance of your network). This journal has been a constant companion by my side for the past eight years; I only teach some of these concepts every second or third year, so I constantly need to refresh commands and concepts and learn new commands and ideas as they are released by Cisco. My journals were the best way for me to review because they were written in my own words—words that I could understand. At least, I had better understand them, because if I didn't, I had only myself to blame.

The journals that I would create for my Academy classes would always be different from the journals I would create when I was teaching from a different curriculum or if I was out in the industry working on some production network. I could understand that the Academy needed to split topics into smaller, more manageable chunks, but for me out in the real world, I needed these concepts to follow a different approach—I needed all the routing protocols together in one place in my journals, and not spread across some two-year outline of knowledge.

This book is my "Industry" edition of the Engineering Journal. It contains a different logical flow to the topics, one more suited to someone working in the field. Like topics are grouped together: routing protocols, switches, troubleshooting. More-complex examples are given. New topics have been added, such as IPv6, wireless, and the Security Device Manager (SDM). The popular "Create Your Own Journal" appendix is still here—blank pages for you to add in your own commands that you need in your specific job. We all recognize the fact that no network administrator's job can be so easily pigeonholed as to being just working with CCNA topics—you all have your own specific jobs and duties assigned to you. That is why you will find those blank pages at the end of the book—make this book your own; personalize it with what you need to make it more effective. That way your journal will not look like mine.

The Cisco Networking Academy Program and This Guide

The first book that I ever published for Cisco Press was a command guide that was specially designed to follow the Cisco Networking Academy Program curriculum. The *CCNA Command Quick Reference* was released in 2005 and was organized in such a way that if you were working on CCNA 3, Chapter 8 in the online curriculum, the commands for that chapter were in Part 3, Chapter 8 of that book. However, the Cisco Networking Academy Program has now released two different *flavors* of the Academy curriculum: CCNA

Discovery and CCNA Exploration. The two courses take decidedly different paths in their delivery of content, but they both end up at the same destination—a place where a student completing either set of courses is ready to take the CCNA certification exam. Because there is such a variety in how the courses teach content, Cisco Press believed that creating two books for the Cisco Academy would not be viable, because most of the content would be the same, just in a different order. Therefore, this book can be used with either CCNA Discovery or CCNA Exploration. A quick perusal of the table of contents, or the inside back cover (where I have my "What Do You Want to Do?" list of the more commonly asked questions), should take you to the section with the command(s) that you are looking for. There is even a section in Chapter 15, "Implementing a Wireless LAN," that deals with topics that are only presented in the Academy curriculum—provisioning a Linksys wireless access point and wireless client card. This topic is not covered on the certification exam, but it is part of the Academy courseware, so I have included it in this book, too.

Networking Devices Used in the Preparation of This Book

To verify the commands in this book, I had to try them out on a few different devices. The following is a list of the equipment I used when writing this book:

- C2620 router running Cisco IOS Software Release 12.3(7)T, with a fixed Fast Ethernet interface, a WIC-2A/S serial interface card, and an NM-1E Ethernet interface
- C2821 ISR with PVDM2, CMME, a WIC-2T, FXS and FXO VICs, running 12.4(10a) IPBase IOS
- WS-C2960-24TT-L Catalyst Switch, running 12.2(25)SE IOS
- WS-C2950-12 Catalyst switch, running version C2950-C3.0(5.3)WC(1) Enterprise Edition software

These devices were not running the latest and greatest versions of Cisco IOS Software. Some of it is quite old.

Those of you familiar with Cisco devices will recognize that a majority of these commands work across the entire range of the Cisco product line. These commands are not limited to the platforms and Cisco IOS Software versions listed. In fact, these devices are in most cases adequate for someone to continue his or her studies into the CCNP level, too.

Private Addressing Used in this Book

This book makes use of RFC 1918 addressing throughout. Because I do not have permission to use public addresses in my examples, I have done everything with private addressing. Private addressing is perfect for use in a lab environment or in a testing situation, because it works exactly like public addressing, with the exception that it cannot be routed across a public network. That is why you will see private addresses in my WAN links between two routers using serial connections, or in my Frame Relay cloud.

Who Should Read This Book

This book is for those people preparing for the CCNA exam, whether through self-study, on-the-job training and practice, or even through study within the Cisco Networking

Academy Program. There are also some handy hints and tips along the way to hopefully make life a bit easier for you in this endeavor. It is small enough that you will find it easy to carry around with you. Big, heavy textbooks might look impressive on your bookshelf in your office, but can you really carry them all around with you when you are working in some server room or equipment closet somewhere?

Optional Sections

A few sections in this book have been marked as "Optional." These sections cover topics that are not on the CCNA certification exam, but they are valuable topics that I believe should be known by someone at a CCNA level. Some of the optional topics might also be concepts that are covered in the Cisco Networking Academy Program courses, either the CCNA Discovery or the CCNA Exploration segments.

Organization of This Book

This book follows what I think is a logical approach to configuring a small to mid-size network. It is an approach that I give to my students when they invariably ask for some sort of outline to plan and then configure a network. Specifically, this approach is as follows:

- Part I: TCP/IP Version 4

  — Chapter 1, "How to Subnet"—An overview of how to subnet, examples of subnetting (both a Class B and a Class C address), the use of the binary AND operation, the Enhanced Bob Maneuver to Subnetting

  — Chapter 2, "VLSM"—An overview of VLSM, an example of using VLSM to make your IP plan more efficient

  — Chapter 3, "Route Summarization"—Using route summarization to make your routing updates more efficient, an example of how to summarize a network, necessary requirements for summarizing your network

- Part II: Introduction to Cisco Devices

  — Chapter 4, "Cables and Connections"—An overview of how to connect to Cisco devices, which cables to use for which interfaces, and the differences between the TIA/EIA 568A and 568B wiring standards for UTP

  — Chapter 5, "The Command-Line Interface"—How to navigate through Cisco IOS Software: editing commands, keyboard shortcuts, and help commands

- Part III: Configuring a Router

  — Chapter 6, "Configuring a Single Cisco Router"—Commands needed to configure a single router: names, passwords, configuring interfaces, MOTD and login banners, IP host tables, saving and erasing your configurations

- Part IV: Routing
    - **Chapter 7, "Static Routing"**—Configuring static routes in your internetwork
    - **Chapter 8, "RIP"**—Configuring and verifying RIPv2, how to see and clear your routing table
    - **Chapter 9, "EIGRP"**—Configuring and verifying EIGRP
    - **Chapter 10, "Single Area OSPF"**—Configuring and verifying Single Area OSPF
- Part V: Switching
    - **Chapter 11, "Configuring a Switch"**—Commands to configure Catalyst 2960 switches: names, passwords, IP addresses, default gateways, port speed and duplex; configuring static MAC addresses; managing the MAC address table; port security
    - **Chapter 12, "VLANs"**—Configuring static VLANs, troubleshooting VLANs, saving and deleting VLAN information.
    - **Chapter 13, "VLAN Trunking Protocol and Inter-VLAN Communication"**—Configuring a VLAN trunk link, configuring VTP, verifying VTP, inter-VLAN communication, router-on-a-stick, and subinterfaces
    - **Chapter 14, "STP and EtherChannel"**—Verifying STP, setting switch priorities, and creating and verifying EtherChannel groups between switches
- Part VI: Extending the LAN
    - **Chapter 15, "Implementing a Wireless LAN"**—Configuring a Linksys wireless access point, configuring a Linksys wireless client card
- Part VII: Network Administration and Troubleshooting
    - **Chapter 16, "Backing Up and Restoring Cisco IOS Software and Configurations"**—Boot commands for Cisco IOS Software, backing up and restoring Cisco IOS Software using TFTP, Xmodem, and ROMmon environmental variables
    - **Chapter 17, "Password-Recovery Procedures and the Configuration Register"**—The configuration register, password-recovery procedure for routers and switches
    - **Chapter 18, "Cisco Discovery Protocol (CDP)"**—Customizing and verifying CDP
    - **Chapter 19, "Telnet and SSH"**—Commands used for Telnet and SSH to remotely connect to other devices
    - **Chapter 20, "The ping and traceroute Commands"**—Commands for both **ping** and extended **ping**; the **traceroute** command
    - **Chapter 21, "SNMP and Syslog"**—Configuring SNMP, working with syslog

— Chapter 22, "Basic Troubleshooting"—Various **show** commands used to view the routing table; interpreting the **show** interface command; verifying your IP settings using different operating systems

- Part VIII: Managing IP Services

  — Chapter 23, "Network Address Translation"—Configuring and verifying NAT and PAT

  — Chapter 24, "DHCP"—Configuring and verifying DHCP

  — Chapter 25, "IPv6"—Transitioning to IPv6; format of IPv6 addresses; configuring IPv6 (interfaces, tunneling, routing with RIPng)

- Part IX: WANs

  — Chapter 26, "HDLC and PPP"—Configuring PPP, authentication of PPP using PAP or CHAP, compression in PPP; multilink in PPP, troubleshooting PPP, returning to HDLC encapsulation

  — Chapter 27, "Frame Relay"—Configuring basic Frame Relay, Frame Relay and subinterfaces, DLCIs, verifying and troubleshooting Frame Relay

- Part X: Network Security

  — Chapter 28, "IP Access Control List Security"—Configuring standard ACLs, wildcard masking, creating extended ACLs, creating named ACLs, using sequence numbers in named ACLs, verifying and troubleshooting ACLs

  — Chapter 29, "Security Device Manager"—Connecting to a router using SDM, SDM user interfaces, SDM wizards, using SDM to configure a router as a DHCP server (or an interface as a DHCP client), using SDM to configure NAT

- Part XI: Appendixes

  — Appendix A, "Binary/Hex/Decimal Conversion Chart"—A chart showing numbers 0 through 255 in the three numbering systems of binary, hexadecimal, and decimal

  — Appendix B, "Create Your Own Journal Here"—Some blank pages for you to add in your own specific commands that might not be in this book

Did I Miss Anything?

I am always interested to hear how my students, and now readers of my books, do on both certification exams and future studies. If you would like to contact me and let me know how this book helped you in your certification goals, please do so. Did I miss anything? Let me know. My e-mail address is ccnaguide@empson.ca.

PART I

TCP/IP Version 4

Chapter 1   **How to Subnet**

Chapter 2   **VLSM**

Chapter 3   **Route Summarization**

How to Subnet

Class A–E Addresses

Class	Leading Bit Pattern	First Octet in Decimal	Notes
A	0xxxxxxx	0–127	0 is invalid 127 reserved for loopback testing
B	10xxxxxx	128–191	
C	110xxxxx	192–223	
D	1110xxxx	224–239	Reserved for multicasting
E	1111xxxx	240–255	Reserved for future use/ testing

Formulae

2^N Where N is equal to number of bits borrowed	Number of total subnets created
$2^N - 2$	Number of valid subnets created
2^H Where H is equal to number of host bits	Number of total hosts per subnet
$2^H - 2$	Number of valid hosts per subnet

Class A Address	N	H	H	H
Class B Address	N	N	H	H
Class C Address	N	N	N	H

N = Network bits
H = Host bits
All 0s in host portion = Network or subnetwork address
All 1s in host portion = Broadcast address
Combination of 1s and 0s in host portion = Valid host address

Converting Between Decimal Numbers and Binary

In any given octet of an IP address, the 8 bits can be defined as follows:

2^7	2^6	2^5	2^4	2^3	2^2	2^1	2^0
128	64	32	16	8	4	2	1

To convert a decimal number into binary, you must turn on the bits (make them a 1) that would add up to that number, as follows:

$$187 = 10111011 = 128+32+16+8+2+1$$
$$224 = 11100000 = 128+64+32$$

To convert a binary number into decimal, you must add the bits that have been turned on (the 1s), as follows:

$$10101010 = 128+32+8+2 = 170$$
$$11110000 = 128+64+32+16 = 240$$

The IP address 138.101.114.250 is represented in binary as

$$10001010.01100101.01110010.11111010$$

The subnet mask of 255.255.255.192 is represented in binary as

$$11111111.11111111.11111111.11000000$$

Subnetting a Class C Network Using Binary

You have a Class C address of 192.168.100.0 /24. You need nine subnets. What is the IP plan of network numbers, broadcast numbers, and valid host numbers? What is the subnet mask needed for this plan?

You cannot use N bits, only H bits. Therefore, ignore 192.168.100. These numbers cannot change.

Step 1   Determine how many H bits you need to borrow to create nine valid subnets.

$$2^N - 2 \geq 9$$

N = 4, so you need to borrow 4 H bits and turn them into N bits.

Start with 8 H bits	HHHHHHHH
Borrow 4 bits	NNNNHHHH

Step 2   Determine the first valid subnet in binary.

0001HHHH	Cannot use subnet 0000 because it is invalid. Therefore, you must start with the bit pattern of 0001
0001**0000**	All 0s in host portion = subnetwork number
0001**0001**	First valid host number
.	
.	
.	
0001**1110**	Last valid host number
0001**1111**	All 1s in host portion = broadcast number

Step 3   Convert binary to decimal.

00010000 = 16	Subnetwork number
00010001 = 17	First valid host number
.	
.	
.	
00011110 = 30	Last valid host number
00011111 = 31	All 1s in host portion = broadcast number

Step 4   Determine the second valid subnet in binary.

0010HHHH	0010 = 2 in binary = second valid subnet
0010**0000**	All 0s in host portion = subnetwork number
0010**0001**	First valid host number
.	
.	
.	
0010**1110**	Last valid host number
0010**1111**	All 1s in host portion = broadcast number

Step 5   Convert binary to decimal.

00100000 = 32	Subnetwork number
00100001 = 33	First valid host number
.	
.	
.	
00101110 = 46	Last valid host number
00101111 = 47	All 1s in host portion = broadcast number

Step 6   Create an IP plan table.

Valid Subnet	Network Number	Range of Valid Hosts	Broadcast Number
1	16	17–30	31
2	32	33–46	47
3	**48**	**49–62**	**63**

Notice a pattern? Counting by 16.

Step 7   Verify the pattern in binary. (The third valid subnet in binary is used here.)

0011HHHH	Third valid subnet
00110000 = **48**	Subnetwork number
00110001 = **49**	First valid host number
.	
.	
.	
00111110 = **62**	Last valid host number
00111111 = **63**	Broadcast number

Step 8   Finish the IP plan table.

Subnet	Network Address (0000)	Range of Valid Hosts (0001–1110)	Broadcast Address (1111)
0 (0000) invalid	192.168.100.0	192.168.100.1– 192.168.100.14	192.168.100.15
1 (0001)	192.168.100.16	192.168.100.17– 192.168.100.30	192.168.100.31
2 (0010)	192.168.100.32	192.168.100.33– 192.168.100.46	192.168.100.47
3 (0011)	192.168.100.48	192.168.100.49– 192.168.100.62	192.168.100.63
4 (0100)	192.168.100.64	192.168.100.65– 192.168.100.78	192.168.100.79
5 (0101)	192.168.100.80	192.168.100.81– 192.168.100.94	192.168.100.95
6 (0110)	192.168.100.96	192.168.100.97– 192.168.100.110	192.168.100.111
7 (0111)	192.168.100.112	192.168.100.113– 192.168.100.126	192.168.100.127
8 (1000)	192.168.100.128	192.168.100.129– 192.168.100.142	192.168.100.143
9 (1001)	192.168.100.144	192.168.100.145– 192.168.100.158	192.168.100.159
10 (1010)	192.168.100.160	192.168.100.161– 192.168.100.174	192.168.100.175
11 (1011)	192.168.100.176	192.168.100.177– 192.168.100.190	192.168.100.191
12 (1100)	192.168.100.192	192.168.100.193– 192.168.100.206	192.168.100.207
13 (1101)	192.168.100.208	192.168.100.209– 192.168.100.222	192.168.100.223
14 (1110)	192.168.100.224	192.168.100.225– 192.168.100.238	192.168.100.239

15 (1111) invalid	192.168.100.**240**	192.168.100.**241**– 192.168.100.**254**	192.168.100.**255**
Quick Check	**Always an even number**	**First valid host is always an odd #** **Last valid host is always an even #**	**Always an odd number**

Use any nine subnets—the rest are for future growth.

Step 9   Calculate the subnet mask.

The default subnet mask for a Class C network is as follows:

Decimal	Binary
255.255.255.0	11111111.11111111.11111111.00000000

1 = Network or subnetwork bit
0 = Host bit

You borrowed 4 bits; therefore, the new subnet mask is the following:

11111111.11111111.11111111.**1111**0000	255.255.255.**240**

> **NOTE:** You subnet a Class B or a Class A network with exactly the same steps as for a Class C network; the only difference is that you start with more H bits.

Subnetting a Class B Network Using Binary

You have a Class B address of 172.16.0.0 /16. You need nine subnets. What is the IP plan of network numbers, broadcast numbers, and valid host numbers? What is the subnet mask needed for this plan?

You cannot use N bits, only H bits. Therefore, ignore 172.16. These numbers cannot change.

Step 1   Determine how many H bits you need to borrow to create nine valid subnets.

$$2^N - 2 \geq 9$$

N = 4, so you need to borrow 4 H bits and turn them into N bits.

Start with 16 H bits	HHHHHHHHHHHHHHHH (Remove the decimal point for now)
Borrow 4 bits	**NNNN**HHHHHHHHHHHH

Step 2   Determine the first valid subnet in binary (without using decimal points).

0001HHHHHHHHHHHH	
0001**000000000000**	Subnet number
0001**000000000001**	First valid host
.	
.	
.	
0001**111111111110**	Last valid host
0001**111111111111**	Broadcast number

Step 3   Convert binary to decimal (replacing the decimal point in the binary numbers).

0001**0000.00000000** = 16.0	Subnetwork number
0001**0000.00000001** = 16.1	First valid host number
.	
.	
.	
0001**1111.11111110** = 31.254	Last valid host number
0001**1111.11111111** = 31.255	Broadcast number

Step 4   Determine the second valid subnet in binary (without using decimal points).

0010HHHHHHHHHHHH	
0010**000000000000**	Subnet number
0010**000000000001**	First valid host
.	
.	
.	
0010**111111111110**	Last valid host
0010**111111111111**	Broadcast number

Step 5   Convert binary to decimal (returning the decimal point in the binary numbers).

00100**000.00000000** = 32.0	Subnetwork number
00100**000.00000001** = 32.1	First valid host number
.	
.	
.	
00101**111.11111110** = 47.254	Last valid host number
00101**111.11111111** = 47.255	Broadcast number

Step 6   Create an IP plan table.

Valid Subnet	Network Number	Range of Valid Hosts	Broadcast Number
1	16.0	16.1–31.254	31.255
2	32.0	32.1–47.254	47.255
3	48.0	48.1–63.254	63.255

Notice a pattern? Counting by 16.

Step 7   Verify the pattern in binary. (The third valid subnet in binary is used here.)

0011HHHHHHHHHHHH	Third valid subnet
00110**000.00000000** = **48.0**	Subnetwork number
00110**000.00000001** = **48.1**	First valid host number
.	
.	
.	
00111**111.11111110** = **63.254**	Last valid host number
00111**111.11111111** = **63.255**	Broadcast number

Step 8   Finish the IP plan table.

Subnet	Network Address (0000)	Range of Valid Hosts (0001–1110)	Broadcast Address (1111)
0 (0000) invalid	172.16.**0.0**	172.16.**0.1**–172.16.**15.254**	172.16.**15.255**
1 (0001)	172.16.**16.0**	172.16.**16.1**–172.16.**31.254**	172.16.**31.255**
2 (0010)	172.16.**32.0**	172.16.**32.1**–172.16.**47.254**	172.16.**47.255**
3 (0011)	172.16.**48.0**	172.16.**48.1**–172.16.**63.254**	172.16.**63.255**
4 (0100)	172.16.**64.0**	172.16.**64.1**–172.16.**79.254**	172.16.**79.255**
5 (0101)	172.16.**80.0**	172.16.**80.1**–172.16.**95.254**	172.16.**95.255**
6 (0110)	172.16.**96.0**	172.16.**96.1**–172.16.**111.254**	172.16.**111.255**
7 (0111)	172.16.**112.0**	172.16.**112.1**–172.16.**127.254**	172.16.**127.255**
8 (1000)	172.16.**128.0**	172.16.**128.1**–172.16.**143.254**	172.16.**143.255**
9 (1001)	172.16.**144.0**	172.16.**144.1**–172.16.**159.254**	172.16.**159.255**
10 (1010)	172.16.**160.0**	172.16.**160.1**–172.16.**175.254**	172.16.**175.255**
11 (1011)	172.16.**176.0**	172.16.**176.1**–172.16.**191.254**	172.16.**191.255**
12 (1100)	172.16.**192.0**	172.16.**192.1**–172.16.**207.254**	172.16.**207.255**
13 (1101)	172.16.**208.0**	172.16.**208.1**–172.16.**223.254**	172.16.**223.255**
14 (1110)	172.16.**224.0**	172.16.**224.1**–172.16.**239.254**	172.16.**239.255**
15 (1111) invalid	172.16.**240.0**	172.16.**240.1**–172.16.**255.254**	172.16.**255.255**
Quick Check	**Always in form even #.0**	**First valid host is always even #.1** **Last valid host is always odd #.254**	**Always odd #.255**

Use any nine subnets—the rest are for future growth.

Step 9   Calculate the subnet mask.

The default subnet mask for a Class B network is as follows:

Decimal	Binary
255.255.0.0	11111111.11111111.00000000.00000000

1 = Network or subnetwork bit
0 = Host bit

You borrowed 4 bits; therefore, the new subnet mask is the following:

11111111.11111111.**1111**0000.00000000	255.255.**240**.0

Binary ANDing

Binary ANDing is the process of performing multiplication to two binary numbers. In the decimal numbering system, ANDing is addition: 2 and 3 equals 5. In decimal, there are an infinite number of answers when ANDing two numbers together. However, in the binary numbering system, the AND function yields only two possible outcomes, based on four different combinations. These outcomes, or answers, can be displayed in what is known as a truth table:

> 0 and 0 = 0
> 1 and 0 = 0
> 0 and 1 = 0
> 1 and 1 = 1

You use ANDing most often when comparing an IP address to its subnet mask. The end result of ANDing these two numbers together is to yield the network number of that address.

Question 1

What is the network number of the IP address 192.168.100.115 if it has a subnet mask of 255.255.255.240?

Answer

Step 1   Convert both the IP address and the subnet mask to binary:

192.168.100.115 = 11000000.10101000.01100100.01110011

255.255.255.240 = 11111111.11111111.11111111.11110000

Step 2   Perform the AND operation to each pair of bits—1 bit from the address ANDed
to the corresponding bit in the subnet mask. Refer to the truth table for the
possible outcomes:

192.168.100.115 = 11000000.10101000.01100100.01110011

255.255.255.240 = <u>11111111.11111111.11111111.1111</u>0000

ANDed result   = 11000000.10101000.01100100.01110000

Step 3   Convert the answer back into decimal:

11000000.10101000.01100100.01110000 = 192.168.100.112

The IP address 192.168.100.115 belongs to the 192.168.100.112 network when
a mask of 255.255.255.240 is used.

Question 2

What is the network number of the IP address 192.168.100.115 if it has a subnet mask of
255.255.255.192?

(Notice that the IP address is the same as in Question 1, but the subnet mask is different.
What answer do you think you will get? The same one? Let's find out!)

Answer

Step 1   Convert both the IP address and the subnet mask to binary:

192.168.100.115 = 11000000.10101000.01100100.01110011

255.255.255.192 = 11111111.11111111.11111111.11000000

Step 2   Perform the AND operation to each pair of bits—1 bit from the address ANDed
to the corresponding bit in the subnet mask. Refer to the truth table for the
possible outcomes:

192.168.100.115 = 11000000.10101000.01100100.01110011

255.255.255.192 = <u>11111111.11111111.11111111.11</u>000000

ANDed result   = 11000000.10101000.01100100.01000000

Step 3   Convert the answer back into decimal:

11000000.10101000.01100100.01110000 = 192.168.100.64

The IP address 192.168.100.115 belongs to the 192.168.100.64 network when a
mask of 255.255.255.192 is used.

So Why AND?

Good question. The best answer is to save you time when working with IP addressing and subnetting. If you are given an IP address and its subnet, you can quickly find out what subnetwork the address belongs to. From here, you can determine what other addresses belong to the same subnet. Remember that if two addresses are in the same network or subnetwork, they are considered to be *local* to each other and can therefore communicate directly with each other. Addresses that are not in the same network or subnetwork are considered to be *remote* to each other and must therefore have a Layer 3 device (like a router or Layer 3 switch) between them to communicate.

Question 3

What is the broadcast address of the IP address 192.168.100.164 if it has a subnet mask of 255.255.255.248?

Answer

Step 1   Convert both the IP address and the subnet mask to binary:

192.168.100.164 = 11000000.10101000.01100100.10100100

255.255.255.248 = 11111111.11111111.11111111.11111000

Step 2   Perform the AND operation to each pair of bits—1 bit from the address ANDed to the corresponding bit in the subnet mask. Refer to the truth table for the possible outcomes:

192.168.100.164 = 11000000.10101000.01100100.10100100

255.255.255.248 = <u>11111111.11111111.11111111.11111000</u>

ANDed result   = 11000000.10101000.01100100.10100000
= 192.168.100.160 (Subnetwork #)

Step 3   Separate the network bits from the host bits:

255.255.255.248 = /29 = The first 29 bits are network/subnetwork bits; therefore,

*11000000.10101000.01100100.10100*000. The last three bits are host bits.

Step 4   Change all host bits to 1. Remember that all 1s in the host portion are the broadcast number for that subnetwork:

*11000000.10101000.01100100.10100*111

Step 5   Convert this number to decimal to reveal your answer:

11000000.10101000.01100100.10100111 = 192.168.100.167

The broadcast address of 192.168.100.164 is 192.168.100.167 when the subnet mask is 255.255.255.248.

Shortcuts in Binary ANDing

Remember when I said that this was supposed to save you time when working with IP addressing and subnetting? Well, there are shortcuts when you AND two numbers together:

- An octet of all 1s in the subnet mask will result in the answer being the same octet as in the IP address.

- An octet of all 0s in the subnet mask will result in the answer being all 0s in that octet.

Question 4

To what network does 172.16.100.45 belong, if its subnet mask is 255.255.255.0?

Answer

172.16.100.0

Proof

Step 1   Convert both the IP address and the subnet mask to binary:

172.16.100.45 = 10101100.00010000.01100100.00101101

255.255.255.0 = 11111111.11111111.11111111.00000000

Step 2   Perform the AND operation to each pair of bits – 1 bit from the address ANDed to the corresponding bit in the subnet mask. Refer to the truth table for the possible outcomes:

172.16.100.45 = 10101100.00010000.01100100.00101101

255.255.255.0 = <u>11111111.11111111.11111111.00000000</u>

10101100.00010000.01100100.00000000

= 172.16.100.0

Notice that the first three octets have the same pattern both before and after they were ANDed. Therefore, any octet ANDed to a subnet mask pattern of 255 is itself! Notice that the last octet is all 0s after ANDing. But according to the truth table, anything ANDed to a 0 is a 0. Therefore, any octet ANDed to a subnet mask pattern of 0 is 0! You should only have to convert those parts of an IP address and subnet mask to binary if the mask is not 255 or 0.

Question 5

To what network does 68.43.100.18 belong, if its subnet mask is 255.255.255.0?

Answer

68.43.100.0 (There is no need to convert here. The mask is either 255s or 0s.)

Question 6

To what network does 131.186.227.43 belong, if its subnet mask is 255.255.240.0?

Answer

Based on the two shortcut rules, the answer should be

131.186.???.0

So now you only need to convert one octet to binary for the ANDing process:

227 =   11100011
240 =   <u>11110000</u>
11100000 = 224

Therefore, the answer is 131.186.224.0.

The Enhanced Bob Maneuver for Subnetting (or How to Subnet Anything in Under a Minute)

Legend has it that once upon a time a networking instructor named Bob taught a class of students a method of subnetting any address using a special chart. This was known as the Bob Maneuver. These students, being the smart type that networking students usually are, added a row to the top of the chart, and the Enhanced Bob Maneuver was born. The chart and instructions on how to use it follow. With practice, you should be able to subnet any address and come up with an IP plan in under a minute. After all, it's *just* math!

The Bob of the Enhanced Bob Maneuver was really a manager/instructor at SHL. He taught this maneuver to Bruce, who taught it to Chad Klymchuk. Chad and a coworker named Troy added the top line of the chart, enhancing it. Chad was first my instructor in Microsoft, then my coworker here at NAIT, and now is one of my Academy instructors—I guess I am now his boss. And the circle is complete.

The Enhanced Bob Maneuver

	192	224	240	248	252	254	255	Subnet Mask
128	64	32	16	8	4	2	1	Target Number
8	7	6	5	4	3	2	1	Bit Place
	126	62	30	14	6	4	N/A	Number of Valid Subnets

Suppose that you have a Class C network and you need nine subnets.

1 On the bottom line (Number of Valid Subnets), move from *right* to *left* and find the closest number that is *bigger* than or *equal* to what you need:

   Nine subnets—move to 14.

2 From that number (14), move up to the line called Bit Place.

   Above 14 is bit place 4.

3 The dark line is called the *high-order line*. If you cross the line, you have to reverse direction.

   You were moving from right to left; now you have to move from left to right.

4 Go to the line called Target Number. Counting *from the left*, move over the number of spaces that the bit place number tells you.

   Starting on 128, moving 4 places takes you to 16.

5 This target number is what you need to count by, starting at 0, and going until you hit 255 or greater. Stop before you get to 256:

   0

   16

   32

   48

   64

   80

   96

   112

128

144

160

176

192

208

224

240

~~256~~ Stop—too far!

6 These numbers are your network numbers. Expand to finish your plan.

Network #	Range of Valid Hosts	Broadcast Number
0 (invalid)	1–14	15
16	17–30 (17 is 1 more than network # 30 is 1 less than broadcast#)	31 (1 less than next network #)
32	33–46	47
48	49–62	63
64	65–78	79
80	81–94	95
96	97–110	111
112	113–126	127
128	129–142	143
144	145–158	159
160	161–174	175
176	177–190	191
192	193–206	207

Network #	Range of Valid Hosts	Broadcast Number
208	209–222	223
224	225–238	239
240 (invalid)	241–254	255

Notice that there are 14 subnets created from .16 to .224.

7 Go back to the Enhanced Bob Maneuver chart and look above your target number to the top line. The number above your target number is your subnet mask.

Above 16 is 240. Because you started with a Class C network, the new subnet mask is 255.255.255.240.

CHAPTER 2

VLSM

Variable-length subnet masking (VLSM) is the more realistic way of subnetting a network to make for the most efficient use of all of the bits.

Remember that when you perform classful (or what I sometimes call classical) subnetting, all subnets have the same number of hosts because they all use the same subnet mask. This leads to inefficiencies. For example, if you borrow 4 bits on a Class C network, you end up with 14 valid subnets of 14 valid hosts. A serial link to another router only needs 2 hosts, but with classical subnetting, you end up wasting 12 of those hosts. Even with the ability to use NAT and private addresses, where you should never run out of addresses in a network design, you still want to ensure that the IP plan that you create is as efficient as possible. This is where VLSM comes in to play.

VLSM is the process of "subnetting a subnet" and using different subnet masks for different networks in your IP plan. What you have to remember is that you need to make sure that there is no overlap in any of the addresses.

IP Subnet Zero

When you work with classical subnetting, you always have to eliminate the subnets that contain either all zeros or all ones in the subnet portion. Hence, you always used the formula $2^N - 2$ to define the number of valid subnets created. However, Cisco devices can use those subnets, as long as the command **ip subnet-zero** is in the configuration. This command is on by default in Cisco IOS Software Release 12.0 and later; if it was turned off for some reason, however, you can re-enable it by using the following command:

```
Router(config)#ip subnet-zero
```

Now you can use the formula 2^N rather than $2^N - 2$.

2^N	Number of total subnets created	
~~$2^N - 2$~~	~~Number of valid subnets created~~	No longer needed because you have the **ip subnet-zero** command enabled
2^H	Number of total hosts per subnet	
$2^H - 2$	Number of valid hosts per subnet	

VLSM Example

You follow the same steps in performing VLSM as you did when performing classical subnetting.

Consider Figure 2-1 as you work through an example.

Figure 2-1   Sample Network Needing a VLSM Address Plan

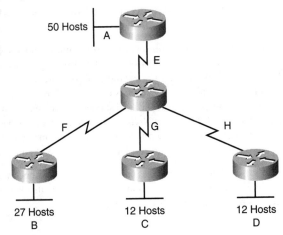

A Class C network—192.168.100.0/24—is assigned. You need to create an IP plan for this network using VLSM.

Once again, you cannot use the N bits—192.168.100. You can use only the H bits. Therefore, ignore the N bits, because they cannot change!

The steps to create an IP plan using VLSM for the network illustrated in Figure 2-1 are as follows:

Step 1   Determine how many H bits will be needed to satisfy the *largest* network.

Step 2   Pick a subnet for the largest network to use.

Step 3   Pick the next largest network to work with.

Step 4   Pick the third largest network to work with.

Step 5   Determine network numbers for serial links.

The remainder of the chapter details what is involved with each step of the process.

Step 1 Determine How Many H Bits Will Be Needed to Satisfy the *Largest* Network

A is the largest network with 50 hosts. Therefore, you need to know how many H bits will be needed:

If $2^H - 2 =$ Number of valid hosts per subnet

Then $2^H - 2 \geq 50$

Therefore H = 6 (6 is the smallest valid value for H)

You need 6 H bits to satisfy the requirements of Network A.

If you need 6 H bits and you started with 8 N bits, you are left with 8 – 6 = 2 N bits to create subnets:

Started with: NNNNNNNN (these are the 8 bits in the fourth octet)

Now have: NNHHHHHH

All subnetting will now have to start at this reference point, to satisfy the requirements of Network A.

Step 2 Pick a Subnet for the Largest Network to Use

You have 2 N bits to work with, leaving you with 2^N or 2^2 or 4 subnets to work with:

NN = 00HHHHHH (The Hs = The 6 H bits you need for Network A)

01HHHHHH

10HHHHHH

11HHHHHH

If you add all zeros to the H bits, you are left with the network numbers for the four subnets:

00**000000** = .0

01**000000** = .64

10**000000** = .128

11**000000** = .192

All of these subnets will have the same subnet mask, just like in classful subnetting.

Two borrowed H bits means a subnet mask of

11111111.11111111.11111111.11000000

or

255.255.255.192

or

/26

The /x notation represents how to show different subnet masks when using VLSM.

/8 means that the first 8 bits of the address are network; the remaining 24 bits are H bits.

/24 means that the first 24 bits are network; the last 8 are host. This is either a traditional default Class C address, or a traditional Class A network that has borrowed 16 bits, or even a traditional Class B network that has borrowed 8 bits!

Pick *one* of these subnets to use for Network A. The rest of the networks will have to use the other three subnets.

For purposes of this example, pick the .64 network.

00**000000** =	.0	
01**000000** =	.64	Network A
10**000000** =	.128	
11**000000** =	.192	

Step 3 Pick the Next Largest Network to Work With

Network B = 27 hosts

Determine the number of H bits needed for this network:

$$2^H - 2 \geq 27$$
$$H = 5$$

You need 5 H bits to satisfy the requirements of Network B.

You started with a pattern of 2 N bits and 6 H bits for Network A. You have to maintain that pattern.

Pick one of the remaining /26 networks to work with Network B.

For the purposes of this example, select the .128/26 network:

10**000000**

But you need only 5 H bits, not 6. Therefore, you are left with

10**N00000**

where

        10 represents the original pattern of subnetting.
        N represents the extra bit.
        00000 represents the 5 H bits you need for Network B.

Because you have this extra bit, you can create two smaller subnets from the original subnet:

10**000000**
10**100000**

Converted to decimal, these subnets are as follows:

10**000000** = .128
10**100000** = .160

You have now subnetted a subnet! This is the basis of VLSM.

Each of these sub-subnets will have a new subnet mask. The original subnet mask of /24 was changed into /26 for Network A. You then take one of these /26 networks and break it into two /27 networks:

10**000000** and 10**100000** both have 3 N bits and 5 H bits.

The mask now equals:

11111111.11111111.11111111.11100000

or

255.255.255.224

or

/27

Pick one of these new sub-subnets for Network B:

10**000000** /27 = Network B

Use the remaining sub-subnet for future growth, or you can break it down further if needed.

You want to make sure the addresses are not overlapping with each other. So go back to the original table.

00**000000** =	.0/26	
01**000000** =	.64/26	Network A
10**000000** =	.128/26	
11**000000** =	.192/26	

You can now break the .128/26 network into two smaller /27 networks and assign Network B.

00**000000** =	.0/26	
01**000000** =	.64/26	Network A
10**000000** =	.128/26	Cannot use because it has been subnetted
10**000000** =	.128/27	Network B
10**100000** =	.160/27	
11**000000** =	.192/26	

The remaining networks are still available to be assigned to networks or subnetted further for better efficiency.

Step 4 Pick the Third Largest Network to Work With

Networks C and Network D = 12 hosts each

Determine the number of H bits needed for these networks:

$$2^H - 2 \geq 12$$
$$H = 4$$

You need 4 H bits to satisfy the requirements of Network C and Network D.

You started with a pattern of 2 N bits and 6 H bits for Network A. You have to maintain that pattern.

You now have a choice as to where to put these networks. You could go to a different /26 network, or you could go to a /27 network and try to fit them into there.

For the purposes of this example, select the other /27 network—.160/27:

> 10**100000** (The 1 in the third bit place is no longer bold, because it is part of the N bits.)

But you only need 4 H bits, not 5. Therefore, you are left with

> 101**N0000**

where

> 10 represents the original pattern of subnetting.
> **N** represents the extra bit you have.
> **0000** represents the 5 H bits you need for Network B.

Because you have this extra bit, you can create two smaller subnets from the original subnet:

> 10**100000**
> 10**110000**

Converted to decimal, these subnets are as follows:

> 10**100000** = .160
> 10**110000** = .176

These new sub-subnets will now have new subnet masks. Each sub-subnet now has 4 N bits and 4 H bits, so their new masks will be

> 11111111.11111111.11111111.11110000

or

> 255.255.255.240

or

> /28

Pick one of these new sub-subnets for Network C and one for Network D.

00**000000** =	.0/26	
01**000000** =	.64/26	Network A
10**000000** =	.128/26	Cannot use because it has been subnetted
10**000000** =	.128/27	Network B
101**00000** =	.160/27	Cannot use because it has been subnetted
101**00000**	.160/28	Network C
1011**0000**	.176/28	Network D
11**000000** =	.192/26	

You have now used two of the original four subnets to satisfy the requirements of four networks. Now all you need to do is determine the network numbers for the serial links between the routers.

Step 5 Determine Network Numbers for Serial Links

All serial links between routers have the same property in that they only need two addresses in a network—one for each router interface.

Determine the number of H bits needed for these networks:

$$2^H - 2 \geq 2$$
$$H = 2$$

You need 2 H bits to satisfy the requirements of Networks E, F, G, and H.

You have two of the original subnets left to work with.

For the purposes of this example, select the .0/26 network:

00**000000**

But you need only 2 H bits, not 6. Therefore, you are left with

00**NNNN00**

where

00 represents the original pattern of subnetting.
NNNN represents the extra bits you have.
00 represents the 2 H bits you need for the serial links.

Because you have 4 **N** bits, you can create 16 sub-subnets from the original subnet:

00**0000**00 = .0/30
00**0001**00 = .4/30
00**0010**00 = .8/30

$$00001100 = .12/30$$
$$00010000 = .16/30$$

.

.

.

$$00111000 = .56/30$$
$$00111100 = .60/30$$

You need only four of them. You can hold the rest for future expansion or recombine them for a new, larger subnet:

$$00010000 = .16/30$$

.

.

.

$$00111000 = .56/30$$
$$00111100 = .60/30$$

All these can be recombined into the following:

$$00010000 = .16/28$$

Going back to the original table, you now have the following:

00000000 =	.0/26	Cannot use because it has been subnetted
00000000 =	.0/30	Network E
00000100 =	.4/30	Network F
00001000 =	.8/30	Network G
00001100 =	.12/30	Network H
00010000 =	.16/28	Future growth
01000000 =	.64/26	Network A
10000000 =	.128/26	Cannot use because it has been subnetted
10000000 =	.128/27	Network B
10100000 =	160/27	Cannot use because it has been subnetted
10100000	160/28	Network C
10110000	176/28	Network D
11000000 =	.192/26	Future growth

Looking at the plan, you can see that no number is used twice. You have now created an IP plan for the network and have made the plan as efficient as possible, wasting no addresses in the serial links and leaving room for future growth. This is the power of VLSM!

CHAPTER 3

Route Summarization

Route summarization, or supernetting, is needed to reduce the number of routes that a router advertises to its neighbor. Remember that for every route you advertise, the size of your update grows. It has been said that if there were no route summarization, the Internet backbone would have collapsed from the sheer size of its own routing tables back in 1997!

Routing updates, whether done with a distance vector or link-state protocol, grow with the number of routes you need to advertise. In simple terms, a router that needs to advertise ten routes needs ten specific lines in its update packet. The more routes you have to advertise, the bigger the packet. The bigger the packet, the more bandwidth the update takes, reducing the bandwidth available to transfer data. But with route summarization, you can advertise many routes with only one line in an update packet. This reduces the size of the update, allowing you more bandwidth for data transfer.

Also, when a new data flow enters a router, the router must do a lookup in its routing table to determine which interface the traffic must be sent out. The larger the routing tables, the longer this takes, leading to more used router CPU cycles to perform the lookup. Therefore, a second reason for route summarization is that you want to minimize the amount of time and router CPU cycles that are used to route traffic.

> **NOTE:** This example is a very simplified explanation of how routers send updates to each other. For a more in-depth description, I highly recommend you go out and read Jeff Doyle's book *Routing TCP/IP,* Volume I, 2nd edition, Cisco Press. This book has been around for many years and is considered by most to be the authority on how the different routing protocols work. If you are considering continuing on in your certification path to try and achieve the CCIE, you need to buy Doyle's book — and memorize it; it's that good.

Example for Understanding Route Summarization

Refer to Figure 3-1 to assist you as you go through the following explanation of an example of route summarization.

Figure 3-1   Four-City Network Without Route Summarization

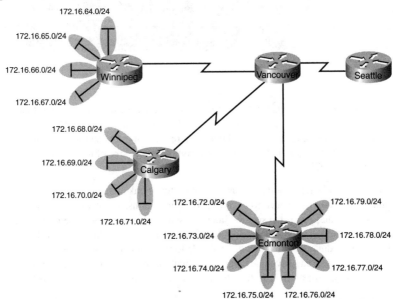

As you can see from Figure 3-1, Winnipeg, Calgary, and Edmonton each have to advertise internal networks to the main router located in Vancouver. Without route summarization, Vancouver would have to advertise 16 networks to Seattle. You want to use route summarization to reduce the burden on this upstream router.

Step 1: Summarize Winnipeg's Routes

To do this, you need to look at the routes in binary to see if there are any specific bit patterns that you can use to your advantage. What you are looking for are common bits on the network side of the addresses. Because all of these networks are /24 networks, you want to see which of the first 24 bits are common to all four networks.

> 172.16.64.0 = *10101100.00010000.01000000*.00000000
> 172.16.65.0 = *10101100.00010000.01000001*.00000000
> 172.16.66.0 = *10101100.00010000.01000010*.00000000
> 172.16.67.0 = *10101100.00010000.01000011*.00000000
> Common bits: *10101100.00010000.010000*xx

You see that the first 22 bits of the four networks are common. Therefore, you can summarize the four routes by using a subnet mask that reflects that the first 22 bits are common. This is a /22 mask, or 255.255.252.0. You are left with the summarized address of

> 172.16.64.0/22

This address, when sent to the upstream Vancouver router, will tell Vancouver: "If you have any packets that are addressed to networks that have the first 22 bits in the pattern of 10101100.00010000.010000xx.xxxxxxxx, then send them to me here in Winnipeg."

By sending one route to Vancouver with this supernetted subnet mask, you have advertised four routes in one line, instead of using four lines. Much more efficient!

Step 2: Summarize Calgary's Routes

For Calgary, you do the same thing that you did for Winnipeg—look for common bit patterns in the routes:

```
172.16.68.0 =   10101100.00010000.01000100.00000000
172.16.69.0 =   10101100.00010000.01000101.00000000
172.16.70.0 =   10101100.00010000.01000110.00000000
172.16.71.0 =   10101100.00010000.01000111.00000000
Common bits:  10101100.00010000.010001xx
```

Once again, the first 22 bits are common. The summarized route is therefore

172.16.68.0/22

Step 3: Summarize Edmonton's Routes

For Edmonton, you do the same thing that we did for Winnipeg and Calgary—look for common bit patterns in the routes:

```
172.16.72.0 =   10101100.00010000.01001000.00000000
172.16.73.0 =   10101100.00010000.01001001.00000000
172.16.74.0 =   10101100.00010000 01001010.00000000
172.16.75.0 =   10101100.00010000 01001011.00000000
172.16.76.0 =   10101100.00010000.01001100.00000000
172.16.77.0 =   10101100.00010000.01001101.00000000
172.16.78.0 =   10101100.00010000.01001110.00000000
172.16.79.0 =   10101100.00010000.01001111.00000000
Common bits:  10101100.00010000.01001xxx
```

For Edmonton, the first 21 bits are common. The summarized route is therefore

172.16.72.0/21

Figure 3-2 shows what the network looks like, with Winnipeg, Calgary, and Edmonton sending their summarized routes to Vancouver.

Figure 3-2   Four-City Network with Edge Cities Summarizing Routes

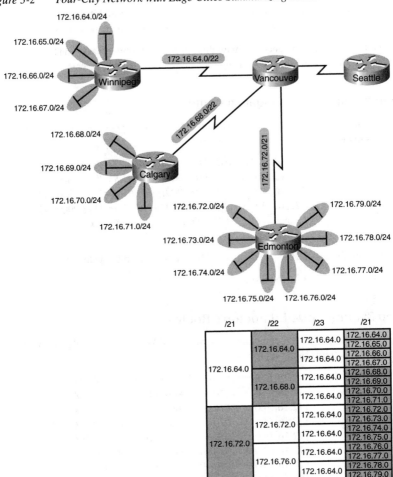

Step 4: Summarize Vancouver's Routes

Yes, you can summarize Vancouver's routes to Seattle. You continue in the same format as before. Take the routes that Winnipeg, Calgary, and Edmonton sent to Vancouver, and look for common bit patterns:

$$172.16.64.0 = \textit{10101100.00010000.01000000.00000000}$$
$$172.16.68.0 = \textit{10101100.00010000.01000100.00000000}$$
$$172.16.72.0 = \textit{10101100.00010000.01001000.00000000}$$
Common bits: *10101100.00010000.0100*xxxx

Because there are 20 bits that are common, you can create one summary route for Vancouver to send to Seattle:

172.16.64.0/20

Vancouver has now told Seattle that in one line of a routing update, 16 different networks are being advertised. This is much more efficient than sending 16 lines in a routing update to be processed.

Figure 3-3 shows what the routing updates would look like with route summarization taking place.

Figure 3-3   Four-City Network with Complete Route Summarization

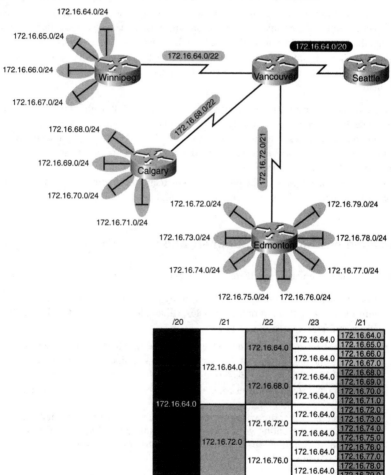

Route Summarization and Route Flapping

Another positive aspect of route summarization has to do with route flapping. *Route flapping* is when a network, for whatever reason (such as interface hardware failure or misconfiguration), goes up and down on a router, causing that router to constantly advertise changes about that network. Route summarization can help insulate upstream neighbors from these problems.

Consider router Edmonton from Figure 3-1. Suppose that network 172.16.74.0/24 goes down. Without route summarization, Edmonton would advertise Vancouver to remove that network. Vancouver would forward that same message upstream to Calgary, Winnipeg, Seattle, and so on. Now assume the network comes back online a few seconds later. Edmonton would have to send another update informing Vancouver of the change. Each time a change needs to be advertised, the router must use CPU resources. If that route were to flap, the routers would constantly have to update their own tables, as well as advertise changes to their neighbors. In a CPU-intensive protocol such as OSPF, the constant hit on the CPU might make a noticeable change to the speed at which network traffic reaches its destination.

Route summarization enables you to avoid this problem. Even though Edmonton would still have to deal with the route constantly going up and down, no one else would notice. Edmonton advertises a single summarized route, 172.16.72.0/21, to Vancouver. Even though one of the networks is going up and down, this does not invalidate the route to the other networks that were summarized. Edmonton will deal with its own route flap, but Vancouver will be unaware of the problem downstream in Edmonton. Summarization can effectively protect or insulate other routers from route flaps.

Requirements for Route Summarization

To create route summarization, there are some necessary requirements:

- Routers need to be running a classless routing protocol, as they carry subnet mask information with them in routing updates. (Examples are RIP v2, OSPF, EIGRP, IS-IS, and BGP.)
- Addresses need to be assigned in a hierarchical fashion for the summarized address to have the same high-order bits. It does no good if Winnipeg has network 172.16.64.0 and 172.16.67.0 while 172.16.65.0 resides in Calgary and 172.16.66.0 is assigned in Edmonton. No summarization could take place from the edge routers to Vancouver.

    TIP: Because most networks use NAT and the ten networks internally, it is important when creating your network design that you assign network subnets in a way that they can be easily summarized. A little more planning now can save you a lot of grief later.

Introduction to Cisco
Devices

Chapter 4 Cables and Connections

Chapter 5 The Command-Line Interface

Cables and Connections

This chapter provides information and commands concerning the following topics:

- Connecting a rollover cable to your router or switch
- Determining what your terminal settings should be
- Understanding the setup of different LAN connections
- Identifying different serial cable types
- Determining which cable to use to connect your router or switch to another device
- 568A versus 568B cables

Connecting a Rollover Cable to Your Router or Switch

Figure 4-1 shows how to connect a rollover cable from your PC to a router or switch.

Figure 4-1   Rollover Cable Connections

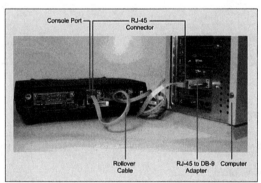

Terminal Settings

Figure 4-2 illustrates the settings that you should configure to have your PC connect to a router or switch.

Figure 4-2   PC Settings to Connect to a Router or Switch

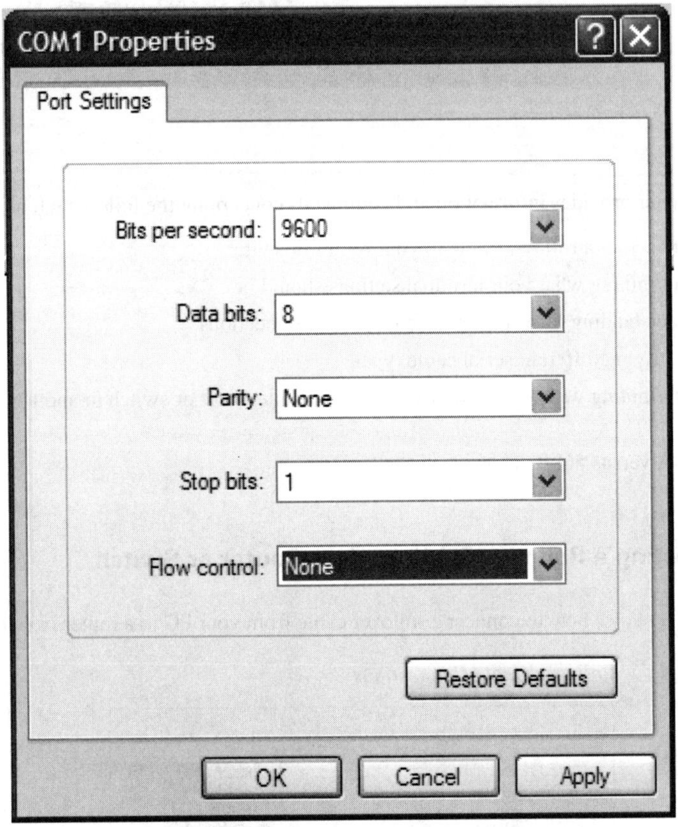

LAN Connections

Table 4-1 shows the various port types and connections between LAN devices.

Table 4-1 LAN Connections

Port or Connection	Port Type	Connected To	Cable
Ethernet	RJ-45	Ethernet switch	RJ-45
T1/E1 WAN	RJ-48C/CA81A	T1 or E1 network	Rollover
Console	8 pin	Computer COM port	Rollover

Table 4-1 LAN Connections (Continued)

Port or Connection	Port Type	Connected To	Cable
AUX	8 pin	Modem	RJ-45
BRI S/T	RJ-48C/CA81A	NT1 device or private integrated network exchange (PINX)	RJ-45
BRI U WAN	RJ-49C/CA11A	ISDN network	RJ-45

Serial Cable Types

Figure 4-3 shows the DB-60 end of a serial cable that connects to a 2500 series router.

Figure 4-4 shows the newer smart serial end of a serial cable that connects to a smart serial port on your router. Smart serial ports are found on modular routers, such as the ISR (x800) series, or on older modular routers such as the 1700 or 2600 series.

Figure 4-5 shows examples of the male DTE and the female DCE ends that are on the other side of a serial or smart serial cable.

Most laptops available today come equipped with USB ports, not serial ports. For these laptops, you need a USB-to-serial connector, as shown in Figure 4-6.

Figure 4-3   Serial Cable (2500)

Figure 4-4   *Smart Serial Cable (1700, 1800, 2600, 2800)*

Figure 4-5   *V.35 DTE and DCE Cables*

NOTE: CCNA focuses on *V.35 cables* for back-to-back connections between routers.

Figure 4-6   USB-to-Serial Connector for Laptops

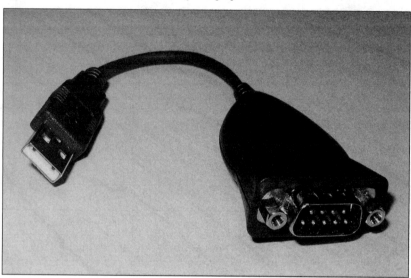

Which Cable to Use?

Table 4-2 describes which cable should be used when wiring your devices together. It is important to ensure you have proper cabling; otherwise, you might be giving yourself problems before you even get started.

Table 4-2 Determining Which Cables to Use When Wiring Devices Together

If Device A Has A:	And Device B Has A:	Then Use This Cable:
Computer COM port	Console of router/switch	Rollover
Computer NIC	Switch	Straight-through
Computer NIC	Computer NIC	Crossover
Switch port	Router's Ethernet port	Straight-through
Switch port	Switch port	Crossover (check for uplink button or toggle switch to defeat this)
Router's Ethernet port	Router's Ethernet port	Crossover
Computer NIC	Router's Ethernet port	Crossover
Router's serial port	Router's serial port	Cisco serial DCE/DTE cables

Table 4-3 lists the pinouts for straight-through, crossover, and rollover cables.

Table 4-3 Pinouts for Different Cables

Straight-Through Cable	Crossover Cable	Rollover Cable
Pin 1 – Pin 1	Pin 1 – Pin 3	Pin 1 – Pin 8
Pin 2 – Pin 2	Pin 2 – Pin 6	Pin 2 – Pin 7
Pin 3 – Pin 3	Pin 3 – Pin 1	Pin 3 – Pin 6
Pin 4 – Pin 4	Pin 4 – Pin 4	Pin 4 – Pin 5
Pin 5 – Pin 5	Pin 5 – Pin 5	Pin 5 – Pin 4
Pin 6 – Pin 6	Pin 6 – Pin 2	Pin 6 – Pin 3
Pin 7 – Pin 7	Pin 7 – Pin 7	Pin 7 – Pin 2
Pin 8 – Pin 8	Pin 8 – Pin 8	Pin 8 – Pin 1

568A Versus 568B Cables

There are two different standards released by the EIA/TIA group about UTP wiring: 568A and 568B. Although 568B is newer and is the recommended standard, either one can be used. The difference between these two standards is pin assignments, not in the use of the different colors (see Table 4-4). The 568A standard is more compatible with voice connections and the Universal Service Order Codes (USOC) standard for telephone infrastructure in the United States. In both 568A and USOC standards, the blue and orange pairs are now on the center four pins; therefore, the colors match more closely with 568A than with the 568B standard. So, which one is preferred? Information here from the standards bodies on this matter is sketchy at best. 568B was traditionally widespread in the United States, whereas places such as Canada and Australia use a lot of 568A. However, 568A is now becoming more dominant in the United States, too.

TIP: Use 568A in new installations, and 568B if connecting to an existing 568B system.

Table 4-4 UTP Wiring Standards

568A Standard				568B Standard			
Pin	**Color**	**Pair**	**Description**	**Pin**	**Color**	**Pair**	**Description**
1	White/green	3	RecvData +	1	White/ orange	2	TxData +
2	Green	3	RecvData -	2	Orange	2	TxData -
3	White/ orange	2	Txdata +	3	White/green	3	RecvData +
4	Blue	1	Unused	4	Blue	1	Unused
5	White/blue	1	Unused	5	White/blue	1	Unused
6	Orange	2	TxData -	6	Green	3	RecvData -
7	White/brown	4	Unused	7	White/ brown	4	Unused
8	Brown	4	Unused	8	Brown	4	Unused

TIP: Odd pin numbers are always the striped wires.

A straight-through cable is one with both ends using the same standard (A or B).

A crossover cable is one that has 568A on one end and 568B on the other end.

CHAPTER 5

The Command-Line Interface

This chapter provides information and commands concerning the following topics:

- Shortcuts for entering commands
- Using the (Tab⇄) key to enter complete commands
- Using the question mark for help
- **enable** command
- **exit** command
- **disable** command
- **logout** command
- Setup mode
- Keyboard help
- History commands
- **show** commands

Shortcuts for Entering Commands

To enhance efficiency, Cisco IOS Software has some shortcuts for entering commands. Although these are great to use in the real world, when it comes time to write a vendor exam, make sure you know the full commands, not just the shortcuts.

Router>**enable** = Router>**enab** = Router>**en**	Entering a shortened form of a command is sufficient as long as there is no confusion about which command you are attempting to enter.
Router#**configure terminal** is the same as Router#**config t**	

Using the (Tab⇄) Key to Complete Commands

When you are entering a command, you can use the (Tab⇄) key to complete the command. Enter the first few characters of a command and press the (Tab⇄) key. If the characters are unique to the command, the rest of the command is entered in for you. This is helpful if you are unsure about the spelling of a command.

Router#sh ⟨Tab⟩ = Router#**show**	

Using the Question Mark for Help

The following output shows you how using the question mark can help you work through a command and all its parameters.

Router#**?**	Lists all commands available in the current command mode
Router#**c?** clear clock	Lists all the possible choices that start with the letter *c*
Router#**cl?** clear clock	Lists all the possible choices that start with the letters *cl*
Router#**clock** % Incomplete Command	Tells you that more parameters need to be entered
Router#**clock ?** Set	Shows all subcommands for this command (in this case, **Set**, which sets the time and date)
Router#**clock set 19:50:00 14** **July 2007 ?** ⟨⏎Enter⟩	Pressing the ⟨⏎Enter⟩ key confirms the time and date configured.
Router#	No error message/Incomplete command message means the command was entered successfully.

enable Command

Router>**enable** Router#	Moves the user from user mode to privileged mode

exit Command

Router#**exit** Or Router>**exit**	Logs a user off
Router(config-if)#**exit** Router(config)#	Moves you back one level
Router(config)#**exit** Router#	Moves you back one level

disable Command

Router#**disable** Router>	Moves you from privileged mode back to user mode

logout Command

Router#**logout**	Performs the same function as **exit**

Setup Mode

Setup mode start automatically if there is no startup configuration present.

Router#**setup**	Enters startup mode from the command line

NOTE: The answer inside the square brackets, [ ], is the default answer. If this is the answer you want, just press ⏎Enter).

Pressing Ctrl-ⒸC at any time will end the setup process, shut down all interfaces, and take you to user mode (Router>).

NOTE: You *cannot* use setup mode to configure an entire router. It does only the basics. For example, you can only turn on either RIPv1 or Interior Gateway Routing Protocol (IGRP), but not Open Shortest Path First Protocol (OSPF) or Enhanced Interior Gateway Routing Protocol (EIGRP). You cannot create access control lists (ACL) here or enable Network Address Translation (NAT). You can assign an IP address to an interface, but not to a subinterface. All in all, setup mode is very limiting.

Entering setup mode is not a recommended practice. Instead, you should use the command-line interface (CLI), which is more powerful:

```
Would you like to enter the initial configuration dialog? [yes] : no
Would you like to enable autoinstall? [yes] : no
```

Autoinstall is a feature that tries to broadcast out all interfaces when attempting to find a configuration. If you answer **yes**, you must wait for a few minutes while it looks for a configuration to load. Very frustrating. Answer **no**.

Keyboard Help

The keystrokes in the following table are meant to help you edit the configuration. Because you'll want to perform certain tasks again and again, Cisco IOS Software provides certain keystroke combinations to help make the process more efficient.

(∧)	Shows you where you made a mistake in entering a command

`Router#config t`
 	
`          ^`
 	
`% Invalid input detected at`
`'^' marker.`
`Router#config t`
`Router(config)#`	

Ctrl-(A)	Moves cursor to beginning of line
Esc-(B)	Moves cursor back one word
Ctrl-(B) (or ←)	Moves cursor back one character
Ctrl-(E)	Moves cursor to end of line
Ctrl-(F) (or →←)	Moves cursor forward one character
Esc-(F)	Moves cursor forward one word
Ctrl-(Z)	Moves you from any prompt back down to privileged mode
($)	Indicates that the line has been scrolled to the left
`Router#terminal no editing` `Router#`	Turns off the ability to use the previous keyboard shortcuts
`Router#terminal editing` `Router#`	Reenables enhanced editing mode (can use above keyboard shortcuts)

History Commands

Ctrl-P (or ↑)	Recalls commands in the history buffer in a backward sequence, beginning with the most recent command
Ctrl-N (or ↓)	Returns to more recent commands in the history buffer after recalling commands with the Ctrl-P key sequence
terminal history size_ *number* See the next row for an example	Sets the number of commands in the buffer that can be recalled by the router (maximum 256)
Router#**terminal history size 25**	Causes the router to now remember the last 25 commands in the buffer
Router#**no terminal history size 25**	Sets the history buffer back to 10 commands, which is the default

NOTE: The **history size** command provides the same function as the **terminal history size** command.

Be careful when you set the size to something larger than the default. By telling the router to keep the last 256 commands in a buffer, you are taking memory away from other parts of the router. What would you rather have: a router that remembers what you last typed in, or a router that routes as efficiently as possible?

show Commands

Router#**show version**	Displays information about the current Cisco IOS Software
Router#**show flash**	Displays information about flash memory
Router#**show history**	Lists all commands in the history buffer

NOTE: The last line of output from the **show version** command tells you what the configuration register is set to.

PART III

Configuring a Router

Chapter 6   Configuring a Single Cisco Router

Configuring a Single Cisco Router

This chapter provides information and commands concerning the following topics:

- Router modes
- Entering global configuration mode
- Configuring a router, specifically
  - Names
  - Passwords
  - Password encryption
  - Interface names
  - Moving between interfaces
  - Configuring a serial interface
  - Configuring a Fast Ethernet interface
  - Creating a message-of-the-day (MOTD) banner
  - Creating a login banner
  - Setting the clock time zone
  - Assigning a local host name to an IP address
  - The **no ip domain-lookup** command
  - The **logging synchronous** command
  - The **exec-timeout** command
  - Saving configurations
  - Erasing configurations
- **show** commands to verify the router configurations
- EXEC commands in configuration mode: the **do** command

Router Modes

Router>	User mode
Router#	Privileged mode (also known as EXEC-level mode)
Router(config)#	Global configuration mode
Router(config-if)#	Interface mode

Router(config-subif)#	Subinterface mode
Router(config-line)#	Line mode
Router(config-router)#	Router configuration mode

TIP: There are other modes than these. Not all commands work in all modes. Be careful. If you type in a command that you know is correct—**show running-config**, for example—and you get an error, make sure that you are in the correct mode.

Entering Global Configuration Mode

Router>	Limited viewing of configuration. You cannot make changes in this mode.
Router#	You can see the configuration and move to make changes.
Router#**configure terminal** Router(config)#	Moves to global configuration mode. This prompt indicates that you can start making changes.

Configuring a Router Name

This command works on both routers and switches.

Router(config)#**hostname Cisco**	The name can be any word you choose.
Cisco(config)#	

Configuring Passwords

These commands work on both routers and switches.

Router(config)#**enable password cisco**	Sets **enable** password
Router(config)#**enable secret class**	Sets **enable secret** password

Router(config)#**line console 0**	Enters console line mode
Router(config-line)#**password console**	Sets console line mode password to **console**
Router(config-line)#**login**	Enables password checking at login
Router(config)#**line vty 0 4**	Enters vty line mode for all five vty lines
Router(config-line)#**password telnet**	Sets vty password to **telnet**
Router(config-line)#**login**	Enables password checking at login
Router(config)#**line aux 0**	Enters auxiliary line mode
Router(config-line)#**password backdoor**	Sets auxiliary line mode password to **backdoor**
Router(config-line)#**login**	Enables password checking at login

CAUTION: The **enable secret** *password* is encrypted by default. The **enable** *password* is not. For this reason, recommended practice is that you *never* use the **enable** *password* command. Use only the **enable secret** *password* command in a router or switch configuration.

You cannot set both **enable secret** *password* and **enable** *password* to the same password. Doing so defeats the use of encryption.

Password Encryption

Router(config)#**service password-encryption**	Applies a weak encryption to passwords
Router(config)#**enable password cisco**	Sets enable password to **cisco**
Router(config)#**line console 0**	Moves to console line mode
Router(config-line)#**password Cisco**	Continue setting passwords as above
	. . .
Router(config)#**no service password-encryption**	Turns off password encryption

CAUTION: If you have turned on service password encryption, used it, and then turned it off, any passwords that you have encrypted will stay encrypted. New passwords will remain unencrypted.

Interface Names

One of the biggest problems that new administrators face is the interface names on the different models of routers. With all the different Cisco devices in production networks today, some administrators are becoming confused about the names of their interfaces.

The following chart is a *sample* of some of the different interface names for various routers. This is by no means a complete list. Refer to the hardware guide of the specific router that you are working on to see the different combinations, or use the following command to see which interfaces are installed on your particular router:

router#**show ip interface brief**

Router Model	Port Location/Slot Number	Slot/Port Type	Slot Numbering Range	Example
2501	On board	Ethernet	Interface-type number	ethernet0 (e0)
	On board	Serial	Interface-type number	serial0 (s0) & s1
2514	On board	Ethernet	Interface-type number	e0 & e1
	On board	Serial	Interface-type number	s0 & s1
1721	On board	Fast Ethernet	Interface-type number	fastethernet0 (fa0)
	Slot 0	WAC (WIN interface card) (serial)	Interface-type number	s0 & s1
1760	On Board	Fast Ethernet	Interface-type 0/port	fa0/0
	Slot 0	WIC/VIC (voice interface card)	Interface-type 0/port	s0/0 & s0/1 v0/0 & v0/1
	Slot 1	WIC/VIC	Interface-type 1/port	s1/0 & s1/1 v1/0 & v1/1

	Slot 2	VIC	Interface-type 2/port	v2/0 & v2/1
	Slot 3	VIC	Interface-type 3/port	v3/0 & v3/1
2610	On board	Ethernet	Interface-type 0/port	e0/0
	Slot 0	WIC (Serial)	Interface-type 0/port	s0/0 & s0/1
2611	On board	Ethernet	Interface-type 0/port	e0/0 & e0/1
	Slot 0	WIC (Serial)	Interface-type 0/port	s0/0 & s0/1
2620	On board	Fast Ethernet	Interface-type 0/port	fa0/0
	Slot 0	WIC (serial)	Interface-type 0/port	s0/0 & s0/1
2621	On board	Fast Ethernet	Interface-type 0/port	fa0/0 & fa0/1
	Slot 0	WIC (serial)	Interface-type 0/port	s0/0 & s0/1
1841	On board	Fast Ethernet	Interface-type 0/port	fa0/0 & fa0/1
	Slot 0	High-speed WAN interface card (HWIC)/ WIC/VWIC	Interface-type 0/slot/ port	s0/0/0 & s0/0/1
1841	Slot 1	HWIC/WIC/ VWIC	Interface-type 0/slot/ port	s0/1/0 & s0/1/1
2801	On board	Fast Ethernet	Interface-type 0/port	fa0/0 & fa0/1
	Slot 0	VIC/VWIC (voice only)	Interface-type 0/slot/ port	voice0/0/0– voice0/0/3
	Slot 1	HWIC/WIC/ VWIC	Interface-type 0/slot/ port	0/1/–0/1/3 (single-wide HWIC) 0/1/0–0/1/7 (double-wide HWIC)

	Slot 2	WIC/VIC/ VWIC	Interface-type 0/slot/ port	0/2/0–0/2/3
	Slot 3	HWIC/WIC/ VWIC	Interface-type 0/slot/ port	0/3/0–0/3/3 (single-wide HWIC) 0/3/0–0/3/7 (double-wide HWIC)
2811	Built in to chassis front	USB	Interface-type port	usb0 & usb 1
	Built in to chassis rear	Fast Ethernet Gigabit Ethernet	Interface-type 0/port	fa0/0 & fa0/1 gi0/0 & gi0/1
	Slot 0	HWIC/HWIC-D/WIC/VWIC/ VIC	Interface-type 0/slot/ port	s0/0/0 & s0/0/1 fa0/0/0 & 0/0/1
	Slot 1	HWIC/HWIC-D/WIC/VWIC/ VIC	Interface-type 0/slot/ port	s0/1/0 & s0/1/1 fa0/1/0 & 0/1/1
	NME slot	NM/NME	Interface-type 1/port	gi1/0 & gi1/1 s1/0 & s1/1

Moving Between Interfaces

What happens in Column 1 is the same thing occurring in Column 3.

Router(config) #interface serial 0/0/0	Moves to serial interface configuration mode	Router(config)# interface serial 0/0/0	Moves to serial interface configuration mode
Router(config-if)#exit	Returns to global configuration mode	Router(config-if)#interface fastethernet 0/0	Moves directly to Fast Ethernet 0/0 configuration mode

`Router(config)`
`# interface`
`fastethernet`
`0/0`
	Moves to Fast Ethernet interface configuration mode	`Router(config-`
		`if)#`
			In Fast Ethernet 0/0 configuration mode now

`Router(config-` `if)#`	In Fast Ethernet 0/0 configuration mode now	`Router(config-` `if)#`	Prompt does not change; be *careful*

Configuring a Serial Interface

`Router(config)#interface s0/0/0`	Moves to serial interface 0/0/0 configuration mode
`Router(config-if)#description Link to ISP`	Optional descriptor of the link is locally significant
`Router(config-if)#ip address 192.168.10.1` `255.255.255.0`	Assigns address and subnet mask to interface
`Router(config-if)#clock rate 56000`	Assigns a clock rate for the interface
`Router(config-if)#no shutdown`	Turns interface on

TIP: The **clock rate** command is used *only* on a *serial* interface that has a *DCE* cable plugged into it. There must be a clock rate set on every serial link between routers. It does not matter which router has the DCE cable plugged into it or which interface the cable is plugged into. Serial 0 on one router can be plugged into Serial 1 on another router.

Configuring a Fast Ethernet Interface

`Router(config)#interface fastethernet 0/0`	Moves to Fast Ethernet 0/0 interface configuration mode
`Router(config-if)#description Accounting` LAN	Optional descriptor of the link is locally significant
`Router(config-if)#ip address 192.168.20.1` `255.255.255.0`	Assigns address and subnet mask to interface
`Router(config-if)#no shutdown`	Turns interface on

Creating a Message-of-the-Day Banner

`Router(config)#banner motd # Building Power`
`will be interrupted next Tuesday evening from`
`8 - 10  PM. #`
`Router(config)#`
	# is known as a *delimiting character*. The delimiting character must surround the banner message and can be any character so long as it is not a character used within the body of the message.

TIP: The MOTD banner is displayed on all terminals and is useful for sending messages that affect all users. Use the **no banner motd** command to disable the MOTD banner. The MOTD banner displays before the login prompt and the login banner, if one has been created.

Creating a Login Banner

`Router(config)#banner login # Authorized`
`Personnel Only! Please enter your username and`
`password. #`
`Router(config)#`
	# is known as a *delimiting character*. The delimiting character must surround the banner message and can be any character so long as it is not a character used within the body of the message.

TIP: The login banner displays before the username and password login prompts. Use the **no banner login** command to disable the login banner. The MOTD banner displays before the login banner.

Setting the Clock Time Zone

`Router(config)#clock timezone EST -5`	Sets the time zone for display purposes. Based on coordinated universal time. (Eastern standard time is 5 hours behind UTC.)

Assigning a Local Host Name to an IP Address

`Router(config)#ip host london 172.16.1.3`	Assigns a host name to the IP address. After this assignment, you can use the host name rather than an IP address when trying to Telnet or ping to that address.

`Router#ping london`
=
`Router#ping 172.16.1.3`
	Both commands execute the same objective: sending a ping to address 172.16.1.3.

TIP: The default port number in the **ip host** command is 23, or Telnet. If you want to Telnet to a device, just enter the IP host name itself:

`Router#london = Router#telnet london = Router#telnet 172.16.1.3`

The no ip domain-lookup Command

`Router(config)#no ip domain-lookup` `Router(config)#`	Turns off trying to automatically resolve an unrecognized command to a local host name

TIP: Ever type in a command incorrectly and are left having to wait for a minute or two as the router tries to *translate* your command to a domain server of 255.255.255.255? The router is set by default to try to resolve any word that is not a command to a Domain Name System (DNS) server at address 255.255.255.255. If you are not going to set up DNS, turn off this feature to save you time as you type, especially if you are a poor typist.

The logging synchronous Command

`Router(config)#line console 0`	Moves to line console configuration mode.
`Router(config-line)#logging synchronous`	Turns on synchronous logging. Information items sent to the console will not interrupt the command you are typing. The command will be moved to a new line.

TIP: Ever try to type in a command and an informational line appears in the middle of what you were typing? Lose your place? Do not know where you are in the command, so you just press ⏎Enter and start all over? The **logging synchronous** command tells the router that if any informational items get displayed on the screen, your prompt and command line should be moved to a new line, so as not to confuse you.

The informational line does not get inserted into the middle of the command you are trying to type. If you were to continue typing, the command would execute properly, even though it looks wrong on the screen.

The exec-timeout Command

`Router(config)#line console 0`	Moves to line console configuration mode.
`Router(config-line)#exec-timeout 0 0`	Sets the time limit when the console automatically logs off. Set to **0 0** (minutes seconds) means the console never logs off.
`Router(config-line)#`	

TIP: The command **exec-timeout 0 0** is great for a lab environment because the console never logs out. This is considered to be bad security and is dangerous in the real world. The default for the **exec-timeout** command is 10 minutes and zero (0) seconds (**exec-timeout 10 0**).

Saving Configurations

`Router#copy running-config startup-config`	Saves the running configuration to local NVRAM
`Router#copy running-config tftp`	Saves the running configuration remotely to a TFTP server

Erasing Configurations

`Router#erase startup-config`	Deletes the startup configuration file from NVRAM

TIP: The running configuration is still in dynamic memory. Reload the router to clear the running configuration.

show Commands

`Router#`**`show`** `?`	Lists all **show** commands available.
`Router#`**`show`** `interfaces`	Displays statistics for all interfaces.
`Router#`**`show`** `interface serial 0/0/0`	Displays statistics for a specific interface (in this case, serial 0/0/0).
`Router#`**`show`** `ip interface brief`	Displays a summary of all interfaces, including status and IP address assigned.
`Router#`**`show`** `controllers serial 0/0/0`	Displays statistics for interface hardware. Statistics display if the clock rate is set and if the cable is DCE, DTE, or not attached.
`Router#`**`show`** `clock`	Displays time set on device.
`Router#`**`show`** `hosts`	Displays local host-to-IP address cache. These are the names and addresses of hosts on the network to which you can connect.
`Router#`**`show`** `users`	Displays all users connected to device.
`Router#`**`show`** `history`	Displays the history of commands used at this edit level.
`Router#`**`show`** `flash`	Displays info about flash memory.
`Router#`**`show`** `version`	Displays info about loaded software version.
`Router#`**`show`** `arp`	Displays the Address Resolution Protocol (ARP) table.
`Router#`**`show`** `protocols`	Displays status of configured Layer 3 protocols.
`Router#`**`show`** `startup-config`	Displays the configuration saved in NVRAM.
`Router#`**`show`** `running-config`	Displays the configuration currently running in RAM.

EXEC Commands in Configuration Mode: The do Command

`Router(config)#do show running-config`	Executes the privileged-level **show running-config** command while in global configuration mode.
`Router(config)#`	The router remains in global configuration mode after the command has been executed.

> **TIP:**   The **do** command is useful when you want to execute EXEC commands, such as **show, clear**, or **debug**, while remaining in global configuration mode or in any configuration submode. You cannot use the **do** command to execute the **configure terminal** command because it is the **configure terminal** command that changes the mode to global configuration mode.

Configuration Example: Basic Router Configuration

Figure 6-1 illustrates the network topology for the configuration that follows, which shows a basic router configuration using the commands covered in this chapter.

Figure 6-1   Network Topology for Basic Router Configuration

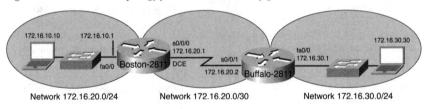

Boston Router

`Router>enable`	Enters privileged mode.
`Router#clock set 18:30:00 15 May 2007`	Sets the local time on the router.
`Router#configure terminal`	Enters global configuration mode.
`Router(config)#hostname Boston`	Sets the router name to Boston.
`Boston(config)#no ip domain-lookup`	Turns off name resolution on unrecognized commands (spelling mistakes).

`Boston(config)#banner motd #`
`This is the Boston Router.`
`Authorized Access Only`
`#`
	Creates an MOTD banner.

`Boston(config)#clock timezone EST -5`	Sets time zone to eastern standard time (–5 from UTC).
`Boston(config)#enable secret cisco`	Enables secret password set to **cisco**.
`Boston(config)#service password-encryption`	Passwords will be given weak encryption.
`Boston(config)#line console 0`	Enters line console mode.
`Boston(config-line)#logging synchronous`	Commands will not be interrupted by unsolicited messages.
`Boston(config-line)#password class`	Sets the password to **class**.
`Boston(config-line)#login`	Enables password checking at login.
`Boston(config-line)#line vty 0 4`	Moves to virtual Telnet lines 0 through 4.
`Boston(config-line)#password class`	Sets the password to **class**.
`Boston(config-line)#login`	Enables password checking at login.
`Boston(config-line)#line aux 0`	Moves to line auxiliary mode.
`Boston(config-line)#password class`	Sets the password to **class**.
`Boston(config-line)#login`	Enables password checking at login.
`Boston(config-line)#exit`	Moves back to global configuration mode.
`Boston(config)#no service password-` `encryption`	Turns off password encryption.
`Boston(config)#interface fastethernet 0/0`	Moves to interface Fast Ethernet 0/0 configuration mode.

`Boston(config-if)#`**`description Engineering`** **LAN**	Sets locally significant description of the interface.
`Boston(config-if)#`**`ip address 172.16.10.1`** **`255.255.255.0`**	Assigns an IP address and subnet mask to the interface.
`Boston(config-if)#`**`no shutdown`**	Turns on the interface.
`Boston(config-if)#`**`interface serial 0/0/0`**	Moves directly to interface serial 0/0/0 configuration mode.
`Boston(config-if)#`**`description Link to`** **`Buffalo Router`**	Sets locally significant description of the interface.
`Boston(config-if)#`**`ip address 172.16.20.1`** **`255.255.255.252`**	Assigns an IP address and subnet mask to the interface.
`Boston(config-if)#`**`clock rate 56000`**	Sets a clock rate for serial transmission. The DCE cable must be plugged into this interface.
`Boston(config-if)#`**`no shutdown`**	Turns on the interface.
`Boston(config-if)#`**`exit`**	Moves back to global configuration mode.
`Boston(config)#`**`ip host buffalo 172.16.20.2`**	Sets a local host name resolution to IP address 172.16.20.2.
`Boston(config)#`**`exit`**	Moves back to privileged mode.
`Boston#`**`copy running-config startup-config`**	Saves the running configuration to NVRAM.

PART IV

Routing

Chapter 7   Static Routing

Chapter 8   RIP

Chapter 9   EIGRP

Chapter 10   Single Area OSPF

Static Routing

This chapter provides information and commands concerning the following topics:

- Configuring a static route on a router
- The **permanent** keyword (optional)
- Static routes and administrative distance (optional)
- Configuring a default route on a router
- Verifying static routes
- Configuration example: Static routes

Configuring a Static Route on a Router

When using the **ip route** command, you can identify where packets should be routed in two ways:

- The next-hop address
- The exit interface

Both ways are shown in the "Configuration Example: Static Routes" and the "Configuring a Default Route on a Router" sections.

`Router(config)#ip route 172.16.20.0 255.255.255.0 172.16.10.2`	172.16.20.0 = destination network. 255.255.255.0 = subnet mask. 172.16.10.2 = next-hop address. Read this to say, "To get to the destination network of 172.16.20.0, with a subnet mask of 255.255.255.0, send all packets to 172.16.10.2."
`Router(config)#ip route 172.16.20.0 255.255.255.0 serial 0/0/0`	172.16.20.0 = destination network. 255.255.255.0 = subnet mask. Serial 0/0/0 = exit interface. Read this to say, "To get to the destination network of 172.16.20.0, with a subnet mask of 255.255.255.0, send all packets out interface serial 0/0/0."

The permanent Keyword (Optional)

Without the **permanent** keyword in a static route statement, a static route will be removed if an interface goes down. A downed interface will cause the directly connected network and any associated static routes to be removed from the routing table. If the interface comes back up, the routes are returned.

Adding the **permanent** keyword to a static route statement will keep the static routes in the routing table even if the interface goes down and the directly connected networks are removed. You *cannot* get to these routes—the interface is down—but the routes remain in the table. The advantage to this is that when the interface comes back up, the static routes do not need to be reprocessed and placed back into the routing table, thus saving time and processing power.

When a static route is added or deleted, this route, along with all other static routes, is processed in one second. Before Cisco IOS Software Release 12.0, this processing time was five seconds.

The routing table processes static routes every minute to install or remove static routes according to the changing routing table.

To specify that the route will not be removed, even if the interface shuts down, enter the following command, for example:

```
Router(config)#ip route 172.16.20.0 255.255.255.0 172.16.10.2 permanent
```

Static Routes and Administrative Distance (Optional)

To specify that an administrative distance of 200 has been assigned to a given route, enter the following command, for example:

```
Router(config)#ip route 172.16.20.0 255.255.255.0 172.16.10.2 200
```

By default, a static route is assigned an administrative distance (AD) of 1. Administrative distance rates the "trustworthiness" of a route. AD is a number from 0 through 255, where 0 is absolutely trusted and 255 cannot be trusted at all. Therefore, an AD of 1 is an extremely reliable rating, with only an AD of 0 being better. An AD of 0 is assigned to a directly connected route. The following table lists the administrative distance for each type of route.

Route Type	Administrative Distance
Connected	0
Static	1
Enhanced Interior Gateway Routing Protocol (EIGRP) summary route	5

Exterior Border Gateway Protocol (eBGP)	20
EIGRP (internal)	90
Open Shortest Path First Protocol (OSPF)	110
Intermediate System-to-Intermediate System Protocol (IS-IS)	115
RIP	120
Exterior Gateway Protocol (EGP)	140
On-Demand Routing	160
EIGRP (external)	170
Internal Border Gateway Protocol (iBGP) (external)	200
Unknown	255

By default, a static route is always used rather than a routing protocol. By adding an AD number to your **ip route** statement, however, you can effectively create a backup route to your routing protocol. If your network is using EIGRP, and you need a backup route, add a static route with an AD greater than 90. EIGRP will be used because its AD is better (lower) than the static route. If EIGRP goes down, however, the static route will be used in its place. This is known as a *floating static route*.

If a static route refers to an exit interface rather than a next-hop address, the destination is considered to be directly connected and is therefore given an AD of 0 rather than 1.

Configuring a Default Route on a Router

Router(config)#**ip route 0.0.0.0 0.0.0.0 172.16.10.2**	Send all packets destined for networks not in my routing table to 172.16.10.2.
Router(config)#**ip route 0.0.0.0 0.0.0.0 serial 0/0/0**	Send all packets destined for networks not in my routing table out my serial 0/0 interface.

Verifying Static Routes

To display the contents of the IP routing table, enter the following command:

Router#**show ip route**

> **NOTE:** The codes to the left of the routes in the table tell you from where the router learned the routes. A static route is described by the letter *S*.

Configuration Example: Static Routes

Figure 7-1 illustrates the network topology for the configuration that follows, which shows how to configure static routes using the commands covered in this chapter.

Figure 7-6 Network Topology for Static Route Configuration

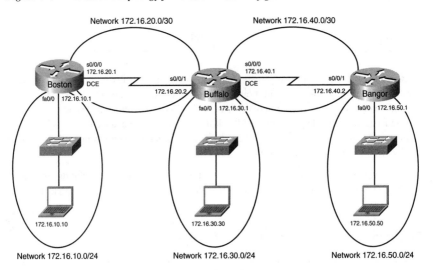

> **NOTE:** The host names, passwords, and interfaces have all been configured using the commands shown in the configuration example in Chapter 6, "Configuring a Single Cisco Router."

Boston Router

Boston>**enable**	Moves to privileged mode
Boston#**configure terminal**	Moves to global configuration mode

Boston(config)#ip route 172.16.30.0 255.255.255.0 172.16.20.2	Configures a static route using the next-hop address
Boston(config)#ip route 172.16.40.0 255.255.255.0 172.16.20.2	Configures a static route using the next-hop address
Boston(config)#ip route 172.16.50.0 255.255.255.0 172.16.20.2	Configures a static route using the next-hop address
Boston(config)#exit	Moves to privileged mode
Boston#copy running-config startup-config	Saves the configuration to NVRAM

Buffalo Router

Buffalo>enable	Moves to privileged mode
Buffalo#configure terminal	Moves to global configuration mode
Buffalo(config)#ip route 172.16.10.0 255.255.255.0 serial 0/0/1	Configures a static route using the exit interface
Buffalo(config)#ip route 172.16.50.0 255.255.255.0 serial 0/0/0	Configures a static route using the exit interface
Buffalo(config)#exit	Moves to privileged mode
Buffalo#copy running-config startup-config	Saves the configuration to NVRAM

Bangor Router

Bangor>enable	Moves to privileged mode
Bangor#configure terminal	Moves to global configuration mode
Bangor(config)#ip route 0.0.0.0 0.0.0.0 serial 0/0/1	Configures a static route using the default route
Bangor(config)#exit	Moves to privileged mode
Bangor#copy running-config startup-config	Saves the configuration to NVRAM

This chapter provides information and commands concerning the following topics:

- The **ip classless** command
- RIP routing: mandatory commands
- RIP routing: optional commands
- Troubleshooting RIP issues
- Configuration example: RIPv2 routing

The ip classless Command

`Router(config)#ip classless`	Instructs Cisco IOS Software to forward packets destined for an unknown subnet to the best supernet route
`Router(config)#no ip classless`	Turns off the **ip classless** command

NOTE: A supernet route is a route that covers a range of subnets with a single entry.

NOTE: The **ip classless** command is enabled by default in Cisco IOS Software Release 11.3 and later.

RIP Routing: Mandatory Commands

`Router(config)#router rip`	Enables RIP as a routing protocol.
`Router(config-router)#network w.x.y.z`	*w.x.y.z* is the network number of the *directly connected* network you want to advertise.

NOTE: You need to advertise only the classful network number, not a subnet:

Router(config-router)#**network 172.16.0.0**

not

Router(config-router)#**network 172.16.10.0**

If you advertise a subnet, you will not receive an error message, because the router will automatically convert the subnet to the classful network address.

RIP Routing: Optional Commands

Router(config)#**no router rip**	Turns off the RIP routing process.
Router(config-router)#**no network** *w.x.y.z*	Removes network *w.x.y.z* from the RIP routing process.
Router(config-router)#**version 2**	RIP will now send and receive RIPv2 packets globally.
Router(config-router)#**version 1**	RIP will now send and receive RIPv1 packets only.
Router(config-if)#**ip rip send version 1**	The interface will send only RIPv1 packets.
Router(config-if)#**ip rip send version 2**	The interface will send only RIPv2 packets.
Router(config-if)#**ip rip send version 1 2**	The interface will send both RIPv1 and RIPv2 packets.
Router(config-if)#**ip rip receive version 1**	The interface will receive only RIPv1 packets.
Router(config-if)#**ip rip receive version 2**	The interface will receive only RIPv2 packets.
Router(config-if)#**ip rip receive version 1 2**	The interface will receive both RIPv1 and RIPv2 packets.
Router(config-router)#**no auto-summary**	RIPv2 summarizes networks at the classful boundary. This command turns auto-summarization off.

`Router(config-router)#`**`passive-interface`** **`s0/0/0`**	RIP updates will not be sent out this interface.
`Router(config-router)#`**`neighbor`** `a.b.c.d`	Defines a specific neighbor with which to exchange information.
`Router(config-router)#`**`no ip split-horizon`**	Turns off split horizon (on by default).
`Router(config-router)#`**`ip split-horizon`**	Reenables split horizon.
`Router(config-router)#`**`timers basic 30 90 180`** **`270 360`**	Changes timers in RIP: 30 = Update timer (in seconds) 90 = Invalid timer (in seconds) 180 = Hold-down timer (in seconds) 270 = Flush timer (in seconds) 360 = Sleep time (in milliseconds)
`Router(config-router)#`**`maximum-paths`** `x`	Limits the number of paths for load balancing to x (4 = default, 6 = maximum).
`Router(config-router)#`**`default-information`** **`originate`**	Generates a default route into RIP.

Troubleshooting RIP Issues

`Router#`**`debug ip rip`**	Displays all RIP activity in real time
`Router#`**`show ip rip database`**	Displays contents of the RIP database

Configuration Example: RIPv2 Routing

Figure 8-1 illustrates the network topology for the configuration that follows, which shows how to configure RIPv2 using the commands covered in this chapter.

Figure 8-1   Network Topology for RIPv2 Routing Configuration

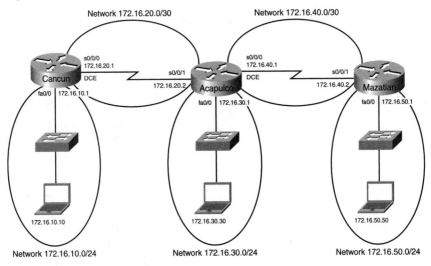

NOTE: The host name, password, and interfaces have all been configured as per the configuration example in Chapter 6, "Configuring a Single Cisco Router."

Cancun Router

Cancun>**enable**	Moves to privileged mode
Cancun#**configure terminal**	Moves to global configuration mode
Cancun(config)#**router rip**	Enables RIP routing
Cancun(config-router)#**version 2**	Enables RIPv2
Cancun(config-router)#**network 172.16.0.0**	Advertises directly connected networks (classful address only)
Cancun(config-router)#**no auto-summary**	Turns off auto-summarization

`Cancun(config-router)#`**`exit`**	Returns to global configuration mode
`Cancun(config)#`**`exit`**	Returns to privileged mode
`Cancun#`**`copy run start`**	Saves the configuration to NVRAM

Acapulco Router

`Acapulco>`**`enable`**	Moves to privileged mode
`Acapulco#`**`configure terminal`**	Moves to global configuration mode
`Acapulco(config)#`**`router rip`**	Enables RIP routing
`Acapulco(config-router)#`**`version 2`**	Enables RIPv2
`Acapulco(config-router)#`**`network 172.16.0.0`**	Advertises directly connected networks (classful address only)
`Acapulco(config-router)#`**`no auto-summary`**	Turns off auto-summarization
`Acapulco(config-router)#`**`exit`**	Moves to global configuration mode
`Acapulco(config)#`**`exit`**	Returns to privileged mode
`Acapulco#`**`copy running-config startup-config`**	Saves the configuration to NVRAM

Mazatlan Router

`Mazatlan>`**`enable`**	Moves to privileged mode
`Mazatlan#`**`configure terminal`**	Moves to global configuration mode
`Mazatlan(config)#`**`router rip`**	Enables RIP routing
`Mazatlan(config-router)#`**`version 2`**	Enables RIPv2
`Mazatlan(config-router)#`**`network 172.16.0.0`**	Advertises directly connected networks (classful address only)

`Mazatlan(config-router)#no auto-summary`	Turns off auto-summarization
`Mazatlan(config-router)#exit`	Moves to global configuration mode
`Mazatlan(config)#exit`	Returns to privileged mode
`Mazatlan#copy running-config startup-config`	Saves the configuration to NVRAM

This chapter provides information and commands concerning the following topics:

- Configuring Enhanced Interior Gateway Routing Protocol (EIGRP)
- EIGRP auto-summarization
- Load balancing: **variance**
- Bandwidth use
- Authentication
- Verifying EIGRP
- Troubleshooting EIGRP
- Configuration example: EIGRP

Configuring Enhanced Interior Gateway Routing Protocol (EIGRP)

`Router(config)#router eigrp 100`	Turns on the EIGRP process. 100 is the autonomous system number, which can be a number between 1 and 65,535.
	All routers in the same autonomous system must use the same autonomous system number.
`Router(config-router)#network 10.0.0.0`	Specifies which network to advertise in EIGRP.
`Router(config-if)#bandwidth x`	Sets the bandwidth of this interface to x kilobits to allow EIGRP to make a better metric calculation.
	TIP: The **bandwidth** command is used for metric calculations only. It does not change interface performance.
`Router(config-router)#no network 10.0.0.0`	Removes the network from the EIGRP process.

Router(config)#no router eigrp 100	Disables routing process 100.
Router(config-router)#network 10.0.0.0 0.255.255.255	Identifies which interfaces or networks to include in EIGRP. Interfaces must be configured with addresses that fall within the wildcard mask range of the **network** statement. A network mask can also be used here.
Router(config-router)#metric weights tos k1 k2 k3 k4 k5	Changes the default k values used in metric calculation. These are the default values: tos=0, k1=1, k2=0, k3=1, k4=0, k5=0

NOTE: *tos* is a reference to the original Interior Gateway Routing Protocol (IGRP) intention to have IGRP perform type-of-service routing. Because this was never adopted into practice, the *tos* field in this command is *always* set to zero (0).

NOTE: With default settings in place, the metric of EIGRP is reduced to the slowest bandwidth plus the sum of all the delays of the exit interfaces from the local router to the destination network.

TIP: For two routers to form a neighbor relationship in EIGRP, the *k* values *must* match.

CAUTION: Unless you are *very* familiar with what is occurring in your network, it is recommended that you *do not* change the *k* values.

EIGRP Auto-Summarization

Router(config-router)#auto-summary	Enables auto-summarization for the EIGRP process.
	NOTE: The default behavior of auto-summarized changed from enabled to disabled was introduced in Cisco IOS Software Release 12.2(8)T.
Router(config-router)#no auto-summary	Turns off the auto-summarization feature.

	NOTE: The behavior of the **auto-summary** command is disabled by default, beginning in Cisco IOS Software Release 12.2(8)T. This means that Cisco IOS Software will now send subprefix routing information across classful network boundaries.
`Router(config)#interface fastethernet 0/0`	Enters interface configuration mode.
`Router(config-if)#ip summary-address eigrp 100 10.10.0.0 255.255.0.0 75`	Enables manual summarization for EIGRP autonomous system 100 on this specific interface for the given address and mask. An administrative distance of 75 is assigned to this summary route.
	NOTE: The *administrative-distance* argument is optional in this command. Without it, an administrative distance of 5 is automatically applied to the summary route.

CAUTION: EIGRP automatically summarizes networks at the classful boundary. A poorly designed network with discontiguous subnets could have problems with connectivity if the summarization feature is left on. For instance, you could have two routers advertise the same network—172.16.0.0/16—when in fact they wanted to advertise two different networks—172.16.10.0/24 and 172.16.20.0/24.

Recommended practice is that you turn off automatic summarization if necessary, use the **ip summary-address** command, and summarize manually what you need to.

Load Balancing: variance

`Router(config)#router eigrp 100`	Creates routing process 100
`Router(config-router)#network 10.0.0.0`	Specifies which network to advertise in EIGRP
`Router(config-router)#variance n`	Instructs the router to include routes with a metric less than or equal to n times the minimum metric route for that destination, where n is the number specified by the **variance** command

NOTE: If a path is not a feasible successor, it is not used in load balancing.

NOTE: EIGRP supports up to six unequal-cost paths.

Bandwidth Use

`Router(config)#interface serial 0/0`	Enters interface configuration mode.
`Router(config-if)#bandwidth 256`	Sets the bandwidth of this interface to 256 kilobits to allow EIGRP to make a better metric calculation.
`Router(config-if)#ip bandwidth-percent eigrp 50 100`	Configures the percentage of bandwidth that may be used by EIGRP on an interface. 50 is the EIGRP autonomous system number. 100 is the percentage value. 100% * 256 = 256 kbps.

NOTE: By default, EIGRP is set to use only up to 50 percent of the bandwidth of an interface to exchange routing information. Values greater than 100 percent can be configured. This configuration option might prove useful if the bandwidth is set artificially low for other reasons, such as manipulation of the routing metric or to accommodate an oversubscribed multipoint Frame Relay configuration.

NOTE: The **ip bandwidth-percent** command relies on the value set by the **bandwidth** command.

Authentication

`Router(config)#interface serial 0/0`	Enters interface configuration mode.
`Router(config-if)#ip authentication mode eigrp 100 md5`	Enables Message Digest 5 algorithm (MD5) authentication in EIGRP packets over the interface.
`Router(config-if)#ip authentication key-chain eigrp 100 romeo`	Enables authentication of EIGRP packets. romeo is the name of the key chain.
`Router(config-if)#exit`	Returns to global configuration mode.

`Router(config)#`**`key chain romeo`**	Identifies a key chain. The name must match the name configured in interface configuration mode above.
`Router(config-keychain)#`**`key 1`**	Identifies the key number.
	NOTE: The range of keys is from 0 to 2147483647. The key identification numbers do not need to be consecutive. At least 1 key must be defined on a key chain.
`Router(config-keychain-key)#`**`key-string shakespeare`**	Identifies the key string.
	NOTE: The string can contain from 1 to 80 uppercase and lowercase alphanumeric characters, except that the first character cannot be a number.
`Router(config-keychain-key)#`**`accept-lifetime`** *`start-time`* `{`**`infinite`** ׀ *`end-time`* ׀ **`duration`** *`seconds`*`}`	Optionally specifies the period during which the key can be received.
	NOTE: The default start time and the earliest acceptable date is January 1, 1993. The default end time is an infinite period.
`Router(config-keychain-key)#`**`send-lifetime`** *`start-time`* `{`**`infinite`** ׀ *`end-time`* ׀ **`duration`** *`seconds`*`}`	Optionally specifies the period during which the key can be sent.
	NOTE: The default start time and the earliest acceptable date is January 1, 1993. The default end time is an infinite period.

NOTE: For the start time and the end time to have relevance, ensure that the router knows the correct time. Recommended practice dictates that you run Network Time Protocol (NTP) or some other time-synchronization method if you intend to set lifetimes on keys.

Verifying EIGRP

`Router#show ip eigrp neighbors`	Displays the neighbor table.
`Router#show ip eigrp neighbors detail`	Displays a detailed neighbor table.
	TIP: The **show ip eigrp neighbors detail** command verifies whether a neighbor is configured as a stub router.
`Router#show ip eigrp interfaces`	Shows information for each interface.
`Router#show ip eigrp interfaces serial 0/0`	Shows information for a specific interface.
`Router#show ip eigrp interfaces 100`	Shows information for interfaces running process 100.
`Router#show ip eigrp topology`	Displays the topology table.
	TIP: The **show ip eigrp topology** command shows you where your feasible successors are.
`Router#show ip eigrp traffic`	Shows the number and type of packets sent and received.
`Router#show ip route eigrp`	Shows a routing table with only EIGRP entries.

Troubleshooting EIGRP

`Router#debug eigrp fsm`	Displays events/actions related to EIGRP feasible successor metrics (FSM)
`Router#debug eigrp packet`	Displays events/actions related to EIGRP packets
`Router#debug eigrp neighbor`	Displays events/actions related to your EIGRP neighbors
`Router#debug ip eigrp neighbor`	Displays events/actions related to your EIGRP neighbors
`Router#debug ip eigrp notifications`	Displays EIGRP event notifications

Configuration Example: EIGRP

Figure 9-1 illustrates the network topology for the configuration that follows, which shows how to configure EIGRP using the commands covered in this chapter.

Figure 9-1   Network Topology for EIGRP Configuration

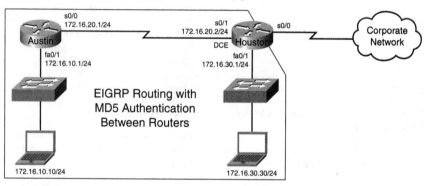

Austin Router

Austin>**enable**	Moves to privileged mode.
Austin#**configure terminal**	Moves to global configuration mode.
Austin(config)#**interface serial 0/0**	Enters interface configuration mode.
Austin(config-if)#**ip address 172.16.20.1 255.255.255.0**	Assigns the IP address and netmask.
Austin(config-if)#**ip authentication mode eigrp 100 md5**	Enables MD5 authentication in EIGRP packets.
Austin(config-if)#**ip authentication key-chain eigrp 100 susannah**	Enables authentication of EIGRP packets. susannah is the name of the key chain.
Austin(config-if)#**no shutdown**	Enables the interface.
Austin(config-if)#**interface fastethernet 0/1**	Enters interface configuration mode.
Austin(config-if)#**ip address 172.16.10.1 255.255.255.0**	Assigns the IP address and netmask.
Austin(config-if)#**no shutdown**	Enables the interface.
Austin(config-if)#**router eigrp 100**	Enables EIGRP routing.

`Austin(config-router)#no auto-summary`	Disables auto-summarization.
`Austin(config-router)#eigrp log-neighbor-changes`	Changes with neighbors will be displayed.
`Austin(config-router)#network 172.16.0.0`	Advertises directly connected networks (classful address only).
`Austin(config-router)#key chain susannah`	Identifies a key chain name, which must match the name configured in interface configuration mode.
`Austin(config-keychain)#key 1`	Identifies the key number.
`Austin(config-keychain-key)#key-string tower`	Identifies the key string.
`Austin(config-keychain-key)#accept-lifetime 06:30:00 Apr 19 2007 infinite`	Specifies the period during which the key can be received.
`Austin(config-keychain-key)#send-lifetime 06:30:00 Apr 19 2007 09:45:00 Apr 19 2007`	Specifies the period during which the key can be sent.
`Austin(config-keychain-key)#exit`	Returns to global configuration mode.
`Austin(config)#exit`	Returns to privileged mode
`Austin#copy running-config startup-config`	Saves the configuration to NVRAM.

Houston Router

`Houston>enable`	Moves to privileged mode.
`Houston#configure terminal`	Moves to global configuration mode.
`Houston(config)#interface serial 0/1`	Enters interface configuration mode.
`Houston(config-if)#ip address 172.16.20.2 255.255.255.0`	Assigns the IP address and netmask.
`Houston(config-if)#ip authentication mode eigrp 100 md5`	Enables MD5 authentication in EIGRP packets.
`Houston(config-if)#ip authentication key-chain eigrp 100 eddie`	Enables authentication of EIGRP packets. eddie is the name of the key chain.

`Houston(config-if)#clock rate 56000`	Sets the clock rate.
`Houston(config-if)#no shutdown`	Enables the interface.
`Houston(config-if)#interface fastethernet 0/1`	Enters interface configuration mode.
`Houston(config-if)#ip address 172.16.30.1 255.255.255.0`	Assigns the IP address and netmask.
`Houston(config-if)#no shutdown`	Enables the interface.
`Houston(config-if)#router eigrp 100`	Enables EIGRP routing.
`Houston(config-router)#no auto-summary`	Disables auto-summarization.
`Houston(config-router)#eigrp log-neighbor-changes`	Changes with neighbors will be displayed.
`Houston(config-router)#network 172.16.0.0`	Advertises directly connected networks (classful address only).
`Houston(config-router)#key chain eddie`	Identifies a key chain name, which must match the name configured in interface configuration mode.
`Houston(config-keychain)#key 1`	Identifies the key number.
`Houston(config-keychain-key)#key-string tower`	Identifies the key string.
`Houston(config-keychain-key)#accept-lifetime 06:30:00 Apr 19 2007 infinite`	Specifies the period during which the key can be received.
`Houston(config-keychain-key)#send-lifetime 06:30:00 Apr 19 2007 09:45:00 Apr 19 2007`	Specifies the period during which the key can be sent.
`Houston(config-keychain-key)#exit`	Returns to global configuration mode.
`Houston(config)#exit`	Returns to privileged mode.
`Houston#copy running-config startup-config`	Saves the configuration to NVRAM.

CHAPTER 10

Single Area OSPF

This chapter provides information and commands concerning the following topics:

- Configuring OSPF: Mandatory commands
- Using wildcard masks with OSPF areas
- Configuring OSPF: Optional commands
  - Loopback interfaces
  - Router ID
  - DR/BDR elections
  - Modifying cost metrics
  - Authentication: Simple
  - Authentication: Using MD5 encryption
  - Timers
  - Propagating a default route
- Verifying OSPF configuration
- Troubleshooting OSPF
- Configuration example: Single area OSPF

Configuring OSPF: Mandatory Commands

`Router(config)#router ospf 123`	Starts OSPF process 123. The process ID is any positive integer value between 1 and 65,535. The process ID *is not related to* the OSPF area. The process ID merely distinguishes one process from another within the device.
`Router(config-router)#network 172.16.10.0 0.0.0.255 area 0`	OSPF advertises interfaces, not networks. Uses the wildcard mask to determine which interfaces to advertise. Read this line to say "Any interface with an address of 172.16.10.x is to be put into area 0."

	NOTE: The process ID number of one router does not have to match the process ID of any other router.
	Unlike Enhanced Interior Gateway Routing Protocol (EIGRP), matching this number across all routers does *not* ensure that network adjacencies will form.
`Router(config-router)#log-adjacency-changes detail`	Configures the router to send a syslog message when there is a change of state between OSPF neighbors.
	TIP: Although the **log-adjacency-changes** command is on by default, only up/down events are reported unless you use the **detail** keyword.

Using Wildcard Masks with OSPF Areas

When compared to an IP address, a wildcard mask identifies which addresses get matched for placement into an area:

- A 0 (zero) in a wildcard mask means to check the corresponding bit in the address for an exact match.
- A 1 (one) in a wildcard mask means to ignore the corresponding bit in the address— can be either 1 or 0.

Example 1: 172.16.0.0 0.0.255.255

$$172.16.0.0 = 10101100.00010000.00000000.00000000$$
$$0.0.255.255 = \underline{00000000.00000000.11111111.11111111}$$
$$result = 10101100.00010000.xxxxxxxx.xxxxxxxx$$

172.16.*x.x* (Anything between 172.16.0.0 and 172.16.255.255 will match the example statement.)

TIP: An octet of all 0s means that the octet has to match exactly to the address. An octet of all 1s means that the octet can be ignored.

Example 2: 172.16.8.0 0.0.7.255

172.168.8.0 = 10101100.00010000.00001000.00000000
0.0.0.7.255 = <u>00000000.00000000.00000111.11111111</u>
result =   10101100.00010000.00001*xxx*.*xxxxxxxx*
00001*xxx* =   00001*000* to 00001*111* = 8–15
xxxxxxxx =   00000000 to 11111111 = 0–255
Anything between 172.16.8.0 and 172.16.15.255 will match the example statement.

`Router(config-router)#network` `172.16.10.1 0.0.0.0 area 0`	Read this line to say "Any interface with an exact address of 172.16.10.1 is to be put into area 0."
`Router(config-router)#network` `172.16.10.0 0.0.255.255 area 0`	Read this line to say "Any interface with an address of 172.16.*x.x* is to be put into area 0."
`Router(config-router)#network 0.0.0.0` `255.255.255.255 area 0`	Read this line to say "Any interface with any address is to be put into area 0."

Configuring OSPF: Optional Commands

The following commands, although not mandatory, enable you to have a more controlled and efficient deployment of OSPF in your network.

Loopback Interfaces

`Router(config)#interface loopback 0`	Creates a virtual interface named loopback 0, and then moves the router to interface configuration mode.
`Router(config-if)#ip address` `192.168.100.1 255.255.255.255`	Assigns the IP address to the interface.
	NOTE: Loopback interfaces are always "up and up" and do not go down unless manually shut down. This makes loopback interfaces great for use as OSPF router IDs.

Router ID

`Router(config)#router ospf 1`	Starts OSPF process 1.
`Router(config-router)#router-id 10.1.1.1`	Sets the router ID to 10.1.1.1. If this command is used on an OSPF router process that is already active (has neighbors), the new router ID is used at the next reload or at a manual OSPF process restart.
`Router(config-router)#no router-id 10.1.1.1`	Removes the static router ID from the configuration. If this command is used on an OSPF router process that is already active (has neighbors), the old router ID behavior is used at the next reload or at a manual OSPF process restart.

DR/BDR Elections

`Router(config)#interface serial 0/0`	Changes the router to interface configuration mode.
`Router(config-if)#ip ospf priority 50`	Changes the OSPF interface priority to 50.
	NOTE: The assigned priority can be between 0 and 255. A priority of 0 makes the router ineligible to become a designated router (DR) or backup designated router BDR). The highest priority wins the election. A priority of 255 guarantees a tie in the election. If all routers have the same priority, regardless of the priority number, they tie. Ties are broken by the highest router ID.

Modifying Cost Metrics

`Router(config)#`**`interface serial 0/0`**	Changes the router to interface configuration mode.
`Router(config-if)#`**`bandwidth 128`**	If you change the bandwidth, OSPF recalculates the cost of the link.
Or	
`Router(config-if)#`**`ip ospf cost 1564`**	Changes the cost to a value of 1564.
	NOTE: The cost of a link is determined by dividing the reference bandwidth by the interface bandwidth. The bandwidth of the interface is a number between 1 and 10,000,000. The unit of measurement is kilobits. The cost is a number between 1 and 65,535. The cost has no unit of measurement—it is just a number.

Authentication: Simple

`Router(config)#`**`router ospf 1`**	Starts OSPF process 1.
`Router(config-router)#`**`area 0`** **`authentication`**	Enables simple authentication; password will be sent in clear text.
`Router(config-router)#`**`exit`**	Returns to global configuration mode.
`Router(config)#`**`interface`** **`fastethernet 0/0`**	Moves to interface configuration mode.
`Router(config-if)#`**`ip ospf`** **`authentication-key fred`**	Sets key (password) to **fred**.
	NOTE: The password can be any continuous string of characters that can be entered from the keyboard, up to 8 bytes in length. To be able to exchange OSPF information, all neighboring routers on the same network must have the same password.

Authentication: Using MD5 Encryption

`Router(config)#router ospf 1`	Starts OSPF process 1.
`Router(config-router)#area 0 authentication message-digest`	Enables authentication with MD5 password encryption.
`Router(config-router)#exit`	Returns to global configuration mode.
`Router(config)#interface fastethernet 0/0`	Moves to interface configuration mode.
`Router(config-if)#ip ospf message-digest-key 1 md5 fred`	1 is the *key-id*. This value must be the same as that of your neighboring router. **md5** indicates that the MD5 hash algorithm will be used. **fred** is the key (password) and must be the same as that of your neighboring router.
	NOTE: If the **service password-encryption** command is not used when implementing OSPF MD5 authentication, the MD5 secret is stored as plain text in NVRAM.

Timers

`Router(config-if)#ip ospf hello-interval timer 20`	Changes the Hello Interval timer to 20 seconds.
`Router(config-if)#ip ospf dead-interval 80`	Changes the Dead Interval timer to 80 seconds.
	NOTE: Hello and Dead Interval timers must match for routers to become neighbors.

Propagating a Default Route

`Router(config)#ip route 0.0.0.0 0.0.0.0 s0/0`	Creates a default route.
`Router(config)#router ospf 1`	Starts OSPF process 1.
`Router(config-router)#default-information originate`	Sets the default route to be propagated to all OSPF routers.

Router(config-router)#**default-information originate always**	The **always** option propagates a default "quad-zero" route even if one is not configured on this router.
	NOTE: The **default-information originate** command or the **default-information originate always** command is usually only to be configured on your "entrance" or "gateway" router, the router that connects your network to the outside world—the Autonomous System Boundary Router (ASBR).

Verifying OSPF Configuration

Router#**show ip protocol**	Displays parameters for all protocols running on the router
Router#**show ip route**	Displays a complete IP routing table
Router#**show ip ospf**	Displays basic information about OSPF routing processes
Router#**show ip ospf interface**	Displays OSPF info as it relates to all interfaces
Router#**show ip ospf interface fastethernet 0/0**	Displays OSPF information for interface fastethernet 0/0
Router#**show ip ospf border-routers**	Displays border and boundary router information
Router#**show ip ospf neighbor**	Lists all OSPF neighbors and their states
Router#**show ip ospf neighbor detail**	Displays a detailed list of neighbors
Router#**show ip ospf database**	Displays contents of the OSPF database
Router#**show ip ospf database nssa-external**	Displays NSSA external link states

Troubleshooting OSPF

Router#**clear ip route ***	Clears entire routing table, forcing it to rebuild
Router#**clear ip route a.b.c.d**	Clears specific route to network a.b.c.d
Router#**clear ip opsf counters**	Resets OSPF counters
Router#**clear ip ospf process**	Resets *entire* OSPF process, forcing OSPF to re-create neighbors, database, and routing table
Router#**debug ip ospf events**	Displays *all* OSPF events
Router#**debug ip ospf adjacency**	Displays various OSPF states and DR/BDR election between adjacent routers
Router#**debug ip ospf packets**	Displays OPSF packets

Configuration Example: Single Area OSPF

Figure 10-1 illustrates the network topology for the configuration that follows, which shows how to configure Single Area OSPF using commands covered in this chapter.

Figure 10-1   Network Topology for Single Area OSPF Configuration

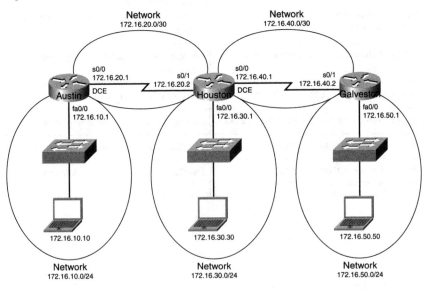

Austin Router

`Router>`**`enable`**	Moves to privileged mode.
`Router#`**`configure terminal`**	Moves to global configuration mode.
`Router(config)#`**`hostname Austin`**	Sets the host name.
`Austin(config)#`**`interface fastethernet 0/0`**	Moves to interface configuration mode.
`Austin(config-if)#`**`ip address 172.16.10.1 255.255.255.0`**	Assigns an IP address and netmask.
`Austin(config-if)#`**`no shutdown`**	Enables the interface.
`Austin(config-if)#`**`interface serial 0/0`**	Moves to interface configuration mode.
`Austin(config-if)#`**`ip address 172.16.20.1 255.255.255.252`**	Assigns an IP address and netmask.
`Austin(config-if)#`**`clock rate 56000`**	DCE cable plugged in this side.
`Austin(config-if)#`**`no shutdown`**	Enables the interface.
`Austin(config-if)#`**`exit`**	Returns to global configuration mode.
`Austin(config)#`**`router ospf 1`**	Starts OSPF process 1.
`Austin(config-router)#`**`network 172.16.10.0 0.0.0.255 area 0`**	Any interface with an address of 172.16.10.x is to be put into area 0.
`Austin(config-router)#`**`network 172.16.20.0 0.0.0.255 area 0`**	Any interface with an address of 172.16.20.x is to be put into area 0.
`Austin(config-router)#`**`<ctrl> z`**	Returns to privileged mode.
`Austin#`**`copy running-config startup-config`**	Saves the configuration to NVRAM.

Houston Router

Router>`enable`	Moves to privileged mode.
Router#`configure terminal`	Moves to global configuration mode.
Router(config)#`hostname Houston`	Sets the host name.
Houston(config)#`interface fastethernet 0/0`	Moves to interface configuration mode.
Houston(config-if)#`ip address 172.16.30.1 255.255.255.0`	Assigns an IP address and netmask.
Houston(config-if)#`no shutdown`	Enables the interface.
Houston(config-if)#`interface serial0/0`	Moves to interface configuration mode.
Houston(config-if)#`ip address 172.16.40.1 255.255.255.252`	Assigns an IP address and netmask.
Houston(config-if)#`clock rate 56000`	DCE cable plugged in this side.
Houston(config-if)#`no shutdown`	Enables the interface.
Houston(config)#`interface serial 0/1`	Moves to interface configuration mode.
Houston(config-if)#`ip address 172.16.20.2 255.255.255.252`	Assigns an IP address and netmask.
Houston(config-if)#`no shutdown`	Enables the interface.
Houston(config-if)#`exit`	Returns to global configuration mode.
Houston(config)#`router ospf 1`	Starts OSPF process 1.
Houston(config-router)#`network 172.16.0.0 0.0.255.255 area 0`	Any interface with an address of 172.16.$x.x$ is to be put into area 0. One statement will now advertise all three interfaces.
Houston(config-router)#`<ctrl> z`	Returns to privileged mode.
Houston#`copy running-config startup-config`	Saves the configuration to NVRAM.

Galveston Router

`Router>`**`enable`**	Moves to privileged mode.
`Router#`**`configure terminal`**	Moves to global configuration mode.
`Router(config)#`**`hostname Galveston`**	Sets the host name.
`Galveston(config)#`**`interface fastethernet 0/0`**	Moves to interface configuration mode.
`Galveston(config-if)#`**`ip address 172.16.50.1 255.255.255.0`**	Assigns an IP address and netmask.
`Galveston(config-if)#`**`no shutdown`**	Enables the interface.
`Galveston(config-if)#`**`interface serial 0/1`**	Moves to interface configuration mode.
`Galveston(config-if)#`**`ip address 172.16.40.2 255.255.255.252`**	Assigns an IP address and netmask.
`Galveston(config-if)#`**`no shutdown`**	Enables the interface.
`Galveston(config-if)#`**`exit`**	Returns to global configuration mode.
`Galveston(config)#`**`router ospf 1`**	Starts OSPF process 1.
`Galveston(config-router)#`**`network 172.16.40.2 0.0.0.0 area 0`**	Any interface with an exact address of 172.16.40.2 is to be put into area 0. This is the most precise way to place an exact address into the OSPF routing process.
`Galveston(config-router)#`**`network 172.16.50.1 0.0.0.0 area 0`**	Any interface with an exact address of 172.16.50.2 is to be put into area 0.
`Galveston(config-router)#`**`<ctrl> z`**	Returns to privileged mode.
`Galveston#`**`copy running-config startup-config`**	Saves the configuration to NVRAM.

Chapter 11   Configuring a Switch

Chapter 12   VLANs

Chapter 13   VLAN Trunking Protocol and Inter-VLAN Routing

Chapter 14   STP and EtherChannel

Configuring a Switch

This chapter provides information and commands concerning the following topics:

- Help commands
- Command modes
- Verifying commands
- Resetting switch configuration
- Setting host names
- Setting passwords
- Setting IP addresses and default gateways
- Setting interface descriptions
- Setting duplex operation
- Setting operation speed
- Managing the MAC address table
- Configuring static MAC addresses
- Switch port security
- Verifying switch port security
- Sticky MAC addresses
- Configuration example

Help Commands

`switch>?`	The **?** works here the same as in a router.

Command Modes

`switch>`**enable**	User mode, same as a router
`switch#`	Privileged mode
`switch#`**disable**	Leaves privileged mode
`switch>`**exit**	Leaves user mode

Verifying Commands

switch#**show version**	Displays information about software and hardware.
switch#**show flash:**	Displays information about flash memory (for the 2900/2950 series only).
switch#**show mac-address-table**	Displays the current MAC address forwarding table.
switch#**show controllers ethernet-controller**	Displays information about the Ethernet controller.
switch#**show running-config**	Displays the current configuration in DRAM.
switch#**show startup-config**	Displays the current configuration in NVRAM.
switch#**show post**	Displays whether the switch passed POST.
switch#**show vlan**	Displays the current VLAN configuration.
switch#**show interfaces**	Displays the interface configuration and status of line: up/up, up/down, admin down.
	NOTE: This command is unsupported in some Cisco IOS Software releases, such as 12.2(25)FX.
switch#**show interface vlan1**	Displays setting of virtual interface VLAN 1, the default VLAN on the switch.
	NOTE: This command is unsupported in some Cisco IOS Software releases, such as 12.2(25)FX.

Resetting Switch Configuration

Switch#**delete flash:vlan.dat**	Removes the VLAN database from flash memory.
Delete filename [vlan.dat]?	Press ⏎Enter.
Delete flash:vlan.dat? [confirm]	Reconfirm by pressing ⏎Enter.
Switch#**erase startup-config**	Erases the file from NVRAM.
<output omitted>	
Switch#**reload**	Restarts the switch.

Setting Host Names

Switch#**configure terminal**	Moves to global configuration mode.
Switch(config)#**hostname 2960Switch**	Creates a locally significant host name of the switch. This is the same command as the router.
2960Switch(config)#	

Setting Passwords

Setting passwords for the 2960 series switches is the same method as used for a router.

2960Switch(config)#**enable password cisco**	Sets the enable password to **cisco**
2960Switch(config)#**enable secret class**	Sets the encrypted secret password to **class**
2960Switch(config)#**line console 0**	Enters line console mode
2960Switch(config-line)#**login**	Enables password checking
2960Switch(config-line)#**password cisco**	Sets the password to **cisco**
2960Switch(config-line)#**exit**	Exits line console mode
2960Switch(config-line)#**line aux 0**	Enters line auxiliary mode

2960Switch(config-line)#**login**	Enables password checking
2960Switch(config-line)#**password cisco**	Sets the password to **cisco**
2960Switch(config-line)#**exit**	Exits line auxiliary mode
2960Switch(config-line)#**line vty 0 4**	Enters line vty mode for all five virtual ports
2960Switch(config-line)#**login**	Enables password checking
2960Switch(config-line)#**password cisco**	Sets the password to **cisco**
2960Switch(config-line)#**exit**	Exits line vty mode
2960Switch(config)#	

Setting IP Addresses and Default Gateways

2960Switch(config)#**interface vlan1**	Enters the virtual interface for VLAN 1, the default VLAN on the switch
2960Switch(config-if)#**ip address 172.16.10.2 255.255.255.0**	Sets the IP address and netmask to allow for remote access to the switch
2960Switch(config-if)#**exit**	
2960Switch(config)#**ip default-gateway 172.16.10.1**	Allows IP information an exit past the local network

TIP: For the 2960 series switches, the IP address of the switch is just that—the IP address for the *entire* switch. That is why you set the address in VLAN 1 (the default VLAN of the switch) and not in a specific Ethernet interface.

Setting Interface Descriptions

2960Switch(config)#**interface fastethernet 0/1**	Enters interface configuration mode
2960Switch(config-if)#**description Finance VLAN**	Adds a description of the interface

TIP: The 2960 series switches have either 12 or 24 Fast Ethernet ports named fa0/1, fa0/2, ... fa0/24—there is no fastethernet 0/0.

Setting Duplex Operation

`2960Switch2960Switch(config)#`**`interface fastethernet 0/1`**	Moves to interface configuration mode
`2960Switch(config-if)#`**`duplex full`**	Forces full-duplex operation
`2960Switch(config-if)#`**`duplex auto`**	Enables auto-duplex config
`2960Switch(config-if)#`**`duplex half`**	Forces half-duplex operation

Setting Operation Speed

`2960Switch(config)#`**`interface fastethernet 0/1`**	
`2960Switch(config-if)#`**`speed 10`**	Forces 10-Mbps operation
`2960Switch(config-if)#`**`speed 100`**	Forces 100-Mbps operation
`2960Switch(config-if)#`**`speed auto`**	Enables autospeed configuration

Managing the MAC Address Table

`switch#`**`show mac address-table`**	Displays current MAC address forwarding table
`switch#`**`clear mac address-table`**	Deletes all entries from current MAC address forwarding table
`switch#`**`clear mac address-table dynamic`**	Deletes only dynamic entries from table

Configuring Static MAC Addresses

`2960Switch(config)#`**`mac address-table static`** `aaaa.aaaa.aaaa` **`vlan 1 interface fastethernet 0/1`**	Sets a permanent address to port fastethernet 0/1 in VLAN 1

2960Switch(config)#**no mac address-table static** *aaaa.aaaa.aaaa* **vlan 1 interface fastethernet 0/1**	Removes the permanent address to port fastethernet 0/1 in VLAN 1

Switch Port Security

Switch(config)#**interface fastethernet 0/1**	Moves to interface configuration mode.
Switch(config-if)#**switchport port-security**	Enables port security on the interface.
Switch(config-if)#**switchport port-security maximum 4**	Sets a maximum limit of four MAC addresses that will be allowed on this port.
	NOTE: The maximum number of secure MAC addresses that you can configure on a switch is set by the maximum number of available MAC addresses allowed in the system.
Switch(config-if)#**switchport port-security mac-address 1234.5678.90ab**	Sets a specific secure MAC address 1234.5678.90ab. You can add additional secure MAC addresses up to the maximum value configured.
Switch(config-if)#**switchport port-security violation shutdown**	Configures port security to shut down the interface if a security violation occurs.
	NOTE: In shutdown mode, the port is errdisabled, a log entry is made, and manual intervention or errdisable recovery must be used to reenable the interface.
Switch(config-if)#**switchport port-security violation restrict**	Configures port security to restrict mode if a security violation occurs.

	NOTE: In restrict mode, frames from a nonallowed address are dropped, and a log entry is made. The interface remains operational.
`Switch(config-if)#switchport port-security violation protect`	Configures port security to protect mode if a security violation occurs.
	NOTE: In protect mode, frames from a nonallowed address are dropped, but no log entry is made. The interface remains operational.

Verifying Switch Port Security

`Switch#show port-security`	Displays security information for all interfaces
`Switch#show port-security interface fastethernet 0/5`	Displays security information for interface fastethernet 0/5
`Switch#show port-security address`	Displays MAC address table security information
`Switch#show mac address-table`	Displays the MAC address table
`Switch#clear mac address-table dynamic`	Deletes all dynamic MAC addresses
`Switch#clear mac address-table dynamic address` *aaaa.bbbb.cccc*	Deletes the specified dynamic MAC address
`Switch#clear mac address-table dynamic interface fastethernet 0/5`	Deletes all dynamic MAC addresses on interface fastethernet 0/5
`Switch#clear mac address-table dynamic vlan 10`	Deletes all dynamic MAC addresses on VLAN 10

Switch#**clear mac address-table notification**	Clears MAC notification global counters
	NOTE: Beginning with Cisco IOS Software Release 12.1(11)EA1, the **clear mac address-table** command (no hyphen in mac address) replaces the **clear mac-address-table** command (with the hyphen in mac-address). The **clear mac-address-table static** command (with the hyphen in mac-address) will become obsolete in a future release.

Sticky MAC Addresses

Sticky MAC addresses are a feature of port security. Sticky MAC addresses limit switch port access to a specific MAC address that can be dynamically learned, as opposed to a network administrator manually associating a MAC address with a specific switch port. These addresses are stored in the running configuration file. If this file is saved, the sticky MAC addresses do not have to be relearned when the switch is rebooted, and thus provide a high level of switch port security.

Switch(config)#**interface fastethernet 0/5**	Moves to interface configuration mode.
Switch(config-if)#**switchport port-security mac-address sticky**	Converts all dynamic port security learned MAC addresses to sticky secure MAC addresses.
Switch(config-if)#**switchport port-security mac-address sticky vlan 10 voice**	Converts all dynamic port security learned MAC addresses to sticky secure MAC addresses on voice VLAN 10.
	NOTE: The **voice** keyword is available only if a voice VLAN is first configured on a port and if that port is not the access VLAN.

Configuration Example

Figure 11-1 shows the network topology for the basic configuration of a 2960 series switch using commands covered in this chapter.

Figure 11-1   Network Topology for 2960 Series Switch Configuration

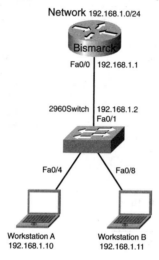

switch>**enable**	Enters privileged mode.
switch#**configure terminal**	Enters global configuration mode.
switch(config)#**no ip domain-lookup**	Turns off Domain Name System (DNS) queries so that spelling mistakes do not slow you down.
switch(config)#**hostname 2960**	Sets the host name.
2960(config)#**enable secret cisco**	Sets the encrypted secret password to **cisco**.
2960(config)#**line console 0**	Enters line console mode.
2960(config-line)#**logging synchronous**	Appends commands to a new line; router information will not interrupt.

`2960(config-line)#login`	User must log in to console before use.
`2960(config-line)#password switch`	Sets the password to **switch**.
`2960(config-line)#exec-timeout 0 0`	Console will never log out.
`2960(config-line)#exit`	Moves back to global configuration mode.
`2960(config)#line aux 0`	Moves to line auxiliary mode.
`2960(config-line)#login`	User must log in to auxiliary port before use.
`2960(config-line)#password class`	Sets the password to **class**.
`2960(config-line)#exit`	Moves back to global configuration mode.
`2960(config)#line vty 0 15`	Moves to configure all 16 vty ports at the same time.
`2960(config-line)#login`	User must log in to vty port before use.
`2960(config-line)#password class`	Sets the password to **class**.
`2960(config-line)#exit`	Moves back to global configuration mode.
`2960(config)#ip default-gateway 192.168.1.1`	Sets default gateway.
`2960(config)#interface vlan 1`	Moves to virtual interface VLAN 1 configuration mode.
`2960(config-if)#ip address 192.168.1.2 255.255.255.0`	Sets the IP address and netmask for switch.
`2960(config-if)#no shutdown`	Turns the virtual interface on.
`2960(config-if)#interface fastethernet 0/1`	Moves to interface configuration mode for fastethernet 0/1.

`2960(config-if)#`**`description Link to Bismarck`** **`Router`**	Sets a local description.
`2960(config-if)#`**`interface fastethernet 0/4`**	Moves to interface configuration mode for fastethernet 0/4.
`2960(config-if)#`**`description Link to`** **`Workstation A`**	Sets a local description.
`2960(config-if)#`**`switchport port-security`**	Activates port security.
`2960(config-if)#`**`switchport port-security`** **`maximum 1`**	Only one MAC address will be allowed in the MAC table.
`2960(config-if)#`**`switchport port-security`** **`violation shutdown`**	Port will be turned off if more than one MAC address is reported.
`2960(config-if)#`**`interface fastethernet 0/8`**	Moves to interface configuration mode for fastethernet 0/8.
`2960(config-if)#`**`description Link to`** **`Workstation B`**	Sets a local description.
`2960(config-if)#`**`switchport port-security`**	Activates port security.
`2960(config-if)#`**`switchport port-security`** **`maximum 1`**	Only one MAC address will be allowed in the MAC table.
`2960(config-if)#`**`switchport port-security`** **`violation shutdown`**	Port will be turned off if more than one MAC address is reported.
`2960(config-if)#`**`exit`**	Returns to global configuration mode.
`2960(config)#`**`exit`**	Returns to privileged mode.
`2960#`**`copy running-config startup-config`**	Saves the configuration to NVRAM.
`2960#`	

This chapter provides information and commands concerning the following topics:

- Creating static VLANs
  - Using VLAN configuration mode
  - Using VLAN database mode
- Assigning ports to VLANs
- Using the **range** command
- Verifying VLAN information
- Saving VLAN configurations
- Erasing VLAN configurations
- Configuration example: VLANs

Creating Static VLANs

Static VLANs occur when a switch port is manually assigned by the network administrator to belong to a VLAN. Each port is associated with a specific VLAN. By default, all ports are originally assigned to VLAN 1. You can create VLANs in two different ways:

- Using the VLAN configuration mode, which is the recommended way to create VLANs
- Using the VLAN database mode (which should not be used but is still available)

Using VLAN Configuration Mode

`Switch(config)#`**`vlan 3`**	Creates VLAN 3 and enters VLAN configuration mode for further definitions.
`Switch(config-vlan)#`**`name Engineering`**	Assigns a name to the VLAN. The length of the name can be from 1 to 32 characters.
`Switch(config-vlan)#`**`exit`**	Applies changes, increases the revision number by 1, and returns to global configuration mode.
`Switch(config)#`	

NOTE: This method is the only way to configure extended-range VLANs (VLAN IDs from 100 to 4094).

NOTE: Regardless of the method used to create VLANs, the VTP revision number is increased by 1 each time a VLAN is created or changed.

Using VLAN Database Mode

CAUTION: The VLAN database mode has been deprecated and will be removed in some future Cisco IOS Software release. It is recommended to use only VLAN configuration mode.

Switch#**vlan database**	Enters VLAN database mode.
Switch(vlan)#**vlan 4 name Sales**	Creates VLAN 4 and names it Sales. The length of the name can be from 1 to 32 characters.
Switch(vlan)#**vlan 10**	Creates VLAN 10 and gives it a name of VLAN0010 as a default.
Switch(vlan)#**apply**	Applies changes to the VLAN database and increases the revision number by 1.
Switch(vlan)#**exit**	Applies changes to the VLAN database, increases the revision number by 1, *and* exits VLAN database mode.
Switch#	

NOTE: You must apply the changes to the VLAN database for the changes to take effect. You must use either the **apply** command or the **exit** command to do so. Using the Ctrl-Z command to exit out of the VLAN database does not work in this mode because it aborts all changes made to the VLAN database—you must either use **exit** or **apply** and then the **exit** command.

Assigning Ports to VLANs

Switch(config)#**interface fastethernet 0/1**	Moves to interface configuration mode
Switch(config-if)#**switchport mode access**	Sets the port to access mode
Switch(config-if)#**switchport access vlan 10**	Assigns this port to VLAN 10

NOTE: When the **switchport mode access** command is used, the port operates as a nontrunking, single VLAN interface that transmits and receives nonencapsulated frames.

An access port can belong to only one VLAN.

Using the range Command

`Switch(config)#interface range fastethernet 0/1 - 9`	Enables you to set the same configuration parameters on multiple ports at the same time.
	NOTE: There is a space before and after the hyphen in the **interface range** command.
`Switch(config-if-range)#switchport mode access`	Sets ports 1–9 as access ports.
`Switch(config-if-range)#switchport access vlan 10`	Assigns ports 1–9 to VLAN 10.

Verifying VLAN Information

`Switch#show vlan`	Displays VLAN information
`Switch#show vlan brief`	Displays VLAN information in brief
`Switch#show vlan id 2`	Displays information about VLAN 2 only
`Switch#show vlan name marketing`	Displays information about VLAN named marketing only
`Switch#show interfaces vlan x`	Displays interface characteristics for the specified VLAN

Saving VLAN Configurations

The configurations of VLANs 1 through 1005 are always saved in the VLAN database. As long as the **apply** or the **exit** command is executed in VLAN database mode, changes are saved. If you are using VLAN configuration mode, the **exit** command saves the changes to the VLAN database, too.

If the VLAN database configuration is used at startup, and the startup configuration file contains extended-range VLAN configuration, this information is lost when the system boots.

If you are using VTP transparent mode, the configurations are also saved in the running configuration and can be saved to the startup configuration using the **copy running-config startup-config** command.

If the VTP mode is transparent in the startup configuration, and the VLAN database and the VTP domain name from the VLAN database matches that in the startup configuration file, the VLAN database is ignored (cleared), and the VTP and VLAN configurations in the startup configuration file are used. The VLAN database revision number remains unchanged in the VLAN database.

Erasing VLAN Configurations

Switch#**delete flash:vlan.dat**	Removes the entire VLAN database from flash.
	WARNING: Make sure there is *no* space between the colon (:) and the characters *vlan.dat*. You can potentially erase the entire contents of the flash with this command if the syntax is not correct. Make sure you read the output from the switch. If you need to cancel, press Ctrl-C to escape back to privileged mode: (Switch#) Switch#**delete flash:vlan.dat** Delete filename [vlan.dat]? Delete flash:vlan.dat? [confirm] Switch#
Switch(config)#**interface fastethernet 0/5**	Moves to interface configuration mode.
Switch(config-if)#**no switchport access vlan 5**	Removes port from VLAN 5 and reassigns it to VLAN 1—the default VLAN.
Switch(config-if)#**exit**	Moves to global configuration mode.
Switch(config)#**no vlan 5**	Removes VLAN 5 from the VLAN database.
Or	
Switch#**vlan database**	Enters VLAN database mode.
Switch(vlan)#**no vlan 5**	Removes VLAN 5 from the VLAN database.
Switch(vlan)#**exit**	Applies changes, increases the revision number by 1, and exits VLAN database mode.

NOTE: When you delete a VLAN from a switch that is in VTP server mode, the VLAN is removed from the VLAN database for all switches in the VTP domain. When you delete a VLAN from a switch that is in VTP transparent mode, the VLAN is deleted only on that specific switch.

NOTE: You cannot delete the default VLANs for the different media types: Ethernet VLAN 1 and FDDI or Token Ring VLANs 1002 to 1005.

CAUTION: When you delete a VLAN, any ports assigned to that VLAN become inactive. They remain associated with the VLAN (and thus inactive) until you assign them to a new VLAN. Therefore, it is recommended that you reassign ports to a new VLAN or the default VLAN before you delete a VLAN from the VLAN database.

Configuration Example: VLANs

Figure 12-1 illustrates the network topology for the configuration that follows, which shows how to configure VLANs using the commands covered in this chapter.

Figure 12-1   Network Topology for VLAN Configuration Example

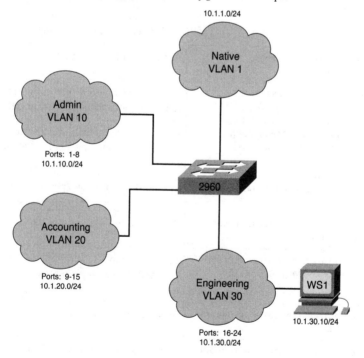

2960 Switch

`Switch>`**`enable`**	Moves to privileged mode.
`Switch#`**`configure terminal`**	Moves to global configuration mode.
`Switch(config)#`**`hostname 2960`**	Sets the host name.
`2960(config)#`**`vlan 10`**	Creates VLAN 10 and enters VLAN configuration mode.
`2960(config-vlan)#`**`name Admin`**	Assigns a name to the VLAN.
`2960(config-vlan)#`**`exit`**	Increases the revision number by 1 and returns to global configuration mode.
`2960(config)#`**`vlan 20`**	Creates VLAN 20 and enters VLAN configuration mode.
`2960(config-vlan)#`**`name Accounting`**	Assigns a name to the VLAN.
`2960(config-vlan)#`**`vlan 30`**	Creates VLAN 30 and enters VLAN configuration mode. Note that you do not have to exit back to global configuration mode to execute this command.
`2960(config-vlan)#`**`name Engineering`**	Assigns a name to the VLAN.
`2960(config-vlan)#`**`exit`**	Increases the revision number by 1 and returns to global configuration mode.
`2960(config)#`**`interface range fasthethernet 0/1 - 8`**	Enables you to set the same configuration parameters on multiple ports at the same time.
`2960(config-if-range)#`**`switchport mode access`**	Sets ports 1–8 as access ports.
`2960(config-if-range)#`**`switchport access vlan 10`**	Assigns ports 1–8 to VLAN 10.
`2960(config-if-range)#`**`interface range fastethernet 0/9 - 15`**	Enables you to set the same configuration parameters on multiple ports at the same time.
`2960(config-if-range)#`**`switchport mode access`**	Sets ports 9–15 as access ports.
`2960(config-if-range)#`**`switchport access vlan 20`**	Assigns ports 9–15 to VLAN 20.

`2960(config-if-range)#`**`interface`** **`range fastethernet 0/16 - 24`**	Enables you to set the same configuration parameters on multiple ports at the same time.
`2960(config-if-range)#`**`switchport`** **`mode access`**	Sets ports 16–24 as access ports.
`2960(config-if-range)#`**`switchport`** **`access vlan 30`**	Assigns ports 16–24 to VLAN 30.
`2960(config-if-range)#`**`exit`**	Returns to global configuration mode.
`2960(config)#`**`exit`**	Returns to privileged mode.
`2960#`**`copy running-config startup-`** **`config`**	Saves the configuration in NVRAM.

CHAPTER 13

VLAN Trunking Protocol and Inter-VLAN Routing

This chapter provides information and commands concerning the following topics:

- Dynamic Trunking Protocol (DTP)
- Setting the encapsulation type
- VLAN Trunking Protocol (VTP)
  - Using global configuration mode
  - Using VLAN database mode
- Verifying VTP
- Inter-VLAN communication using an external router: Router-on-a-stick
- Inter-VLAN communication tips
- Configuration example: Inter-VLAN communication

Dynamic Trunking Protocol (DTP)

`Switch (config)#interface fastethernet 0/1`	Moves to interface configuration mode.
`Switch(config-if) #switchport mode dynamic desirable`	Makes the interface actively attempt to convert the link to a trunk link.
	NOTE: With the **switchport mode dynamic desirable** command set, the interface becomes a trunk link if the neighboring interface is set to **trunk**, **desirable**, or **auto**.
`Switch(config-if) #switchport mode dynamic auto`	Makes the interface able to convert into a trunk link.
	NOTE: With the **switchport mode dynamic auto** command set, the interface becomes a trunk link if the neighboring interface is set to **trunk** or **desirable**.
`Switch(config-if) #switchport nonegotiate`	Prevents the interface from generating DTP frames.

	NOTE: Use the **switchport mode nonegotiate** command only when the interface switchport mode is **access** or **trunk**. You must manually configure the neighboring interface to establish a trunk link.
`Switch(config-if)` `#switchport mode trunk`	Puts the interface into permanent trunking mode and negotiates to convert the link into a trunk link.
	NOTE: With the **switchport mode trunk** command set, the interface becomes a trunk link even if the neighboring interface is not a trunk link.

TIP: The default mode is dependent on the platform. For the 2960, the default mode is dynamic auto.

TIP: On a 2960 switch, the default for all ports is to be an access port. However, with the default DTP mode being dynamic auto, an access port can be converted into a trunk port if that port receives DTP information from the other side of the link if that side is set to **trunk** or **desirable**. It is therefore recommended to hard-code all access ports as access ports with the **switchport mode access** command. This way, DTP information will not inadvertently change an access port to a trunk port. Any port set with the **switchport mode access** command ignores any DTP requests to convert the link.

Setting the Encapsulation Type

Depending on the series of switch that you are using, you might have a choice as to what type of VLAN encapsulation you want to use: the Cisco proprietary Inter-Switch Link (ISL) or the IEEE Standard 802.1q (dot1q). The 2960 switch supports only dot1q trunking.

`3560Switch(config)#interface` `fastethernet 0/1`	Moves to interface configuration mode
`3560Switch(config-if)` `#switchport mode trunk`	Puts the interface into permanent trunking mode and negotiates to convert the link into a trunk link
`3560Switch(config-if)` `#switchport trunk` `encapsulation isl`	Specifies ISL encapsulation on the trunk link
`3560Switch(config-if)` `#switchport trunk` `encapsulation dot1q`	Specifies 802.1q encapsulation on the trunk link

3560Switch(config-if) #**switchport trunk** **encapsulation negotiate**	Specifies that the interface negotiate with the neighboring interface to become either an ISL or dot1q trunk, depending on the capabilities or configuration of the neighboring interface

TIP: With the **switchport trunk encapsulation negotiate** command set, the preferred trunking method is ISL.

CAUTION: The 2960 series switch supports only dot1q trunking.

VLAN Trunking Protocol (VTP)

VTP is a Cisco proprietary protocol that allows for VLAN configuration (addition, deletion, or renaming of VLANs) to be consistently maintained across a common administrative domain.

Using Global Configuration Mode

Switch(config)#**vtp mode** **client**	Changes the switch to VTP client mode.
Switch(config)#**vtp mode** **server**	Changes the switch to VTP server mode.
Switch(config)#**vtp mode** **transparent**	Changes the switch to VTP transparent mode.
	NOTE: By default, all Catalyst switches are in server mode.
Switch(config)#**no vtp mode**	Returns the switch to the default VTP server mode.
Switch(config)#**vtp domain** *domain-name*	Configures the VTP domain name. The name can be from 1 to 32 characters long.
	NOTE: All switches operating in VTP server or client mode must have the same domain name to ensure communication.
Switch(config)#**vtp password** *password*	Configures a VTP password. In Cisco IOS Software Release 12.3 and later, the password is an ASCII string from 1 to 32 characters long. If you are using a Cisco IOS Software release earlier than 12.3, the password length ranges from 8 to 64 characters long.

	NOTE: To communicate with each other, all switches must have the same VTP password set.
`Switch(config)#`**`vtp v2-mode`**	Sets the VTP domain to Version 2. This command is for Cisco IOS Software Release 12.3 and later. If you are using a Cisco IOS Software release earlier than 12.3, the command is **vtp version 2**.
	NOTE: VTP Versions 1 and 2 are not interoperable. All switches must use the same version. The biggest difference between Versions 1 and 2 is that Version 2 has support for Token Ring VLANs.
`Switch(config)#`**`vtp pruning`**	Enables VTP pruning.
	NOTE: By default, VTP pruning is disabled. You need to enable VTP pruning on only 1 switch in VTP server mode.

NOTE: Only VLANs included in the pruning-eligible list can be pruned. VLANs 2 through 1001 are pruning eligible by default on trunk ports. Reserved VLANs and extended-range VLANs cannot be pruned. To change which eligible VLANs can be pruned, use the interface-specific **switchport trunk pruning vlan** command:

```
Switch(config-if)#switchport trunk pruning vlan remove 4, 20-30
! Removes VLANs 4 and 20-30
Switch(config-if)#switchport trunk pruning vlan except 40-50
! All VLANs are added to the pruning list except for 40-50
```

Using VLAN Database Mode

CAUTION: The VLAN database mode has been deprecated and will be removed in some future Cisco IOS release. Recommended practice dictates using only the VLAN configuration mode.

`Switch#`**`vlan database`**	Enters VLAN database mode.
`Switch(vlan)#`**`vtp client`**	Changes the switch to VTP client mode.
`Switch(vlan)#`**`vtp server`**	Changes the switch to VTP server mode.
`Switch(vlan)#`**`vtp transparent`**	Changes the switch to VTP transparent mode.
	NOTE: By default, all Catalyst switches are in server mode.

Switch(vlan)#**vtp domain domain-name**	Configures the VTP domain name. The name can be from 1 to 32 characters long.
	NOTE: All switches operating in VTP server or client mode must have the same domain name to ensure communication.
Switch(vlan)#**vtp password password**	Configures a VTP password. In Cisco IOS Software Release 12.3 and later, the password is an ASCII string from 1 to 32 characters long. If you are using a Cisco IOS release earlier than 12.3, the password length ranges from 8 to 64 characters long.
	NOTE: All switches must have the same VTP password set to communicate with each other.
Switch(vlan)#**vtp v2-mode**	Sets the VTP domain to Version 2. This command is for Cisco IOS Release 12.3 and later. If you are using a Cisco IOS release earlier than 12.3, the command is **vtp version 2**.
	NOTE: VTP Versions 1 and 2 are not interoperable. All switches must use the same version. The biggest difference between Versions 1 and 2 is that Version 2 has support for Token Ring VLANs.
Switch(vlan)#**vtp pruning**	Enables VTP pruning.
	NOTE: By default, VTP pruning is disabled. You need to enable VTP pruning on only one switch in VTP server mode.
	NOTE: Only VLANs included in the pruning-eligible list can be pruned. VLANs 2 through 1001 are pruning eligible by default on trunk ports. Reserved VLANs and extended-range VLANs cannot be pruned. To change which eligible VLANs can be pruned, use the interface-specific **switchport trunk pruning vlan** command: Switch(config-if)#**switchport trunk pruning vlan remove 4, 20-30** Removes VLANs 4 and 20 through 30. Switch(config-if)#**switchport trunk pruning vlan except 40-50** All VLANs are added to the pruning list except for 40 through 50.
Switch(vlan)#**exit**	Applies changes to the VLAN database, increases the revision number by 1, and exits back to privileged mode.

Verifying VTP

Switch#**show vtp status**	Displays general information about VTP configuration
Switch#**show vtp counters**	Displays the VTP counters for the switch

NOTE: If trunking has been established before VTP is set up, VTP information is propagated throughout the switch fabric almost immediately. However, because VTP information is advertised only every 300 seconds (5 minutes), unless a change has been made to force an update, it can take several minutes for VTP information to be propagated.

Inter-VLAN Communication Using an External Router: Router-on-a-Stick

Router(config)#**interface fastethernet 0/0**	Moves to interface configuration mode.
Router(config-if)#**duplex full**	Sets the interface to full duplex.
Router(config-if)#**no shutdown**	Enables the interface.
Router(config-if)#**interface fastethernet 0/0.1**	Creates subinterface 0/0.1 and moves to subinterface configuration mode.
Router(config-subif)#**description Management VLAN 1**	(Optional) Sets the locally significant description of the subinterface.
Router(config-subif) #**encapsulation dot1q 1 native**	Assigns VLAN 1 to this subinterface. VLAN 1 will be the native VLAN. This subinterface will use the 802.1q trunking protocol.
Router(config-subif)#**ip address 192.168.1.1 255.255.255.0**	Assigns the IP address and netmask.
Router(config-subif)#**interface fastethernet 0/0.10**	Creates subinterface 0/0.10 and moves to subinterface configuration mode.
Router(config-subif)#**description Accounting VLAN 10**	(Optional) Sets the locally significant description of the subinterface.
Router(config-subif) #**encapsulation dot1q 10**	Assigns VLAN 10 to this subinterface. This subinterface will use the 802.1q trunking protocol.

`Router(config-subif)#ip address` `192.168.10.1 255.255.255.0`	Assigns the IP address and netmask.
`Router(config-subif)#exit`	Returns to interface configuration mode.
`Router(config-if)#exit`	Returns to global configuration mode.
`Router(config)#`	

NOTE: The subnets of the VLANs are directly connected to the router. Routing between these subnets does not require a dynamic routing protocol. In a more complex topology, these routes need to either be advertised with whatever dynamic routing protocol is being used or be redistributed into whatever dynamic routing protocol is being used.

NOTE: Routes to the subnets associated with these VLANs appear in the routing table as directly connected networks.

Inter-VLAN Communication Tips

- Although most routers support both ISL and dot1q encapsulation, some switch models only support dot1q (the 2950 and 2960 series, for example).
- If you need to use ISL as your trunking protocol, use the command **encapsulation isl** *x*, where *x* is the number of the VLAN to be assigned to that subinterface.
- Recommended best practice is to use the same number of the VLAN number for the subinterface number. It is easier to troubleshoot VLAN 10 on subinterface fa0/0.10 than on fa0/0.2.
- The native VLAN (usually VLAN 1) cannot be configured on a subinterface for Cisco IOS Software releases that are earlier than 12.1(3)T. Native VLAN IP addresses therefore need to be configured on the physical interface. Other VLAN traffic is configured on subinterfaces:

```
Router(config)#interface fastethernet 0/0
Router(config-if)#encapsulation dot1q 1 native
Router(config-if)#ip address 192.168.1.1 255.255.255.0
Router(config-if)#interface fastethernet 0/0.10
Router(config-subif)#encapsulation dot1q 10
Router(config-subif)#ip address 192.168.10.1 255.255.255.0
```

Configuration Example: Inter-VLAN Communication

Figure 13-1 illustrates the network topology for the configuration that follows, which shows how to configure inter-VLAN communication using commands covered in this chapter. Some commands used in this configuration are from previous chapters.

Figure 13-1   Network Topology for Inter-VLAN Communication Configuration

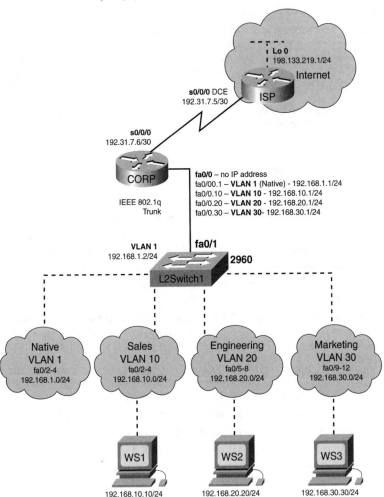

ISP Router

`Router>`**`enable`**	Moves to privileged mode
`Router>#`**`configure terminal`**	Moves to global configuration mode
`Router(config)#`**`hostname ISP`**	Sets the host name
`ISP(config)#`**`interface loopback 0`**	Moves to interface configuration mode
`ISP(config-if)#`**`description simulated address representing remote website`**	Sets the locally significant interface description
`ISP(config-if)#`**`ip address 198.133.219.1 255.255.255.0`**	Assigns the IP address and netmask
`ISP(config-if)#`**`interface serial 0/0/0`**	Moves to interface configuration mode
`ISP(config-if)#`**`description WAN link to the Corporate Router`**	Sets the locally significant interface description
`ISP(config-if)#`**`ip address 192.31.7.5 255.255.255.252`**	Assigns the IP address and netmask
`ISP(config-if)#`**`clock rate 56000`**	Assigns a clock rate to the interface—the DCE cable is plugged into this interface
`ISP(config-if)#`**`no shutdown`**	Enables the interface
`ISP(config-if)#`**`exit`**	Returns to global configuration mode
`ISP(config-if)#`**`router eigrp 10`**	Creates Enhanced Interior Gateway Routing Protocol (EIGRP) routing process 10
`ISP(config-router)#`**`network 198.133.219.0`**	Advertises directly connected networks (classful address only)
`ISP(config-router)#`**`network 192.31.7.0`**	Advertises directly connected networks (classful address only)
`ISP(config-router)#`**`no auto-summary`**	Disables auto summarization
`ISP(config-router)#`**`exit`**	Returns to global configuration mode
`ISP(config)#`**`exit`**	Returns to privileged mode
`ISP#`**`copy running-config startup-config`**	Saves the configuration to NVRAM

CORP Router

`Router>`**`enable`**	Moves to privileged mode.
`Router>#`**`configure terminal`**	Moves to global configuration mode.
`Router(config)#`**`hostname CORP`**	Sets the host name.
`CORP(config)#`**`no ip domain-lookup`**	Turns off Domain Name System (DNS) resolution to avoid wait time due to DNS lookup of spelling errors.
`CORP(config)#`**`interface serial 0/0/0`**	Moves to interface configuration mode.
`CORP(config-if)#`**`description link to ISP`**	Sets the locally significant interface description.
`CORP(config-if)#`**`ip address 192.31.7.6 255.255.255.252`**	Assigns the IP address and netmask.
`CORP(config-if)#`**`no shutdown`**	Enables the interface.
`CORP(config-if)#`**`exit`**	Returns to global configuration mode.
`CORP(config)#`**`interface fastethernet 0/0`**	Enters interface configuration mode.
`CORP(config-if)#`**`duplex full`**	Enables full-duplex operation to ensure trunking takes effect between here and L2Switch1.
`CORP(config-if)#`**`no shutdown`**	Enables the interface.
`CORP(config-if)#`**`interface fastethernet 0/0.1`**	Creates a virtual subinterface and moves to subinterface configuration mode.
`CORP(config-subif)#`**`description Management VLAN 1 - Native VLAN`**	Sets the locally significant interface description.
`CORP(config-subif)#`**`encapsulation dot1q 1 native`**	Assigns VLAN 1 to this subinterface. VLAN 1 will be the native VLAN. This subinterface will use the 802.1q trunking protocol.
`CORP(config-subif)#`**`ip address 192.168.1.1 255.255.255.0`**	Assigns the IP address and netmask.
`CORP(config-subif)#`**`interface fastethernet 0/0.10`**	Creates a virtual subinterface and moves to subinterface configuration mode.

`CORP(config-subif)#description` `Sales VLAN 10`	Sets the locally significant interface description.
`CORP(config-subif)#encapsulation` `dot1q 10`	Assigns VLAN 10 to this subinterface. This subinterface will use the 802.1q trunking protocol.
`CORP(config-subif)#ip address` `192.168.10.1 255.255.255.0`	Assigns the IP address and netmask.
`CORP(config-subif)#interface` `fastethernet 0/0.20`	Creates a virtual subinterface and moves to subinterface configuration mode.
`CORP(config-subif)#description` `Engineering VLAN 20`	Sets the locally significant interface description.
`CORP(config-subif)#encapsulation` `dot1q 20`	Assigns VLAN 20 to this subinterface. This subinterface will use the 802.1q trunking protocol.
`CORP(config-subif)#ip address` `192.168.20.1 255.255.255.0`	Assigns the IP address and netmask.
`CORP(config-subif)#interface` `fastethernet 0/0.30`	Creates a virtual subinterface and moves to subinterface configuration mode.
`CORP(config-subif)#description` `Marketing VLAN 30`	Sets the locally significant interface description.
`CORP(config-subif)#encapsulation` `dot1q 30`	Assigns VLAN 30 to this subinterface. This subinterface will use the 802.1q trunking protocol.
`CORP(config-subif)#ip add` `192.168.30.1 255.255.255.0`	Assigns the IP address and netmask.
`CORP(config-subif)#exit`	Returns to interface configuration mode.
`CORP(config-if)#exit`	Returns to global configuration mode.
`CORP(config)#router eigrp 10`	Creates EIGRP routing process 10 and moves to router configuration mode.
`CORP(config-router)#network` `192.168.1.0`	Advertises the 192.168.1.0 network.
`CORP(config-router)#network` `192.168.10.0`	Advertises the 192.168.10.0 network.
`CORP(config-router)#network` `192.168.20.0`	Advertises the 192.168.20.0 network.

CORP(config-router)#**network 192.168.30.0**	Advertises the 192.168.30.0 network.
CORP(config-router)#**network 192.31.7.0**	Advertises the 192.31.7.0 network.
CORP(config-router)#**no auto-summary**	Turns off automatic summarization at the classful boundary.
CORP(config-router)#**exit**	Returns to global configuration mode.
CORP(config)#**exit**	Returns to privileged mode.
CORP#**copy running-config startup-config**	Saves the configuration in NVRAM.

L2Switch1 (Catalyst 2960)

Switch>**enable**	Moves to privileged mode.
Switch#**configure terminal**	Moves to global configuration mode.
Switch(config)#**hostname L2Switch1**	Sets the host name.
L2Switch1(config)#**no ip domain-lookup**	Turns off DNS resolution.
L2Switch1(config)#**vlan 10**	Creates VLAN 10 and enters VLAN configuration mode.
L2Switch1(config-vlan)#**name Sales**	Assigns a name to the VLAN.
L2Switch1(config-vlan)#**exit**	Returns to global configuration mode.
L2Switch1(config)#**vlan 20**	Creates VLAN 20 and enters VLAN configuration mode.
L2Switch1(config-vlan)#**name Engineering**	Assigns a name to the VLAN.
L2Switch1(config-vlan)#**vlan 30**	Creates VLAN 30 and enters VLAN configuration mode. Note that you do not have to exit back to global configuration mode to execute this command.
L2Switch1(config-vlan)#**name Marketing**	Assigns a name to the VLAN.
L2Switch1(config-vlan)#**exit**	Returns to global configuration mode.

`L2Switch1(config)#interface range fastethernet 0/2 - 4`	Enables you to set the same configuration parameters on multiple ports at the same time.
`L2Switch1(config-if-range)#switchport mode access`	Sets ports 2–4 as access ports.
`L2Switch1(config-if-range)#switchport access vlan 10`	Assigns ports 2–4 to VLAN 10.
`L2Switch1(config-if-range)#interface range fastethernet 0/5 - 8`	Enables you to set the same configuration parameters on multiple ports at the same time.
`L2Switch1(config-if-range)#switchport mode access`	Sets ports 5–8 as access ports.
`L2Switch1(config-if-range)#switchport access vlan 20`	Assigns ports 5–8 to VLAN 20.
`L2Switch1(config-if-range)#interface range fastethernet 0/9 - 12`	Enables you to set the same configuration parameters on multiple ports at the same time
`L2Switch1(config-if-range)#switchport mode access`	Sets ports 9–12 as access ports.
`L2Switch1(config-if-range)#switchport access vlan 30`	Assigns ports 9–12 to VLAN 30.
`L2Switch1(config-if-range)#exit`	Returns to global configuration mode.
`L2Switch1(config)#interface fastethernet 0/1`	Moves to interface configuration mode.
`L2Switch1(config)#description Trunk Link to CORP Router`	Sets the locally significant interface description.
`L2Switch1(config-if)#switchport mode trunk`	Puts the interface into trunking mode and negotiates to convert the link into a trunk link
`L2Switch1(config-if)#exit`	Returns to global configuration mode.
`L2Switch1(config)#interface vlan 1`	Creates the virtual interface for VLAN 1 and enters interface configuration mode.

L2Switch1(config-if)#ip address 192.168.1.2 255.255.255.0	Assigns the IP address and netmask.
L2Switch1(config-if)#no shutdown	Enables the interface.
L2Switch1(config-if)#exit	Returns to global configuration mode.
L2Switch1(config)#ip default-gateway 192.168.1.1	Assigns the default gateway address.
L2Switch1(config)#exit	Returns to privileged mode.
L2Switch1#copy running-config startup-config	Saves the configuration in NVRAM.

This chapter provides information and commands concerning the following topics:

- Spanning Tree Protocol
  - Enabling Spanning Tree Protocol
  - Configuring the root switch
  - Configuring a secondary root switch
  - Configuring port priority
  - Configuring the path cost
  - Configuring the switch priority of a VLAN
  - Configuring STP timers
  - Verifying STP
  - Optional STP configurations
  - Changing the spanning-tree mode
  - Extended System ID
  - Enabling Rapid Spanning Tree
  - Troubleshooting Spanning Tree
  - Configuration example: STP
- EtherChannel
  - Interface modes in EtherChannel
  - Guidelines for configuring EtherChannel
  - Configuring Layer 2 EtherChannel
  - Verifying EtherChannel
  - Configuration example: EtherChannel

Spanning Tree Protocol

Enabling Spanning Tree Protocol

`Switch(config)#spanning-tree vlan 5`	Enables STP on VLAN 5
`Switch(config)#no spanning-tree vlan 5`	Disables STP on VLAN 5

NOTE: If more VLANs are defined in the VLAN Trunking Protocol (VTP) than there are spanning-tree instances, you can only have STP on 64 VLANs. If you have more than 128 VLANs, it is recommended that you use Multiple STP.

Configuring the Root Switch

`Switch(config)#`**`spanning-tree vlan 5`** **`root`**	Modifies the switch priority from the default 32768 to a lower value to allow the switch to become the root switch for VLAN 5.
	NOTE: If all other switches have extended system ID support, this switch resets its priority to 24576. If any other switch has a priority set to below 24576 already, this switch sets its own priority to 4096 *less* than the lowest switch priority. If by doing this the switch would have a priority of less than 1, this command fails.
`Switch(config)#`**`spanning-tree vlan`** **`5 root primary`**	Switch recalculates timers along with priority to allow the switch to become the root switch for VLAN 5.
	TIP: The root switch should be a backbone or distribution switch.
`Switch(config)#`**`spanning-tree vlan 5`** **`root primary diameter 7`**	Configures the switch to be the root switch for VLAN 5 and sets the network diameter to 7.
	TIP: The **diameter** keyword is used to define the maximum number of switches between any two end stations. The range is from 2 to 7 switches.
`Switch(config)#`**`spanning-tree vlan 5`** **`root primary hello-time 4`**	Configures the switch to be the root switch for VLAN 5 and sets the hello-delay timer to 4 seconds.
	TIP: The **hello-time** keyword sets the hello-delay timer to any amount between 1 and 10 seconds. The default time is 2 seconds.

Configuring a Secondary Root Switch

`Switch(config)#`**`spanning-tree vlan 5`** **`root secondary`**	Switch recalculates timers along with priority to allow the switch to become the root switch for VLAN 5 should the primary root switch fail.
	NOTE: If all other switches have extended system ID support, this switch resets its priority to 28672. Therefore, if the root switch fails, and all other switches are set to the default priority of 32768, this becomes the new root switch. For switches without extended system ID support, the switch priority is changed to 16384.
`Switch(config)#`**`spanning-tree vlan`** **`5 root secondary diameter 7`**	Configures the switch to be the secondary root switch for VLAN 5 and sets the network diameter to 7.
`Switch(config)#`**`spanning-tree vlan 5`** **`root secondary hello-time 4`**	Configures the switch to be the secondary root switch for VLAN 5 and sets the hello-delay timer to 4 seconds.

Configuring Port Priority

`Switch(config)#`**`interface`** **`gigabitethernet 0/1`**	Moves to interface configuration mode.
`Switch(config-if)#`**`spanning-tree`** **`port-priority 64`**	Configures the port priority for the interface that is an access port.
`Switch(config-if)#`**`spanning-tree`** **`vlan 5 port-priority 64`**	Configures the VLAN port priority for an interface that is a trunk port.
	NOTE: Port priority is used to break a tie when 2 switches have equal priorities for determining the root switch. The number can be between 0 and 255. The default port priority is 128. The lower the number, the higher the priority.

Configuring the Path Cost

Switch(config)#**interface gigabitethernet 0/1**	Moves to interface configuration mode.
Switch(config-if)#**spanning-tree cost 100000**	Configures the cost for the interface that is an access port.
Switch(config-if)#**spanning-tree vlan 5 cost 1000000**	Configures the VLAN cost for an interface that is a trunk port.
	NOTE: If a loop occurs, STP uses the path cost when trying to determine which interface to place into the forwarding state. A higher path cost means a lower speed transmission. The range of the **cost** keyword is 1 through 200000000. The default is based on the media speed of the interface.

Configuring the Switch Priority of a VLAN

Switch(config)#**spanning-tree vlan 5 priority 12288**	Configures the switch priority of VLAN 5 to 12288

NOTE: With the **priority** keyword, the range is 0 to 61440 in increments of 4096. The default is 32768. The lower the priority, the more likely the switch will be chosen as the root switch.

Only the following numbers can be used as a priority value:

0	4096	8192	12288
16384	20480	24576	28672
32768	36864	40960	45056
49152	53248	57344	61440

CAUTION: Cisco recommends caution when using this command. Cisco further recommends that the **spanning-tree vlan** *x* **root primary** or the **spanning-tree vlan** *x* **root secondary** command be used instead to modify the switch priority.

Configuring STP Timers

`Switch(config)#spanning-tree vlan 5 hello-time 4`	Changes the hello-delay timer to 4 seconds on VLAN 5
`Switch(config)#spanning-tree vlan 5 forward-time 20`	Changes the forward-delay timer to 20 seconds on VLAN 5
`Switch(config)#spanning-tree vlan 5 max-age 25`	Changes the maximum-aging timer to 25 seconds on VLAN 5

NOTE: For the **hello-time** command, the range is 1 to 10 seconds. The default is 2 seconds.

For the **forward-time** command, the range is 4 to 30 seconds. The default is 15 seconds.

For the **max-age** command, the range is 6 to 40 seconds. The default is 20 seconds.

CAUTION: Cisco recommends caution when using this command. Cisco further recommends that the **spanning-tree vlan** *x* **root primary** or the **spanning-tree vlan** *x* **root secondary** command be used instead to modify the switch timers.

Verifying STP

`Switch#show spanning-tree`	Displays STP information
`Switch#show spanning-tree active`	Displays STP information on active interfaces only
`Switch#show spanning-tree brief`	Displays a brief status of the STP
`Switch#show spanning-tree detail`	Displays a detailed summary of interface information
`Switch#show spanning-tree interface gigabitethernet 0/1`	Displays STP information for interface gigabitethernet 0/1
`Switch#show spanning-tree summary`	Displays a summary of port states
`Switch#show spanning-tree summary totals`	Displays the total lines of the STP section
`Switch#show spanning-tree vlan 5`	Displays STP information for VLAN 5

Optional STP Configurations

Although the following commands are not mandatory for STP to work, you might find these helpful to fine-tune your network.

PortFast

`Switch(config)#interface fastethernet 0/10`	Moves to interface configuration mode.
`Switch(config-if)#spanning-tree portfast`	Enables PortFast on an access port.
`Switch(config-if)#spanning-tree portfast trunk`	Enables PortFast on a trunk port.
	WARNING: Use the **portfast** command only when connecting a single end station to an access or trunk port. Using this command on a port connected to a switch or hub could prevent spanning tree from detecting loops.
	NOTE: If you enable the voice VLAN feature, PortFast is enabled automatically. If you disable voice VLAN, PortFast is still enabled.
`Switch#show spanning-tree interface fastethernet 0/10 portfast`	Displays PortFast information on interface fastethernet 0/10.

BPDU Guard

`Switch(config)#spanning-tree portfast bpduguard default`	Globally enables BPDU Guard.
`Switch(config)#interface range fastethernet 0/1 - 5`	Enters interface range configuration mode.
`Switch(config-if-range)#spanning-tree portfast`	Enables PortFast on all interfaces in the range.
	NOTE: By default, BPDU Guard is disabled.
`Switch(config)#errdisable recovery cause bpduguard`	Allows port to reenable itself if the cause of the error is BPDU Guard by setting a recovery timer.

`Switch(config)#errdisable recovery interval 400`	Sets recovery timer to 400 seconds. The default is 300 seconds. The range is from 30 to 86400 seconds.
`Switch#show spanning-tree summary totals`	Verifies whether BPDU Guard is enabled or disabled.
`Switch#show errdisable recovery`	Displays errdisable recovery timer information.

Changing the Spanning-Tree Mode

Different types of spanning tree can be configured on a Cisco switch. The options vary according to the platform:

- **Per-VLAN Spanning Tree (PVST)**—There is one instance of spanning tree for each VLAN. This is a Cisco proprietary protocol.
- **Per-VLAN Spanning Tree Plus (PVST+)**—Also Cisco proprietary. Has added extensions to the PVST protocol.
- **Rapid PVST+**—This mode is the same as PVST+ except that it uses a rapid convergence based on the 802.1w standard.
- **Multiple Spanning Tree Protocol (MSTP)**—IEEE 802.1s. Extends the 802.1w Rapid Spanning Tree (RST) algorithm to multiple spanning trees. Multiple VLANs can map to a single instance of RST. You cannot run MSTP and PVST at the same time.

`Switch(config)#spanning-tree mode mst`	Enables MSTP. This command is available only on a switch running the EI software image.
`Switch(config)#spanning-tree mode pvst`	Enables PVST. This is the default setting.
`Switch(config)#spanning-tree mode rapid-pvst`	Enables Rapid PVST+.

Extended System ID

Switch(config)#**spanning-tree extend system-id**	Enables extended system ID, also known as MAC address reduction.
	NOTE: Catalyst switches running software earlier than Cisco IOS Software Release 12.1(8) EA1 do not support the extended system ID.
Switch#**show spanning-tree summary**	Verifies extended system ID is enabled.
Switch#**show running-config**	Verifies extended system ID is enabled.

Enabling Rapid Spanning Tree

Switch(config)#**spanning-tree mode rapid-pvst**	Enables Rapid PVST+.
Switch(config)#**interface fastethernet 0/1**	Moves to interface configuration mode.
Switch(config-if)#**spannisng-tree link-type point-to-point**	Sets the interface to be a point-to-point interface.
	NOTE: By setting the link type to point to point, this means that if you connect this port to a remote port, and this port becomes a designated port, the switch negotiates with the remote port and transitions the local port to a forwarding state.
Switch(config-if)#**exit**	
Switch(config)#**clear spanning-tree detected-protocols**	
	NOTE: The **clear spanning-tree detected-protocols** command restarts the protocol-migration process on the switch if any port is connected to a port on a legacy 802.1D switch.

Troubleshooting Spanning Tree

Switch#**debug spanning-tree all**	Displays all spanning-tree debugging events
Switch#**debug spanning-tree events**	Displays spanning-tree debugging topology events
Switch#**debug spanning-tree backbonefast**	Displays spanning-tree debugging BackboneFast events
Switch#**debug spanning-tree uplinkfast**	Displays spanning-tree debugging UplinkFast event
Switch#**debug spanning-tree mstp all**	Displays all MST debugging events
Switch#**debug spanning-tree switch state**	Displays spanning-tree port state changes
Switch#**debug spanning-tree pvst+**	Displays PVST+ events

Configuration Example: STP

Figure 14-1 illustrates the network topology for the configuration that follows, which shows how to configure STP using commands covered in this chapter.

Figure 14-1   Network Topology for STP Configuration Example

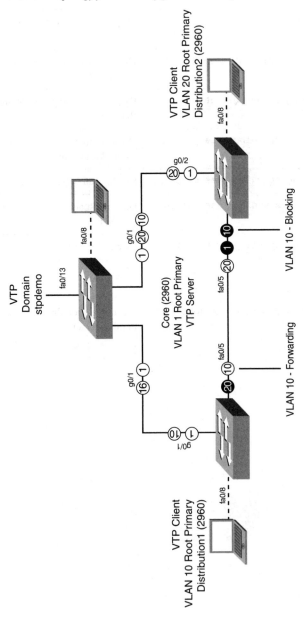

Core Switch (2960)

Switch>**enable**	Moves to privileged mode.
Switch#**configure terminal**	Moves to global configuration mode.
Switch(config)#**hostname Core**	Sets the host name.
Core(config)#**no ip domain-lookup**	Turns off Dynamic Name System (DNS) queries so that spelling mistakes do not slow you down.
Core(config)#**vtp mode server**	Changes the switch to VTP server mode. This is the default mode.
Core(config)#**vtp domain stpdemo**	Configures the VTP domain name to stpdemo.
Core(config)#**vlan 10**	Creates VLAN 10 and enters VLAN configuration mode.
Core(config-vlan)#**name Accounting**	Assigns a name to the VLAN.
Core(config-vlan)#**exit**	Returns to global configuration mode.
Core(config)#**vlan 20**	Creates VLAN 20 and enters VLAN configuration mode.
Core(config-vlan)#**name Marketing**	Assigns a name to the VLAN.
Core(config-vlan)#**exit**	Returns to global configuration mode.
Core(config)#**spanning-tree vlan 1 root primary**	Configures the switch to become the root switch for VLAN 1.
Core(config)#**exit**	Returns to privileged mode.
Core#**copy running-config startup-config**	Saves the configuration to NVRAM.

Distribution 1 Switch (2960)

Switch>**enable**	Moves to privileged mode.
Switch#**configure terminal**	Moves to global configuration mode.
Switch(config)#**hostname Distribution1**	Sets the host name.
Distribution1(config)#**no ip domain-lookup**	Turns off DNS queries so that spelling mistakes do not slow you down.

`Distribution1(config)#vtp domain stpdemo`	Configures the VTP domain name to stpdemo.
`Distribution1(config)#vtp mode client`	Changes the switch to VTP client mode.
`Distribution1(config)#spanning-tree vlan 10 root primary`	Configures the switch to become the root switch of VLAN 10.
`Distribution1(config)#exit`	Returns to privileged mode.
`Distribution1#copy running-config startup-config`	Saves the configuration to NVRAM.

Distribution 2 Switch (2960)

`Switch>enable`	Moves to privileged mode.
`Switch#configure terminal`	Moves to global configuration mode.
`Switch(config)#hostname Distribution2`	Sets the host name.
`Distribution2(config)#no ip domain-lookup`	Turns off DNS queries so that spelling mistakes do not slow you down.
`Distribution2(config)#vtp domain stpdemo`	Configures the VTP domain name to stpdemo.
`Distribution2(config)#vtp mode client`	Changes the switch to VTP client mode.
`Distribution2(config)#spanning-tree vlan 20 root primary`	Configures the switch to become the root switch of VLAN 20.
`Distribution2(config)#exit`	Returns to privileged mode.
`Distribution2#copy running-config startup-config`	Saves the configuration to NVRAM.

EtherChannel

EtherChannel provides fault-tolerant, high-speed links between switches, routers, and servers. An EtherChannel consists of individual Fast Ethernet or Gigabit Ethernet links bundled into a single logical link. If a link within an EtherChannel fails, traffic previously carried over that failed link changes to the remaining links within the EtherChannel.

Interface Modes in EtherChannel

Mode	Protocol	Description
On	None	Forces the interface into an EtherChannel without PAgP or LACP. Channel only exists if connected to another interface group also in On mode.
Auto	PAgP	Places the interface into a passive negotiating state—will respond to PAgP packets but will not initiate PAgP negotiation.
Desirable	PAgP	Places the interface into an active negotiating state—will send PAgP packets to start negotiations.
Passive	LACP	Places the interface into a passive negotiating state—will respond to LACP packets but will not initiate LACP negotiation.
Active	LACP	Places the interface into an active negotiating state—will send LACP packets to start negotiations.

Guidelines for Configuring EtherChannel

- PAgP is Cisco proprietary.
- LACP is defined in 802.3ad.
- You can combine from two to eight parallel links.
- All ports must be identical:
  - Same speed and duplex
  - Cannot mix Fast Ethernet and Gigabit Ethernet
  - Cannot mix PAgP and LACP
  - Must all be VLAN trunk or nontrunk operational status
- All links must be either Layer 2 or Layer 3 in a single channel group.
- To create a channel in PAgP, sides must be set to
  - Auto-Desirable
  - Desirable-Desirable
- To create a channel in LACP, sides must be set to
  - Active-Active
  - Active-Passive
- To create a channel without using PAgP or LACP, sides must be set to On-On.
- Do *not* configure a GigaStack gigabit interface converter (GBIC) as part of an EtherChannel.

- An interface that is already configured to be a Switched Port Analyzer (SPAN) destination port will not join an EtherChannel group until SPAN is disabled.
- Do *not* configure a secure port as part of an EtherChannel.
- Interfaces with different native VLANs cannot form an EtherChannel.
- When using trunk links, ensure all trunks are in the same mode—Inter-Switch Link (ISL) or dot1q.

Configuring Layer 2 EtherChannel

`Switch(config)#interface range fastethernet 0/1 - 4`	Moves to interface range configuration mode.
`Switch(config-if-range)#channel-protocol pagp`	Specifies the PAgP protocol to be used in this channel.
Or	
`Switch(config-if-range)#channel-protocol lacp`	Specifies the LACP protocol to be used in this channel.
`Switch(config-if-range)#channel-group 1 mode {desirable I auto I on I passive I active }`	Creates channel group 1 and assigns interfaces 01–04 as part of it. Use whichever mode is necessary, depending on your choice of protocol.

Verifying EtherChannel

`Switch#show running-config`	Displays list of what is currently running on the device
`Switch#show running-config interface fastethernet 0/12`	Displays interface fastethernet 0/12 information
`Switch#show etherchannel`	Displays all EtherChannel information
`Switch#show etherchannel 1 port-channel`	Displays port channel information
`Switch#show etherchannel summary`	Displays a summary of EtherChannel information
`Switch#show pagp neighbor`	Shows PAgP neighbor information
`Switch#clear pagp 1 counters`	Clears PAgP channel group 1 information
`Switch#clear lacp 1 counters`	Clears LACP channel group 1 information

Configuration Example: EtherChannel

Figure 14-2 illustrates the network topology for the configuration that follows, which shows how to configure EtherChannel using commands covered in this chapter.

Figure 14-2   Network Topology for EtherChannel Configuration

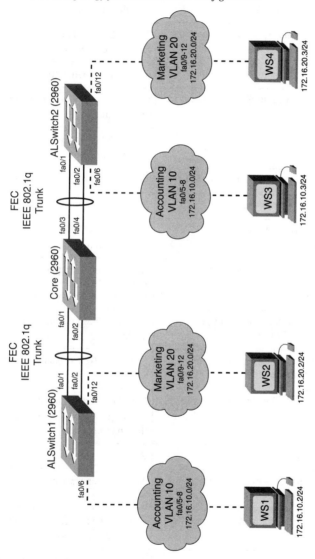

Core (2960)

`Switch>`**`enable`**	Moves to privileged mode
`Switch#`**`configure terminal`**	Moves to global configuration mode
`Switch(config)#`**`hostname Core`**	Sets the host name
`Core(config)#`**`no ip domain-lookup`**	Turns off DNS queries so that spelling mistakes do not slow you down
`Core(config)#`**`vtp mode server`**	Changes the switch to VTP server mode
`Core(config)#`**`vtp domain testdomain`**	Configures the VTP domain name to testdomain
`Core(config)#`**`vlan 10`**	Creates VLAN 10 and enters VLAN configuration mode
`Core(config-vlan)#`**`name Accounting`**	Assigns a name to the VLAN
`Core(config-vlan)#`**`exit`**	Returns to global configuration mode
`Core(config)#`**`vlan 20`**	Creates VLAN 20 and enters VLAN configuration mode
`Core(config-vlan)#`**`name Marketing`**	Assigns a name to the VLAN
`Core(config-vlan)#`**`exit`**	Returns to global configuration mode
`Core(config)#`**`interface range fastethernet 0/1 - 4`**	Moves to interface range configuration mode
`Core(config-if)#`**`switchport trunk encapsulation dot1q`**	Specifies 802.1q encapsulation on the trunk link
`Core(config-if)#`**`switchport mode trunk`**	Puts the interface into permanent trunking mode and negotiates to convert the link into a trunk link
`Core(config-if)#`**`exit`**	Returns to global configuration mode
`Core(config)#`**`interface range fastethernet 0/1 - 2`**	Moves to interface range configuration mode
`Core(config-if)#`**`channel-group 1 mode desirable`**	Creates channel group 1 and assigns interfaces 01–02 as part of it
`Core(config-if)#`**`exit`**	Moves to global configuration mode

Core(config)#**interface range fastethernet 0/3 - 4**	Moves to interface range configuration mode
Core(config-if)#**channel-group 2 mode desirable**	Creates channel group 2 and assigns interfaces 03–04 as part of it
Core(config-if)#**exit**	Moves to global configuration mode
Core(config)#**exit**	Moves to privileged mode
Core#**copy running-config startup-config**	Saves the configuration to NVRAM

ALSwitch1 (2960)

Switch>**enable**	Moves to privileged mode
Switch#**configure terminal**	Moves to global configuration mode
Switch(config)#**hostname ALSwitch1**	Sets the host name
ALSwitch1(config)#**no ip domain-lookup**	Turns off DNS queries so that spelling mistakes do not slow you down
ALSwitch1(config)#**vtp mode client**	Changes the switch to VTP client mode
ALSwitch1(config)#**vtp domain testdomain**	Configures the VTP domain name to testdomain
ALSwitch1(config)#**interface range fastethernet 0/5 - 8**	Moves to interface range configuration mode
ALSwitch1(config-if-range)#**switchport mode access**	Sets ports 5–8 as access ports
ALSwitch1(config-if-range)#**switchport access vlan 10**	Assigns ports to VLAN 10
ALSwitch1(config-if-range)#**exit**	Moves to global configuration mode
ALSwitch1(config)#**interface range fastethernet 0/9 - 12**	Moves to interface range configuration mode
ALSwitch1(config-if-range)#**switchport mode access**	Sets ports 9–12 as access ports
ALSwitch1(config-if-range)#**switchport access vlan 20**	Assigns ports to VLAN 20

`ALSwitch1(config-if-range)#exit`	Moves to global configuration mode
`ALSwitch1(config)#interface range fastethernet 0/1 - 2`	Moves to interface range configuration mode
`ALSwitch1(config-if-range)#switchport mode trunk`	Puts the interface into permanent trunking mode and negotiates to convert the link into a trunk link
`ALSwitch1(config-if-range)#channel-group 1 mode desirable`	Creates channel group 1 and assigns interfaces 01–02 as part of it
`ALSwitch1(config-if-range)#exit`	Moves to global configuration mode
`ALSwitch1(config)#exit`	Moves to privileged mode
`ALSwitch1#copy running-config startup-config`	Saves the configuration to NVRAM

ALSwitch2 (2960)

`Switch>enable`	Moves to privileged mode
`Switch#configure terminal`	Moves to global configuration mode
`Switch(config)#hostname ALSwitch2`	Sets the host name
`ALSwitch2(config)#no ip domain-lookup`	Turns off DNS queries so that spelling mistakes do not slow you down
`ALSwitch2(config)#vtp mode client`	Changes the switch to VTP client mode
`ALSwitch2(config)#vtp domain testdomain`	Configures the VTP domain name to testdomain
`ALSwitch2(config)#interface range fastethernet 0/5 - 8`	Moves to interface range configuration mode
`ALSwitch2(config-if-range)#switchport mode access`	Sets ports 5–8 as access ports
`ALSwitch2(config-if-range)#switchport access vlan 10`	Assigns ports to VLAN 10
`ALSwitch2(config-if-range)#exit`	Moves to global configuration mode

`ALSwitch2(config)#`**`interface range`** **`fastethernet 0/9 - 12`**	Moves to interface range configuration mode
`ALSwitch2(config-if-range)#`**`switchport`** **`mode access`**	Sets ports 9–12 as access ports
`ALSwitch2(config-if-range)#`**`switchport`** **`access vlan 20`**	Assigns ports to VLAN 20
`ALSwitch2(config-if-range)#`**`exit`**	Moves to global configuration mode
`ALSwitch2(config)#`**`interface range`** **`fastethernet 0/1 - 2`**	Moves to interface range configuration mode
`ALSwitch2(config-if-range)#`**`switchport`** **`mode trunk`**	Puts the interface into permanent trunking mode and negotiates to convert the link into a trunk link
`ALSwitch2(config-if-range)#`**`channel-`** **`group 1 mode desirable`**	Creates channel group 1 and assigns interfaces 01–02 as part of it.
`ALSwitch2(config-if-range)#`**`exit`**	Moves to global configuration mode
`ALSwitch2(config)#`**`exit`**	Moves to privileged mode
`ALSwitch2#`**`copy running-config`** **`startup-config`**	Saves the configuration to NVRAM

PART VI

Extending the LAN

Chapter 15   Implementing a Wireless LAN

Implementing a Wireless LAN

This chapter provides information and commands concerning the following topics:

- Wireless access point configuration: Linksys 300N access point
- Wireless client configuration: Linksys Wireless-N Notebook Adapter

  NOTE: This chapter contains information that is *not* part of the objective list of knowledge needed for passing the CCNA 640-901 certification exam. However, the Cisco Networking Academy Program has included these topics as part of its curriculum. Therefore, this chapter is provided to you as valuable reference information only—the configuration of a wireless access point or a wireless client is not evaluated on the CCNA certification exam.

Wireless Access Point Configuration: Linksys 300N Access Point

  NOTE: The wireless access point (AP) used in this chapter is the Linksys Wireless-N Broadband Router. If you are using a different AP, the screen captures shown here may differ.

  It is important to use the most up-to-date firmware or drivers. This is especially true for the 300N AP because the 802.11n technology is still in draft stage. Therefore, check the AP manufacturer website for available updates. In the case of Linksys, its website for updates is http://www.linksys.com/download.

Figure 15-1 shows the initial screen of the Setup Wizard, which runs automatically when you use the installation CD provided with the AP. Run the Setup Wizard on the computer before you plug in any cables to your AP or cable modem.

Figure 15-2 shows the license agreement for the device. After you have read the agreement, click **Next** to continue, or **Exit** to exit the setup program.

Figure 15-1 GUI Setup Wizard

Figure 15-2 License Agreement

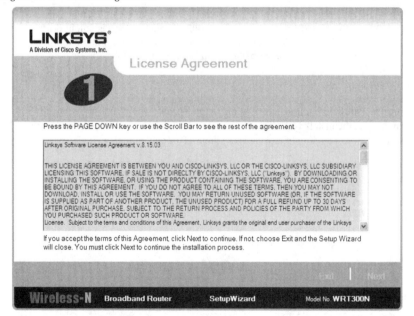

Figure 15-3 shows the wizard asking you to unplug the power from your modem. When you have finished, click **Next**.

Figure 15-3   Unplugging Power to the Modem

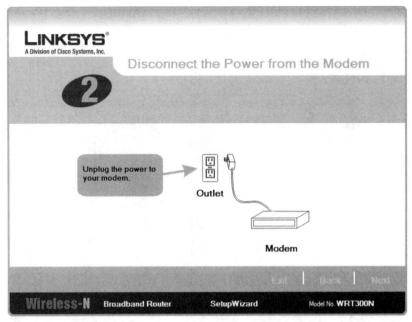

Figure 15-4 shows the wizard asking you to unplug the modem from your computer. When you have finished, click **Next**.

Figure 15-4   Disconnecting the Modem from the Computer

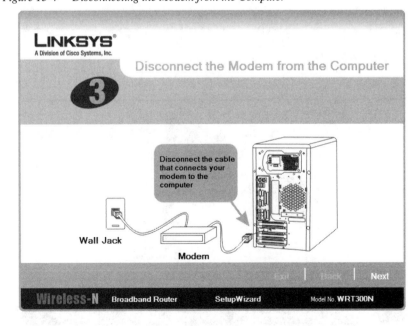

In the next screen, shown in Figure 15-5, the wizard directs you to connect the modem to the router.

Figure 15-5   Connect the Modem to the Router

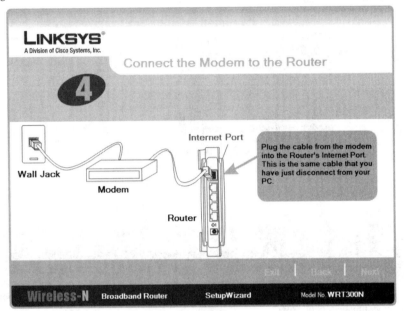

The screen in Figure 15-6 shows the wizard asking you to plug power back into the modem.

Figure 15-6   Connect the Power to the Modem

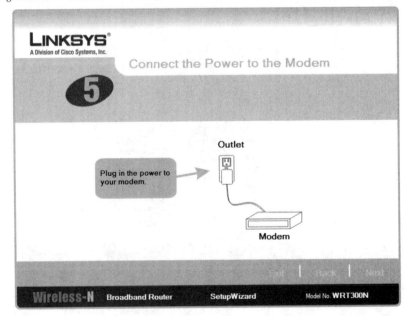

In the screens shown in Figure 15-7 and Figure 15-8, the wizard asks you to connect your router to a computer. To install this device correctly, you must have a wired connection to it. After this, you can configure the device to accept wireless clients.

The 300N has the RJ45 ports colored coded for ease of use—the port to connect to the modem is blue, and the four ports that you can use to connect to devices are yellow. Check with your device to make sure you are plugged into the correct ports.

Figure 15-7   Connect the Router to a Computer

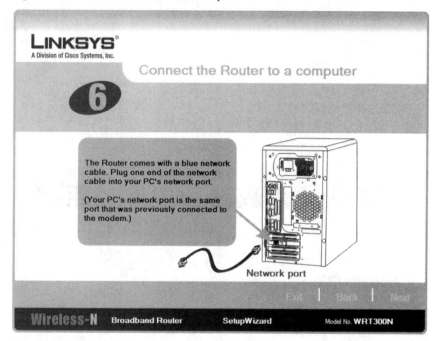

Now that you have wired the Linksys router to your computer and modem, connect the power cord to the router and plug it into the wall, as instructed in the screen shown in Figure 15-9.

Figure 15-8   Connect the Router to a Computer

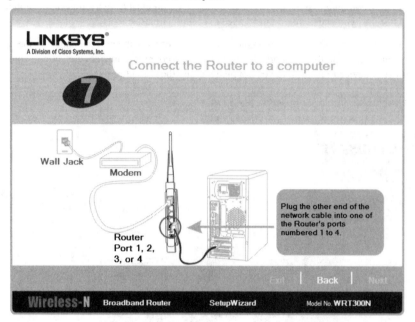

Figure 15-9   Power on the Router

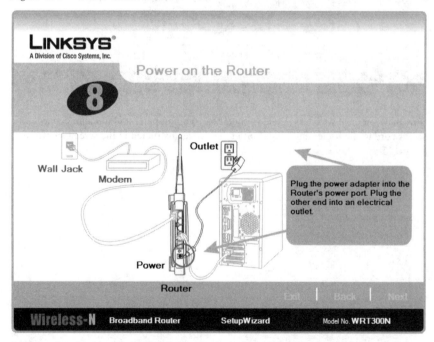

At this point, the wizard asks for you to check the status of the router to verify that the correct LEDs are lit. At this point, if you need to start over, or if you need to review your steps, you can click **Review instructions** from the screen in Figure 15-10 to start over. If not, click **Next** to continue. The Setup Wizard checks your computer settings, so you will see a timer bar appear over the top of the wizard, as shown in Figure 15-11.

Figure 15-10   Check the Router's Status

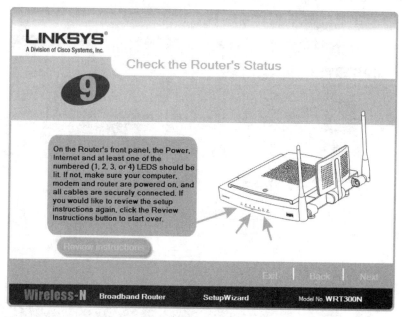

Figure 15-11   Checking Your Computer's Settings

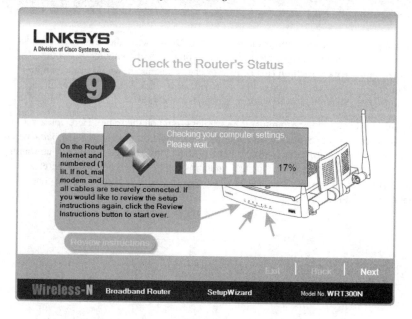

Next, you need to set up the different parameters of the router to connect different devices to it. The first parameter is DHCP. The screen in Figure 15-12 shows a few different options from which to select. If you are unsure about what to select, do not select anything. This example assumes that you are plugged into a cable modem, so you leave this setting at the default, Cable (DHCP).

Figure 15-12   Configure Cable or DHCP Settings

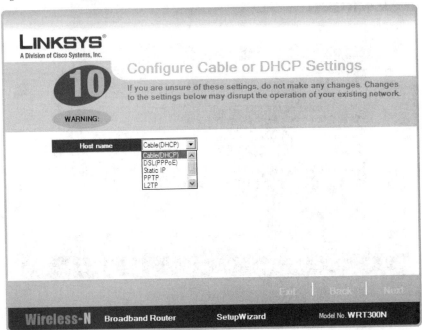

The next step is to set an administrative password. Do not leave the password at the default setting. If you want to have this password saved on the local computer, select the **Remember my password on this computer** check box, as shown on the screen in Figure 15-13. After you set and confirm the password, click **Next**. The router checks settings and then progresses to the next screen in the wizard.

Figure 15-14 shows the beginning of the wireless setup on the router. Here you are asked for the name of your wireless network and what channel you want to use. The name will be your service set identification (SSID), and this name must be used by any device wanting to connect to this AP. To ensure the least amount of interference from other wireless installations, limit your choices of channel number to 1, 6, or 11, because these channels do not overlap with each other.

Figure 15-13   Set the Router's Administrative Password

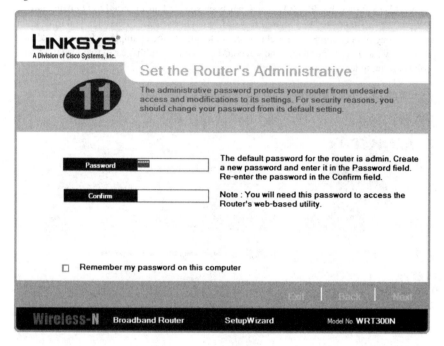

Figure 15-14   Wireless Settings

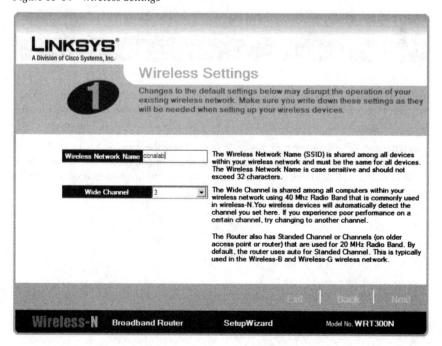

The next part of the wireless setup is to choose security settings. This part is optional. Figure 15-15 shows that PSK2 Personal has been selected, as opposed to not using any settings. PSK2 stands for Pre-Shared Key 2. If you choose PSK2 Personal, you must enter a shared key of between 8 and 63 characters in length. In the example in Figure 15-15, the shared key has letters, numbers, and keyboard characters—in this case, two exclamation points are included.

Figure 15-15   Configure Wireless Security Settings (Optional)

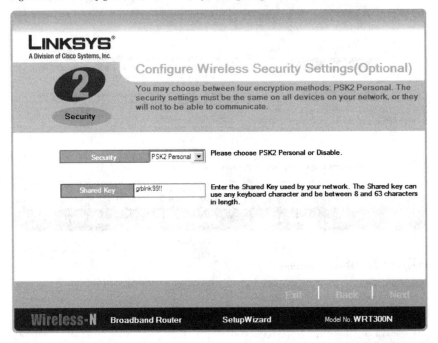

After you finish entering the wireless configuration, you will see the confirmation screen shown in Figure 15-16. If you want, you can save these settings to a text file by clicking the **Save Settings** button. After saving a copy of your settings, click **Yes** to continue.

This is the end of the Setup Wizard. You are presented with the screen in Figure 15-17, from which you can install Norton Internet Security on your computer if desired. If you choose not to install this, click **Finish** to exit the wizard; you will see the Congratulations screen shown in Figure 15-18.

Figure 15-16   Confirm New Settings

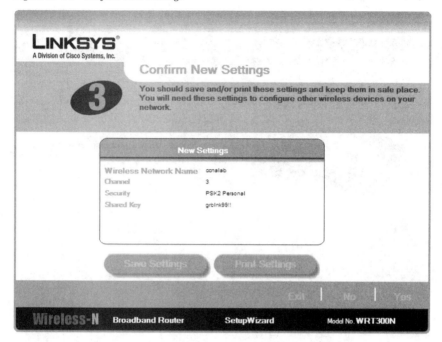

Figure 15-17   Option to Install Norton Internet Security

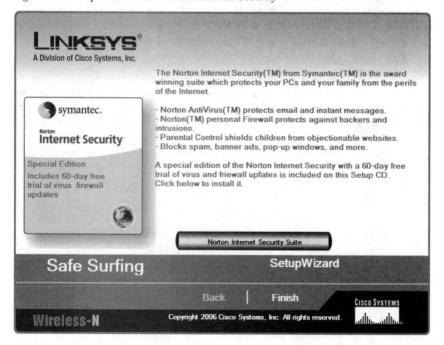

Figure 15-18   End of Wizard

After you have completed the Setup Wizard, you can use your Internet browser to connect to the AP for management of the device. The default IP address is 192.168.1.1. Enter this address in the address bar of your browser, and you will be prompted for a username and password—the ones you set previously. Figure 15-19 shows the username/password challenge window, and Figure 15-20 shows the main screen of the Linksys web-based management utility.

Figure 15-21 shows the menu bar present in the web-based management utility. Selecting any one of the main items—Setup, Wireless, Security, Access Restrictions, Applications & Gaming, Administration, Status—will take you to a new screen with submenus for additional management tasks. In Figure 15-21, the main button, Setup, has been selected, and there are four screens that can be chosen: Basic Setup, DDNS, MAC Address Clone, or Advanced Routing.

Figure 15-19   Username/Password Challenge

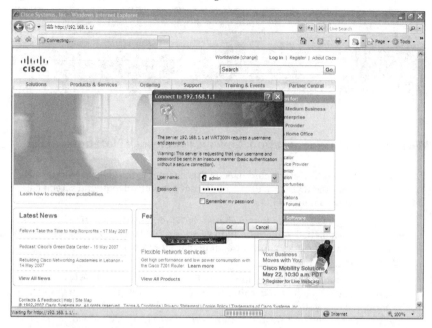

Figure 15-20   Main Screen of Web-Based Management Utility

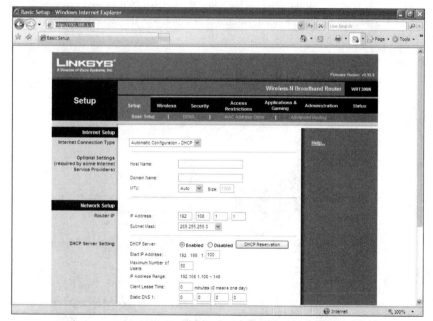

Figure 15-21 Web-Based Management Utility Menu Bar

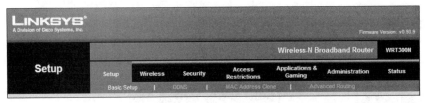

Wireless Client Configuration: Linksys Wireless-N Notebook Adapter

NOTE: The wireless client card used in this chapter is the Linksys Wireless-N Notebook Adapter. If you are using a different network adapter, the screen captures shown here might differ.

The operating system used in this chapter is Windows XP Professional, with Service Pack 2 installed. If you are running Windows 2000, refer to the Linksys Quick Start Handout that came with your adapter card for instructions on installing the adapter card.

It is important to use the most up-to-date firmware or drivers. This is especially true for the 300N client card because the 802.11n technology is still in draft stage. Therefore, check your client card's website for available updates. In the case of Linksys, its website for updates is http://www.linksys.com/download.

Figure 15-22 shows the initial screen of the Setup Wizard, which runs automatically when you use the installation CD provided with the client card. Run the Setup Wizard on the computer before you plug in your client card to the PC.

Figure 15-22 GUI Setup Wizard

Figure 15-23 shows the license agreement for the device. After you have read the agreement, click on **Next** to continue, or **Cancel** to exit the setup program.

Figure 15-23   License Agreement

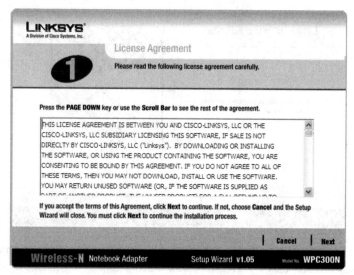

The Setup Wizard then installs some files onto your computer. A window might appear saying that this software has not passed Windows Logo Testing, as shown in Figure 15-24. Click **Continue Anyway** to continue with the setup.

Figure 15-24   Software Installation

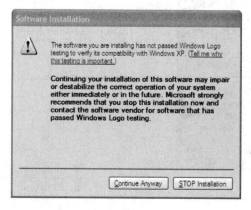

Figure 15-25 shows the next screen of the Setup Wizard, in which you are asked to insert the adapter into either the PCMCIA or CardBus slot of your PC. Insert the card, and then click **Next**.

Figure 15-25   Connecting the Adapter

A Found New Hardware Wizard pop-up window will appear, as shown in Figure 15-26. Select **Yes, this time only** to the question "Can Windows connect to Windows Update to search for software?" Then click **Next** to continue.

Figure 15-26   Found New Hardware Wizard

Figure 15-27 is the second screen of the Found New Hardware Wizard. Because you want to install the software automatically for this adapter, you only have to click the **Next** button, because that option is already highlighted in the wizard.

Figure 15-27   Found New Hardware Wizard Second Screen

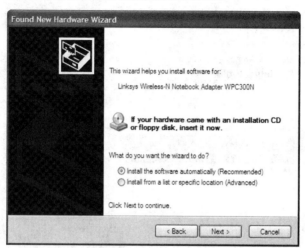

A window may appear saying that this software has not passed Windows Logo Testing, as shown previously in Figure 15-24. Click **Continue Anyway** to continue with the setup. After the files have been successfully copied onto your hard drive, and the drivers have been installed, the last screen of the Found New Hardware Wizard appears, as shown in Figure 15-28. Click **Finish** to exit the wizard.

Figure 15-28   Completing the Found New Hardware Wizard

The next screen is the Creating a Profile screen, shown in Figure 15-29. Here you should see all the available networks to which you can connect. If you do not see your network listed, click the **Refresh** button. The network named lander78 in this screen shot is a neighbor's network. Notice that his security is disabled.

Figure 15-29   Creating a Profile: Available Wireless Networks

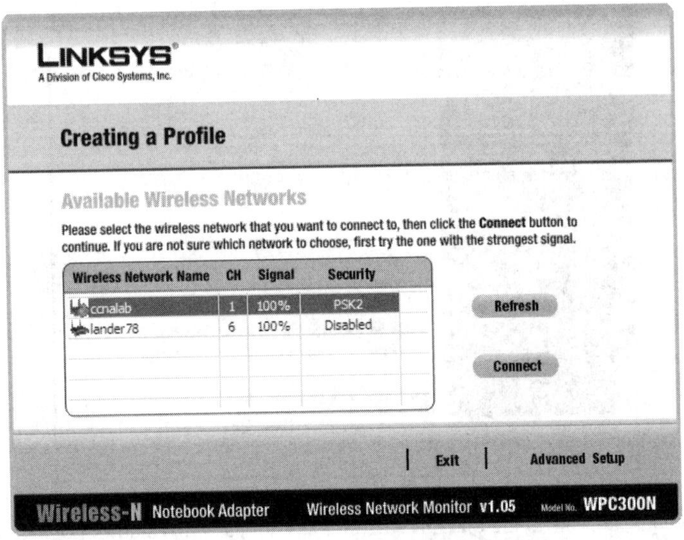

Because you set up security on the AP earlier in this chapter, you see the pop-up warning shown in Figure 15-30. To connect to this network, you must enter your security settings—the same settings you configured on the AP earlier in this chapter. Figure 15-31 shows the screen in which you enter the pre-shared key: grblnk99!!. Continue by clicking the **Connect** button.

Figure 15-30   Security Warning

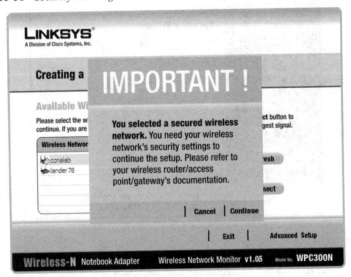

Figure 15-31   Security Connection

WPA2-Personal Needed for Connection

This wireless network has PSK2 enabled. To connect to this network, enter the required Pre-Shared Key in the appropriate field below. Then click the **Connect** button.

| Security | PSK2 | Please select the wireless security method used by your existing wireless network. |

| Pre-shared Key | grblnk99!! | Please enter a Pre-shared Key that is 8 to 63 characters in length. |

| Cancel | Connect

After connecting to your network, you will see the final screen of the wizard, the Congratulations screen, shown in Figure 15-32. Click **Finish** to end the wizard.

Figure 15-32   Congratulations: End of Wizard

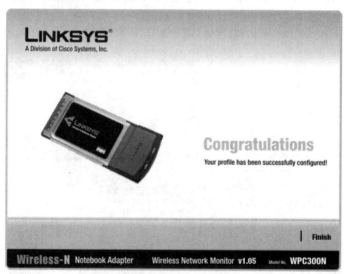

Congratulations

Your profile has been successfully configured!

| Finish

Wireless-N Notebook Adapter   Wireless Network Monitor **v1.05**   Model No. **WPC300N**

Figure 15-33 shows that the connection to the network is strong—you have solid signal strength and solid link quality. Signal strength is a measurement of the overall connection between the client and the AP. Link quality is a measurement of bandwidth after removing any noise/interference.

Figure 15-33   Link Information

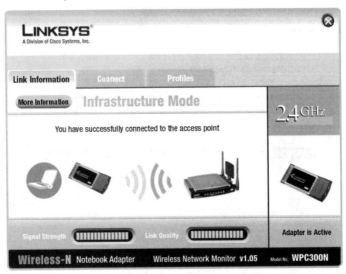

From the screen shown in Figure 15-33, you can also choose to go to two other screens:

- **Connect**—Displays a list of available networks to join (see Figure 15-34)
- **Profile**—Displays the profiles created for this adapter (see Figure 15-35)

Figure 15-34   Connect Screen

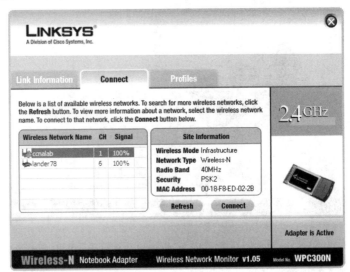

Figure 15-35   Profiles Screen

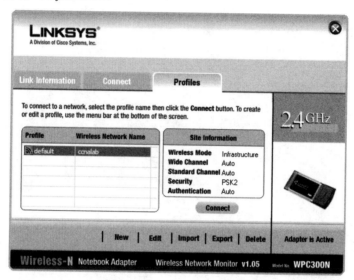

Figure 15-36 shows the status of your wireless connection. In this case, it is Connection 2 because a built-in wireless adapter on this laptop is Connection 1. Note that with the draft 802.11n technology, the connection achieves a speed of 216 Mbps in the local LAN.

Figure 15-36   Wireless Network Connection Status

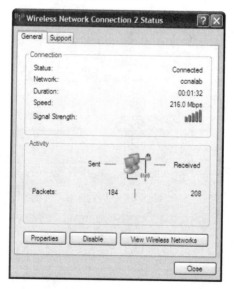

Chapter 16   Backing Up and Restoring Cisco IOS Software and Configurations

Chapter 17   Password Recovery Procedures and the Configuration Register

Chapter 18   Cisco Discovery Protocol (CDP)

Chapter 19   Telnet and SSH

Chapter 20   The ping and traceroute Commands

Chapter 21   SNMP and Syslog

Chapter 22   Basic Troubleshooting

Backing Up and Restoring Cisco IOS Software and Configurations

This chapter provides information and commands concerning the following topics:

- Boot system commands
- The Cisco IOS File System
- Backing up configurations to a TFTP server
- Restoring configurations from a TFTP server
- Backing up the Cisco IOS Software to a TFTP server
- Restoring/upgrading the Cisco IOS Software from a TFTP server
- Restoring the Cisco IOS Software from ROM Monitor mode using Xmodem
- Restoring the Cisco IOS Software using the ROM Monitor environmental variables and **tftpdnld** command

Boot System Commands

Router(config)#**boot system flash** *image-name*	Loads the Cisco IOS Software with *image-name*.
Router(config)#**boot system tftp** *image-name* **172.16.10.3**	Loads the Cisco IOS Software with *image-name* from a TFTP server.
Router(config)#**boot system rom**	Loads the Cisco IOS Software from ROM.
Router(config)#**exit**	
Router#**copy running-config startup-config**	Saves the running configuration to NVRAM. The router will execute commands in their order on the next reload.

If you enter **boot system flash** first, that is the first place the router will go to look for the Cisco IOS Software. If you want to go to a TFTP server first, make sure that the **boot system tftp** command is the first one you enter.

The Cisco IOS File System

NOTE: The Cisco IOS File System (IFS) provides a single interface to all the file systems available on a routing device, including the flash memory file system; network file systems such as TFTP, Remote Copy Protocol (RCP), and File Transfer Protocol (FTP); and any other endpoint for reading and writing data, such as NVRAM, or the running configuration.

The Cisco IFS minimizes the required prompting for many commands. Instead of entering in an EXEC-level **copy** command and then having the system prompt you for more information, you can enter a single command on one line with all necessary information.

Cisco IOS Software Commands	IFS Commands
`copy tftp running-config`	`copy tftp: system:running-config`
`copy tftp startup-config`	`copy tftp: nvram:startup-config`
`show startup-config`	`more nvram:startup-config`
`erase startup-config`	`erase nvram:`
`copy running-config startup-config`	`copy system:running-config nvram:startup-config`
`copy running-config tftp`	`copy system:running-config tftp:`
`show running-config`	`more system:running-config`

Backing Up Configurations to a TFTP Server

`Denver#copy running-config startup-config`	Saves the running configuration from DRAM to NVRAM (locally).
`Denver#copy running-config tftp`	Copies the running configuration to the remote TFTP server.
`Address or name of remote host[ ]?` `192.168.119.20`	The IP address of the TFTP server.

Destination Filename [Denver-confg]?⏎Enter	The name to use for the file saved on the TFTP server.
!!!!!!!!!!!!!!!	Each bang symbol (!) = 1 datagram of data.
624 bytes copied in 7.05 secs	
Denver#	File has been transferred successfully.

NOTE: You can also use the preceding sequence for a **copy startup-config tftp** command sequence.

Restoring Configurations from a TFTP Server

Denver#**copy tftp running-config**	Copies the configuration file from the TFTP server to DRAM.
Address or name of remote host[ ]? 192.168.119.20	The IP address of the TFTP server.
Source filename [ ]?Denver-confg	Enter the name of the file you want to retrieve.
Destination filename [running-config]? ⏎Enter	
Accessing tftp://192.168.119.20/Denver-confg…	
Loading Denver-confg from 192.168.119.02 (via Fast Ethernet 0/0):	
!!!!!!!!!!!!!!	
[OK-624 bytes]	
624 bytes copied in 9.45 secs	
Denver#	File has been transferred successfully.

NOTE: You can also use the preceding sequence for a **copy tftp startup-config** command sequence.

Backing Up the Cisco IOS Software to a TFTP Server

Denver#`copy flash tftp`	
Source filename [ ]? **c2600-js-1_121-3.bin**	Name of the Cisco IOS Software image.
Address or name of remote host [ ]? **192.168.119.20**	The address of the TFTP server.
Destination filename [c2600-js-1_121-3.bin]? 〔↵Enter〕	The destination filename is the same as the source filename, so just press 〔↵Enter〕.
!! !!!	
8906589 bytes copied in 263.68 seconds	
Denver#	

Restoring/Upgrading the Cisco IOS Software from a TFTP Server

Denver#`copy tftp flash`	
Address or name of remote host [ ]? **192.168.119.20**	
Source filename [ ]? **c2600-js-1_121-3.bin**	
Destination filename [c2600-js-1_121-3.bin]? 〔↵Enter〕	
Accessing tftp://192.168.119.20/c2600-js-1_121-3.bin	
Erase flash: before copying? [confirm] 〔↵Enter〕	If flash memory is full, erase it first.
Erasing the flash file system will remove all files	
Continue? [confirm] 〔↵Enter〕	Press 〔Ctrl〕-〔C〕 if you want to cancel.

`Erasing device  eeeeeeeeeeeeeeeeee...erased`	Each *e* represents data being erased.
`Loading c2600-js-l_121-3.bin from` `192.168.119.20`	

`    (via) FastEthernet 0/0):`
`!!!!!!!!!!!!!!!!!!!!!!!!!!!!!!!!!!!!!!!!!!!!!!!`
`!!!!!!!!!!!!!!!!!!!!!!!!!!!!!!!!!!!!!!!!!!!!!!!`
`!!!`
	Each bang symbol (!) = 1 datagram of data.

`Verifying Check sum ............... OK`	
`[OK - 8906589 Bytes]`	
`8906589 bytes copied in 277.45 secs`	
`Denver#`	Success.

Restoring the Cisco IOS Software from ROM Monitor Mode Using Xmodem

The output that follows was taken from a 1720 router. Some of this output might vary from yours, depending on the router model that you are using.

`rommon 1 >confreg`	Shows the configuration summary. Step through the questions, answering defaults until you can change the console baud rate. Change it to **115200**; it makes transfer go faster.

`    Configuration Summary`
`enabled are:`
`load rom after netboot fails`
`console baud: 9600`
`boot: image specified by the boot system`
`commands`
`        or default to: cisco2-c1700`	

do you wish to change the configuration? y/n [n]: **y** enable "diagnostic mode"? y/n [n]: **n** enable "use net in IP bcast address"? y/n [n]: **n** disable "load rom after netboot fails"? y/n [n]: **n** enable "use all zero broadcast"? y/n [n]: **n** enable "break/abort has effect"? y/n [n]: **n** enable "ignore system config info"? y/n [n]: **n** change console baud rate? y/n [n]: **y** enter rate: 0=9600, 1=4800, 2=1200, 3=2400 4=19200, 5=38400, 6=57600, 7=115200 [0]: **7** change the boot characteristics? y/n [n]: **n**	Prompts begin to ask a series of questions that allow you to change the configuration register. Answer **n** to all questions except the one that asks you to change the console baud rate. For the enter rate, choose **7** because that is the number that represents a baud rate of 115200.
Configuration Summary enabled are: load rom after netboot fails console baud: 115200 boot: image specified by the boot system commands or default to: cisco2-c1700 do you wish to change the configuration? y/n [n]: **n** rommon2>	After the summary is shown again, choose **n** to not change the configuration and go to the rommon> prompt again.
rommon 2>**reset**	Reloads the router at the new com speed. Change the HyperTerminal setting to **115200** to match the router's new console setting.
Rommon 1>**xmodem c1700-js-l_121-3.bin**	Asking to transfer this image using Xmodem.
...<output cut>...	

`Do you wish to continue? y/n [n ]:y`	Choose **y** to continue.
	In HyperTerminal, go to Transfer, then Send File (see Figure 16-1). Locate the Cisco IOS Software file on the hard drive and click **Send** (see Figure 16-2).
Router will reload when transfer is completed.	
Reset baud rate on router.	
`Router(config)#line con 0`	
`Router(config-line)#speed 9600`	
`Router(config-line)#exit`	HyperTerminal will stop responding. Reconnect to the router using 9600 baud, 8-N-1.

Figure 16-1   Finding the Cisco IOS Software Image File

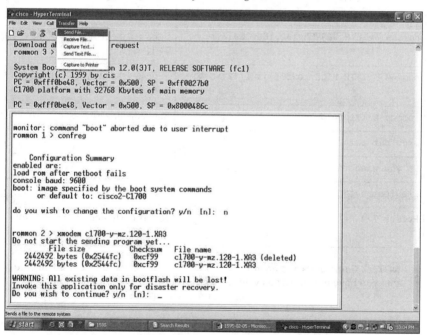

Figure 16-2   Sending the Cisco IOS Software Image File to the Router

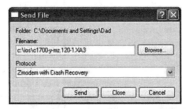

Restoring the Cisco IOS Software Using the ROM Monitor Environmental Variables and tftpdnld Command

rommon 1>IP_ADDRESS=192.168.100.1	Indicates the IP address for this unit.
rommon 2>IP_SUBNET_MASK=255.255.255.0	Indicates the subnet mask for this unit.
rommon 3>DEFAULT_GATEWAY=192.168.100.1	Indicates the default gateway for this unit.
rommon 4>TFTP_SERVER=192.168.100.2	Indicates the IP address of the TFTP server.
rommon 5>TFTP_FILE= c2600-js-l_121-3.bin	Indicates the filename to fetch from the TFTP server.
rommon 6>**tftpdnld**	Starts the process.
...<output cut>...	
Do you wish to continue? y/n: [n]:**y**	
...<output cut>...	
Rommon 7>**i**	Resets the router. The *i* stands for initialize.

NOTE: Commands and environmental variables are case sensitive, so be sure that you have not accidentally added spaces between variables and answers.

CHAPTER 17

Password-Recovery Procedures and the Configuration Register

This chapter provides information and commands concerning the following topics:

- The configuration register
  - A visual representation
  - What the bits mean
  - The boot field
  - Console terminal baud rate settings
  - Changing the console line speed: CLI
  - Changing the console line speed: ROM Monitor mode
- Password-recovery procedures for Cisco routers
- Password-recovery procedures for 2960 series switches

The Configuration Register

router#**show version**	The last line of output tells you what the configuration register is set to.
router#**configure terminal**	Moves to global configuration mode.
router(config)#**config-register 0x2142**	Changes the configuration register to 2142.

A Visual Representation

The configuration register is a 16-bit field stored in NVRAM. The bits are numbered from 15 to 0 looking at the bit stream from left to right. Bits are split up into groups of 4, and each group is represented by a hexadecimal digit.

15 14 13 12	11 10 9 8	7 6 5 4	3 2 1 0	Bit places
0 0 1 0	0 0 0 1	0 1a0 0	0 0 1 0	Register bits
2	1	4	2	Bits represented in hex

What the Bits Mean

Bit Number	Hexadecimal	Meaning
00–03	0x0000–0x000F	Boot field.
06	0x0040	Ignore NVRAM contents.
07	0x0080	OEM bit enabled.
08	0x0100	Break disabled.
09	0x0200	Causes system to use secondary bootstrap (typically not used).
10	0x0400	IP broadcast with all 0s.
5, 11, 12	0x0020, 0x0800, 0x1000	Console line speed.
13	0x2000	Boots default ROM software if network boot fails.
14	0x4000	IP broadcasts do not have net numbers.
15	0x8000	Enables diagnostic messages and ignores NVRAM contents.

The Boot Field

> **NOTE:** Even though there are 16 possible combinations in the boot field, only 3 are used.

Boot Field	Meaning
00	Stays at the ROM Monitor on a reload or power cycle
01	Boots the first image in flash memory as a system image
02–F	Enables default booting from flash memory Enables **boot system** commands that override default booting from flash memory

> **TIP:** Because the default boot field has 14 different ways to represent it, a configuration register setting of 0x2102 is the same as 0x2109, or 210F. The **boot system** command is described in Chapter 16, "Backing Up and Restoring Cisco IOS Software and Configurations."

Console Terminal Baud Rate Settings

Baud	Bit 5	Bit 12	Bit 11
115200	1	1	1
57600	1	1	0
38400	1	0	1
19200	1	0	0
9600	0	0	0
4800	0	0	1
2400	0	1	1
1200	0	1	0

Changing the Console Line Speed: CLI

router#**configure terminal**	
router(config)#**line console 0**	Enters console line mode
router(config-line)#**speed 19200**	Changes speed to 19200 baud

TIP: Cisco IOS Software does not allow you to change the console speed bits directly with the **config-register** command.

Changing the Console Line Speed: ROM Monitor Mode

rommon1>**confreg**	Shows configuration summary. Step through the questions, answering with the defaults until you can change the console baud rate.
Configuration Summary enabled are: load rom after netboot fails console baud: 9600 boot: image specified by the boot system commands or default to: *x* (name of system image)	

do you wish to change the configuration? y/n [n]: **y** enable "diagonstic mode"? y/n [n]: **n** enable "use net in IP bcast address"? y/n [n]: **n** disable "load rom after netboot fails"? y/n [n]: **n** enable "use all zero broadcast"? y/n [n]: **n** enable "break/abort has effect"? y/n [n]: **n** enable "ignore system config info"? y/n [n]: **n** change console baud rate? y/n [n]: **y** enter rate: 0=9600, 1=4800, 2=1200, 3=2400 4=19200, 5=38400, 6=57600, 7=115200 [0]: **7**	
Configuration Summary enabled are: load rom after netboot fails console baud: 115200 boot: image specified by the boot system commands or default to: *x* (name of system image)	
change the boot characteristics? y/n [n]: **n**	After the summary is shown again, choose **n** to not change the configuration and go to the rommon>prompt again.
rommon2>	

TIP: Make sure that after you change the console baud rate, you change your terminal program to match the same rate!

Password-Recovery Procedures for Cisco Routers

Step	2500 Series Commands	1700/2600/ISR Series Commands
Step 1: Boot the router and interrupt the boot sequence as soon as text appears on the screen.	Press Ctrl-Break >	Press Ctrl-Break rommon 1>

Step 2: Change the configuration register to ignore contents of NVRAM.	`>o/r 0x2142`	`rommon 1>confreg 0x2142`
	`>`	`rommon 2>`
Step 3: Reload the router.	`>i`	`rommon 2>reset`
Step 4: Enter privileged mode. (Do not enter setup mode.)	`Router>enable`	`Router>enable`
	`Router#`	`Router#`
Step 5: Copy the startup configuration into the running configuration.	`Router#copy startup-config running-config`	`Router#copy startup-config running-config`
	`...<output cut>...`	`...<output cut>...`
	`Denver#`	`Denver#`
Step 6: Change the password.	`Denver#configure terminal`	`Denver#configure terminal`
	`Denver(config)#enable secret new`	`Denver(config)#enable secret new`
	`Denver(config)#`	`Denver(config)#`
Step 7: Reset the configuration register back to its default value.	`Denver(config)#config-register 0x2102`	`Denver(config)#config-register 0x2102`
	`Denver(config)#`	`Denver(config)#`
Step 8: Save the configuration.	`Denver(config)#exit`	`Denver(config)#exit`
	`Denver#copy running-config startup-config`	`Denver#copy running-config startup-config`
	`Denver#`	`Denver#`

Step 9: Verify the configuration register.	Denver#**show version**	Denver#**show version**
	...<output cut>...	...<output cut>...
	Configuration register is 0x2142 (will be 0x2102 at next reload)	Configuration register is 0x2142 (will be 0x2102 at next reload)
	Denver#	Denver#
Step 10: Reload the router.	Denver#**reload**	Denver#**reload**

Password Recovery for 2960 Series Switches

Unplug the power supply from the back of the switch.	
Press and hold the Mode button on the front of the switch.	
Plug the switch back in.	
Release the Mode button when the SYST LED blinks amber and then turns solid green. When you release the Mode button, the SYST LED blinks green.	
Issue the following commands:	
switch: **flash_init**	Initializes the flash memory.
switch: **load_helper**	
switch: **dir flash:**	Do not forget the colon. This displays which files are in flash memory.
switch: **rename flash:config.text flash:config.old**	You are renaming the configuration file. The config.text file contains the password.
switch: **boot**	Boots the switch.

When asked whether you want to enter the configuration dialog, enter **n** to exit out to the switch prompt.	Takes you to user mode.
switch>`enable`	Enters privileged mode.
switch#`rename flash:config.old flash:config.text`	Renames the configuration file back to the original name.
Destination filename [config.text]	Press ⏎Enter.
switch#`copy flash:config.text system:running-config`	Copies the configuration file into memory.
768 bytes copied in 0.624 seconds	
2960Switch#	The configuration file is now reloaded. Notice the new prompt.
2960Switch#`configure terminal`	Enters global configuration mode.
2960Switch(config)#	
Proceed to change the passwords as needed	
2900Switch(config)#`exit`	
2900Switch#`copy running-config startup-config`	Saves the configuration into NVRAM with new passwords.

CHAPTER 18

Cisco Discovery Protocol (CDP)

This chapter provides information and commands concerning the following topic:

- Cisco Discovery Protocol (CDP)

Cisco Discovery Protocol

Router#**show cdp**	Displays global CDP information (such as timers)
Router#**show cdp neighbors**	Displays information about neighbors
Router#**show cdp neighbors detail**	Displays more detail about the neighbor device
Router#**show cdp entry word**	Displays information about the device named word
Router#**show cdp entry ***	Displays information about all devices
Router#**show cdp interface**	Displays information about interfaces that have CDP running
Router#**show cdp interface** *x*	Displays information about specific interface *x* running CDP
Router#**show cdp traffic**	Displays traffic information—packets in/out/version
Router(config)#**cdp holdtime** *x*	Changes the length of time to keep CDP packets
Router(config)#**cdp timer** *x*	Changes how often CDP updates are sent
Router(config)#**cdp run**	Enables CDP globally (on by default)
Router(config)#**no cdp run**	Turns off CDP globally
Router(config-if)#**cdp enable**	Enables CDP on a specific interface

`Router(config-if)#no cdp enable`	Turns off CDP on a specific interface
`Router#clear cdp counters`	Resets traffic counters to 0
`Router#clear cdp table`	Deletes the CDP table
`Router#debug cdp adjacency`	Monitors CDP neighbor information
`Router#debug cdp events`	Monitors all CDP events
`Router#debug cdp ip`	Monitors CDP events specifically for IP
`Router#debug cdp packets`	Monitors CDP packet-related information

CAUTION: Although CDP is necessary for some management applications, CDP should still be disabled in some instances.

Disable CDP globally if

• CDP is not required at all.

• The device is located in an insecure environment.

Use the command **no cdp run** to disable CDP globally:

```
RouterOrSwitch(config)#no cdp run
```

Disable CDP on any interface if

• Management is not being performed.

• The switch interface is a nontrunk interface.

• The interface is connected to a nontrusted network.

Use the interface configuration command **no cdp enable** to disable CDP on a specific interface:

```
RouterOrSwitch(config)#interface fastethernet 0/1
RouterOrSwitch(config-if)#no cdp enable
```

CHAPTER 19

Telnet and SSH

This chapter provides information and commands concerning the following topics:

- Using Telnet to remotely connect to other devices
- Configuring the Secure Shell Protocol (SSH)

Using Telnet to Remotely Connect to Other Devices

The following five commands all achieve the same result: the attempt to connect remotely to the router named Paris at IP address 172.16.20.1.

Denver>`telnet paris`	Enter if **ip host** command was used previously to create a mapping of an IP address to the word *paris*.
Denver>`telnet 172.16.20.1`	
Denver>`paris`	Enter if **ip host** command is using default port #.
Denver>`connect paris`	
Denver>`172.16.20.1`	

Any of the preceding commands lead to the following configuration sequence:

Paris>	As long as vty password is set. See the Caution following this table.
Paris>`exit`	Terminates the Telnet session and returns you to the Denver prompt.
Denver>	
Paris>`logout`	Terminates the Telnet session and returns you to the Denver prompt.

`Denver>`	
`Paris>` Ctrl - ⬆Shift - 6 , `release, then press` x	Suspends the Telnet session but does not terminate it, and returns you to the Denver prompt.
`Denver>`	
`Denver>`⏎Enter	Resumes the connection to Paris.
`Paris>`	
`Denver>`**resume**	Resumes the connection to Paris.
`Paris>`	
`Denver>`**disconnect paris**	Terminates the session to Paris.
`Denver>`	
`Denver#`**show sessions**	Displays connections you opened to other sites.
`Denver#`**show users**	Displays who is connected remotely to you.
`Denver#`**clear line** *x*	Disconnects the remote user connected to you on line *x*. The line number is listed in the output gained from the **show users** command.
`Denver(config)#`**line vty 0 4**	Moves to line configuration mode for vty lines 0–4.
`Denver(config-line)` **session-limit** *x*	Limits the number of simultaneous sessions per vty line to *x* number.

CAUTION: The following configuration creates a big security hole. Never use it in a live production environment. Use it in the lab only!

`Denver(config)#line vty 0 4`	Moves you to line configuration mode for vty lines 0–4.
`Denver(config-line)#no password`	The remote user is not challenged when Telnetting to this device.
`Denver(config-line)#no login`	The remote user moves straight to user mode.

NOTE: A device must have two passwords for a remote user to be able to make changes to your configuration:

- Line vty password (or have it explicitly turned off; see the preceding Caution)
- **Enable** or **enable secret** password

Without the **enable** or **enable secret** password, a remote user will only be able to get to user mode, not to privileged mode. This is extra security.

Configuring the Secure Shell Protocol (SSH)

CAUTION: SSH Version 1 implementations have known security issues. It is recommended to use SSH Version 2 whenever possible.

NOTE: To work, SSH requires a local username database, a local IP domain, and an RSA key to be generated.

The Cisco implementation of SSH requires Cisco IOS Software to support Rivest-Shamir-Adleman (RSA) authentication and minimum Data Encryption Standard (DES) encryption—a cryptographic software image.

`Router(config)#username Roland password tower`	Creates a locally significant username/password combination. These are the credentials needed to be entered when connecting to the router with SSH client software.
`Router(config)#ip domain-name test.lab`	Creates a host domain for the router.
`Router(config)#crypto key generate rsa`	Enables the SSH server for local and remote authentication on the router and generates an RSA key pair.

CHAPTER 20

The ping and traceroute Commands

This chapter provides information and commands concerning the following topics:

- ICMP redirect messages
- The **ping** command
- Examples of using the **ping** and the extended **ping** commands
- The **traceroute** command

ICMP Redirect Messages

`Router(config-if)#no ip redirects`	Disables ICMP redirects from this specific interface
`Router(config-if)#ip redirects`	Reenables ICMP redirects from this specific interface

The ping Command

`Router#ping w.x.y.z`	Checks for Layer 3 connectivity with device at address *w.x.y.z*
`Router#ping`	Enters extended ping mode, which provides more options

The following table describes the possible ping output characters.

Character	Meaning
!	Successful receipt of a reply.
.	Device timed out while waiting for a reply.
U	A destination unreachable error protocol data unit (PDU) was received.
Q	Source quench (destination too busy).

M	Could not fragment.
?	Unknown packet type.
&	Packet lifetime exceeded.

Examples of Using the ping and the Extended ping Commands

Router#**ping 172.168.20.1**	Performs a basic Layer 3 test to address.
Router#**ping paris**	Same as above but through the IP host name.
Router#**ping**	Enters extended ping mode; can now change parameters of ping test.
Protocol [ip]: ⏎Enter	Press ⏎Enter to use ping for IP.
Target IP address: **172.16.20.1**	Enter the target IP address.
Repeat count [5]: **100**	Enter the number of echo requests you want to send. The default is 5.
Datagram size [100]: ⏎Enter	Enter the size of datagrams being sent. The default is 100.
Timeout in Seconds [2]: ⏎Enter	Enter the timeout delay between sending echo requests.
Extended commands [n]: **yes**	Allows you to configure extended commands.
Source address or interface: **10.0.10.1**	Allows you to explicitly set where the pings are originating from.
Type of Service [0]	Allows you to set the TOS field in the IP header.

`Set DF bit in IP header [no]`	Allows you to set the DF bit in the IP header.
`Validate reply data? [no]`	Allows you to set whether you want validation.
`Data Pattern [0xABCD]`	Allows you to change the data pattern in the data field of the ICMP echo request packet.

`Loose, Strict, Record, Timestamp,`
`Verbose[none]:` ⏎Enter
 	
`Sweep range of sizes [no]:` ⏎Enter
 	
`Type escape sequence to abort`
 	
`Sending 100, 100-byte ICMP Echos to`
`172.16.20.1, timeout is 2 seconds:`
 	
`!!!!!!!!!!!!!!!!!!!!!!!!!!!!!!!!!!!!!!!!!!!!!`
`!!!!!!!!!!!!!!!!!!!!!!!!!!!!!!!!!!!!!!!!!!!!!`
`!!!!!!!!!!!!!!!!!!!!!!!!!!!!!!!!!!!!!!!`
 	
`Success rate is 100 percent (100/100) round-`
`trip min/avg/max = 1/1/4 ms`	

The traceroute Command

`Router#traceroute 172.168.20.1`	Discovers the route taken to travel to the destination
`Router#traceroute paris`	Command with IP host name rather than IP address
`Router#trace 172.16.20.1`	Common shortcut spelling of the **traceroute** command

CHAPTER 21

SNMP and Syslog

This chapter provides information and commands concerning the following topics:

- Configuring SNMP
- Configuring Syslog

Configuring SNMP

Router(config)#**snmp-server community academy ro**	Sets a read-only (**ro**) community string called **academy**
Router(config)#**snmp-server community academy rw**	Sets a read-write (**rw**) community string called **academy**
Router(config)#**snmp-server location 2nd Floor IDF**	Defines an SNMP string that describes the physical location of the SNMP server
Router(config)#**snmp-server contact Scott Empson 555-5236**	Defines an SNMP string that describes the sysContact information

NOTE: A community string is like a password. In the case of the first command, the community string grants you access to SNMP.

Configuring Syslog

Router(config)#**logging on**	Enables logging to all supported destinations.
Router(config)#**logging 192.168.10.53**	Logging messages will be sent to a syslog server host at address 192.168.10.53.

`Router(config)#logging sysadmin`	Logging messages will be sent to a syslog server host named sysadmin.
`Router(config)#logging trap x`	Sets the syslog server logging level to value *x*, where *x* is a number between 0 and 7 or a word defining the level. The table that follows provides more details.
`Router(config)#service timestamps log datetime`	Syslog messages will now have a timestamp included.

There are eight levels of severity in logging messages, as follows:

0	Emergencies	System is unusable
1	Alerts	Immediate action needed
2	Critical	Critical conditions
3	Errors	Error conditions
4	Warnings	Warning conditions
5	Notifications	Normal but significant conditions
6	Informational	Informational messages (default level)
7	Debugging	Debugging messages

Setting a level means you will get that level and everything below it. Level 6 means you will receive level 6 and 7 messages. Level 4 means you will get levels 4 through 7.

CHAPTER 22

Basic Troubleshooting

This chapter provides information and commands concerning the following topics:

- Viewing the routing table
- Determining the gateway of last resort
- Determining the last routing update
- OSI Layer 3 testing
- OSI Layer 7 testing
- Interpreting the **show interface** command
- Clearing interface counters
- Using CDP to troubleshoot
- The **traceroute** command
- The **show controllers** command
- **debug** commands
- Using time stamps
- Operating system IP verification commands
- The **ip http server** command
- The **netstat** command

Viewing the Routing Table

Router#**show ip route**	Displays the entire routing table
Router#**show ip route** *protocol*	Displays a table about a specific protocol (for example, RIP or IGRP)
Router#**show ip route** *w.x.y.z*	Displays information about route *w.x.y.z*
Router#**show ip route connected**	Displays a table of connected routes
Router#**show ip route static**	Displays a table of static routes
Router#**show ip route summary**	Displays a summary of all routes

Determining the Gateway of Last Resort

Router(config)#ip default-network w.x.y.z	Sets network *w.x.y.z* to be the default route. All routes not in the routing table will be sent to this network.
Router(config)#ip route 0.0.0.0 0.0.0.0 172.16.20.1	Specifies that all routes not in the routing table will be sent to 172.16.20.1.

NOTE: The **ip default-network** command is for use with the deprecated Cisco proprietary Interior Gateway Routing Protocol (IGRP). Although you can use it with Enhanced Interior Gateway Routing Protocol (EIGRP) or RIP, it is not recommended. Use the **ip route 0.0.0.0 0.0.0.0** command instead.

Routers that use the **ip default-network** command must have either a specific route to that network or a **0.0.0.0 /0** default route.

Determining the Last Routing Update

Router#show ip route	Displays the entire routing table
Router#show ip route w.x.y.z	Displays information about route *w.x.y.z*
Router#show ip protocols	Displays the IP routing protocol parameters and statistics
Router#show ip rip database	Displays the RIP database

OSI Layer 3 Testing

Router#ping w.x.y.z	Checks for Layer 3 connectivity with the device at address *w.x.y.z*
Router#ping	Enters extended ping mode, which provides more options

NOTE: See Chapter 20, "The **ping** and **traceroute** Commands," for all applicable **ping** commands.

OSI Layer 7 Testing

NOTE: See Chapter 19, "Telnet and SSH," for all applicable Telnet commands.

`Router#`**`debug telnet`**	Displays the Telnet negotiation process

Interpreting the show interface Command

`Router#`**`show interface serial 0/0/0`**	Displays the status and stats of the interface.
`Serial 0/0/0 is` *`up`*`, line protocol is` *`up`*	The first part refers to the physical status. The second part refers to the logical status.
`…<output cut>…`	
`Possible output results:`	
`Serial 0/0/0 is` *`up`*`, line protocol is` *`up`*	The interface is up and working.
`Serial 0/0/0 is` *`up`*`, line protocol is` *`down`*	Keepalive or connection problem (no clock rate, bad encapsulation).
`Serial 0/0/0 is` *`down`*`, line protocol is` *`down`*	Interface problem, or other end has not been configured.
`Serial 0/0/0 is administratively` *`down`*`, line protocol is` *`down`*	Interface is disabled—shut down.

Clearing Interface Counters

`Router#`**`clear counters`**	Resets all interface counters to 0
`Router#`**`clear counters`** *`interface type/slot`*	Resets specific interface counters to 0

Using CDP to Troubleshoot

NOTE: See Chapter 19 for all applicable CDP commands.

The traceroute Command

Router#traceroute *w.x.y.z*	Displays all routes used to reach the destination of *w.x.y.z*

NOTE: See Chapter 20 for all applicable **traceroute** commands.

The show controllers Command

Router#show controllers serial 0/0/0	Displays the type of cable plugged into the serial interface (DCE or DTE) and what the clock rate is, if it was set

debug Commands

Router#debug all	Turns on all possible debugging.
Router#u all (short form of **undebug all**)	Turns off all possible debugging.
Router#show debug	Lists what **debug** commands are on.
Router#terminal monitor	Debug output will now be seen through a Telnet session (default is to only send output on the console screen)

CAUTION: Turning all possible debugging on is extremely CPU intensive and will probably cause your router to crash. Use *extreme caution* if you try this on a production device. Instead, be selective about which **debug** commands you turn on.

Do not leave debugging turned on. After you have gathered the necessary information from debugging, turn all debugging off. If you want to turn off only one specific **debug** command and leave others on, issue the **no debug** *x* command, where *x* is the specific **debug** command you want to disable.

Using Time Stamps

`Router(config)#service timestamps`	Adds a time stamp to all system logging messages
`Router(config)#service timestamps debug`	Adds a time stamp to all debugging messages
`Router(config)#service timestamps debug uptime`	Adds a time stamp along with the total uptime of the router to all debugging messages
`Router(config)#service timestamps debug datetime localtime`	Adds a time stamp displaying the local time and the date to all debugging messages
`Router(config)#no service timestamps`	Disables all time stamps

TIP: Make sure you have the date and time set with the **clock** command at privileged mode so that the time stamps are more meaningful.

Operating System IP Verification Commands

The following are commands that you should use to verify what your IP settings are. Different operating systems have different commands.

- **ipconfig** (Windows 2000/XP):

  Click **Start > Run > Command > ipconfig** or **ipconfig/all**.

- **winipcfg** (Windows 95/98/Me):

  Click **Start > Run > winipcfg**.

- **ifconfig** (Mac/Linux):

  `#ifconfig`

The ip http server Command

`Router(config)#ip http server`	Enables the HTTP server, including the Cisco web browser user interface
`Router(config-if)#no ip http server`	Disables the HTTP server

CAUTION: The HTTP server was introduced in Cisco IOS Software Release 11.0 to extend router management to the web. You have limited management capabilities to your router through a web browser if the **ip http server** command is turned on.

Do not turn on the **ip http server** command unless you plan to use the browser interface for the router. Having it on creates a potential security hole because another port is open.

The netstat Command

`C\>netstat`	Used in Windows and UNIX/Linux to display TCP/IP connection and protocol information; used at the command prompt in Windows

PART VIII

Managing IP Services

Chapter 23   Network Address Translation

Chapter 24   DHCP

Chapter 25   IPv6

Network Address Translation

This chapter provides information and commands concerning the following topics:

- Private IP addresses: RFC 1918
- Configuring dynamic NAT: One private to one public address translation
- Configuring Port Address Translation (PAT): Many private to one public address translation
- Configuring static NAT: One private to one permanent public address translation
- Verifying NAT and PAT configurations
- Troubleshooting NAT and PAT configurations
- Configuration example: PAT

Private IP Addresses: RFC 1918

The following table lists the address ranges as specified in RFC 1918 that can be used by anyone as internal private addresses. These will be your "inside-the-LAN" addresses that will have to be translated into public addresses that can be routed across the Internet. Any network is allowed to use these addresses; however, these addresses are not allowed to be routed onto the public Internet.

Private Addresses		
Class	**RFC 1918 Internal Address Range**	**CIDR Prefix**
A	10.0.0.0–10.255.255.255	10.0.0.0/8
B	172.16.0.0–172.31.255.255	172.16.0.0/12
C	192.168.0.0–192.168.255.255	192.168.0.0/16

Configuring Dynamic NAT: One Private to One Public Address Translation

> **NOTE:** For a complete configuration of NAT/PAT with a diagram for visual assistance, see the sample configuration at the end of this chapter.

Step 1: Define a static route on the remote router stating where the public addresses should be routed.	`ISP(config)#ip route`
	`64.64.64.64 255.255.255.128`
	`s0/0/0`
		Informs the ISP router where to send packets with addresses destined for 64.64.64.64 255.255.255.128.

Step 2: Define a pool of usable public IP addresses on your router that will perform NAT.		The private address will receive the first available public address in the pool.

	`Corp(config)#ip nat pool`
	`scott 64.64.64.70`
	`64.64.64.126 netmask`
	`255.255.255.128`
		Defines the following:
		
		The name of the pool is scott. (The name of the pool can be anything.)
		
		The start of the pool is 64.64.64.70.
		
		The end of the pool is 64.64.64.126.
		
		The subnet mask is 255.255.255.128.

Step 3: Create an access control list (ACL) that will identify which private IP addresses will be translated.	`Corp(config)#access-list 1` `permit 172.16.10.0 0.0.0.255`	
Step 4: Link the ACL to the pool of addresses (create the translation).	`Corp(config)#ip nat inside` `source list 1 pool scott`	Defines the following: The source of the private addresses is from ACL 1. The pool of available public addresses is named scott.

Step 5: Define which interfaces are inside (contain the private addresses).	`Router(config)#interface fastethernet 0/0`	Moves to interface configuration mode.
	`Router(config-if)#ip nat inside`	You can have more than one inside interface on a router. Addresses from each inside interface are then allowed to be translated into a public address.
	`Router(config-if)#exit`	Returns to global configuration mode.
Step 6: Define the outside interface (the interface leading to the public network).	`Router(config)#interface serial 0/0/0`	
	`Router(config-if)#ip nat outside`	

Configuring PAT: Many Private to One Public Address Translation

All private addresses use a single public IP address and numerous port numbers for translation.

Step 1: Define a static route on the remote router stating where public addresses should be routed.	`ISP(config)#ip route 64.64.64.64 255.255.255.128 s0/0`	Informs the Internet service provider (ISP) where to send packets with addresses destined for 64.64.64.64 255.255.255.128.

Step 2: Define a pool of usable public IP addresses on your router that will perform NAT (optional).		Use this step if you have many private addresses to translate. A single public IP address can handle thousands of private addresses. Without using a pool of addresses, you can translate all private addresses into the IP address of the exit interface (the serial link to the ISP, for example).
	`Corp(config)#ip nat pool scott 64.64.64.70 64.64.64.70 netmask 255.255.255.128`	Defines the following: The name of the pool is scott. (The name of the pool can be anything.) The start of the pool is 64.64.64.70. The end of the pool is 64.64.64.70. The subnet mask is 255.255.255.128.
Step 3: Create an ACL that will identify which private IP addresses will be translated.	`Corp(config)#access-list 1 permit 172.16.10.0 0.0.0.255`	
Step 4 (Option 1): Link the ACL to the outside public interface (create the translation).	`Corp(config)#ip nat inside source list 1 interface serial 0/0/0 overload`	The source of the private addresses is from ACL 1. The public address to be translated into is the one assigned to serial 0/0/0. The **overload** keyword states that port numbers will be used to handle many translations.

Step 4 (Option 2): Link the ACL to the pool of addresses (create the translation).		If using the pool created in Step 1 . . .
	`Corp(config)#ip nat inside source list 1 pool scott overload`	The source of the private addresses is from ACL 1. The pool of the available addresses is named scott. The **overload** keyword states that port numbers will be used to handle many translations.
Step 5: Define which interfaces are inside (contain the private addresses).	`Corp(config)#interface fastethernet 0/0`	Moves to interface configuration mode.
	`Corp(config-if)#ip nat inside`	You can have more than one inside interface on a router.
	`Corp(config-if)#exit`	Returns to global configuration mode.
Step 6: Define the outside interface (the interface leading to the public network).	`Corp(config)#interface serial 0/0/0`	Moves to interface configuration mode.
	`Corp(config-if)#ip nat outside`	Defines which interface is the outside interface for NAT.

NOTE: You can have an IP NAT pool of more than one address, if needed. The syntax for this is as follows:

`Corp(config)#ip nat pool scott 64.64.64.70 74.64.64.128 netmask 255.255.255.128`

You would then have a pool of 63 addresses (and all of their ports) available for translation.

Configuring Static NAT: One Private to One Permanent Public Address Translation

Step 1: Define a static route on the remote router stating where the public addresses should be routed.	`ISP(config)#ip route`
	`64.64.64.64`
	`255.255.255.128 s0/0`
		Informs the ISP where to send packets with addresses destined for 64.64.64.64 255.255.255.128.

Step 2: Create a static mapping on your router that will perform NAT.	`Corp(config)#ip nat inside`
	`source static 172.16.10.5`
	`64.64.64.65`
		Permanently translates the inside address of 172.16.10.5 to a public address of 64.64.64.65.
		
		Use the command for each of the private IP addresses you want to statically map to a public address.

Step 3: Define which interfaces are inside (contain the private addresses).	`Corp(config)#interface` `fastethernet 0/0`	Moves to interface configuration mode.
	`Corp(config-if)#ip nat` `inside`	You can have more than one inside interface on a router.
Step 4: Define the outside interface (the interface leading to the public network).	`Corp(config-if)#interface` `serial 0/0/0`	Moves to interface configuration mode.
	`Corp(config-if)#ip nat` `outside`	Defines which interface is the outside interface for NAT.

CAUTION: Make sure that you have in your router configurations a way for packets to travel back to your NAT router. Include a static route on the ISP router advertising your NAT pool and how to travel back to your internal network. Without this in place, a packet can leave your network with a public address, but it will not be able to return if your ISP router does not know where the pool of public addresses exists in the network. You should be advertising the pool of public addresses, not your private addresses.

Verifying NAT and PAT Configurations

Router#show ip nat translations	Displays the translation table
Router#show ip nat statistics	Displays NAT statistics
Router#clear ip nat translations inside *a.b.c.d* outside *e.f.g.h*	Clears a specific translation from the table before it times out
Router#clear ip nat translations*	Clears the entire translation table before entries time out

Troubleshooting NAT and PAT Configurations

Router#debug ip nat	Displays information about every packet that is translated. Be careful with this command. The router's CPU might not be able to handle this amount of output and might therefore hang the system.
Router#debug ip nat detailed	Displays greater detail about packets being translated.

Configuration Example: PAT

Figure 23-1 shows the network topology for the PAT configuration that follows using the commands covered in this chapter.

Figure 23-1   Port Address Translation Configuration

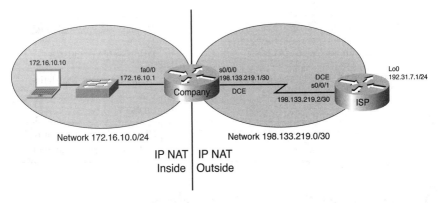

Network 172.16.10.0/24   Network 198.133.219.0/30

IP NAT | IP NAT
Inside | Outside

ISP Router

`router>`**enable**	Moves to privileged mode.
`router#`**configure terminal**	Moves to global configuration mode.
`router(config)#`**host ISP**	Sets the host name.
`ISP(config)#`**no ip domain-lookup**	Turns off Domain Name System (DNS) resolution to avoid wait time due to DNS lookup of spelling errors.
`ISP(config)#`**enable secret cisco**	Sets the encrypted password to **cisco**.
`ISP(config)#`**line console 0**	Moves to line console mode.
`ISP(config-line)#`**login**	User must log in to be able to access the console port.
`ISP(config-line)#`**password class**	Sets the console line password to **class**.
`ISP(config-line)#`**logging synchronous**	Commands will be appended to a new line.
`ISP(config-line)#`**exit**	Returns to global configuration mode.

`ISP(config)#interface serial 0/0/1`	Moves to interface configuration mode.
`ISP(config-if)#ip address 198.133.219.2 255.255.255.252`	Assigns an IP address and netmask.
`ISP(config-if)#clock rate 56000`	Assigns the clock rate to the DCE cable on this side of the link.
`ISP(config-if)#no shutdown`	Enables the interface.
`ISP(config-if)#interface loopback 0`	Creates loopback interface 0 and moves to interface configuration mode.
`ISP(config-if)#ip address 192.31.7.1255.255.255.255`	Assigns an IP address and netmask.
`ISP(config-if)#exit`	Returns to global configuration mode.
`ISP(config)#exit`	Returns to privileged mode.
`ISP#copy running-config startup-config`	Saves the configuration to NVRAM.

Company Router

`router>enable`	Moves to privileged mode.
`router#configure terminal`	Moves to global configuration mode.
`router(config)#host Company`	Sets the host name.
`Company(config)#no ip domain-lookup`	Turns off DNS resolution to avoid wait time due to DNS lookup of spelling errors.
`Company(config)#enable secret cisco`	Sets the secret password to **cisco**.
`Company(config)#line console 0`	Moves to line console mode.
`Company(config-line)#login`	User must log in to be able to access the console port.
`Company(config-line)#password class`	Sets the console line password to **class**.
`Company(config-line)#logging synchronous`	Commands will be appended to a new line.

`Company(config-line)#exit`	Returns to global configuration mode.
`Company(config)#interface` `fastethernet 0/0`	Moves to interface configuration mode.
`Company(config-if)#ip address` `172.16.10.1 255.255.255.0`	Assigns an IP address and netmask.
`Company(config-if)#no shutdown`	Enables the interface.
`Company(config-if)#interface serial` `0/0/0`	Moves to interface configuration mode.
`Company(config-if)#ip address` `198.133.219.1 255.255.255.252`	Assigns an IP address and netmask.
`Company(config-if)#no shutdown`	Enables the interface.
`Company(config-if)#exit`	Returns to global configuration mode.
`Company(config)#ip route 0.0.0.0` `0.0.0.0 198.133.219.2`	Sends all packets not defined in the routing table to the ISP router.
`Company(config)#access-list 1 permit` `172.16.10.0 0.0.0.255`	Defines which addresses are permitted through; these addresses are those that will be allowed to be translated with NAT.
`Company(config)#ip nat inside source` `list 1 interface serial 0/0/0 overload`	Creates NAT by combining list 1 with the interface serial 0/0/0. Overloading will take place.
`Company(config)#interface` `fastethernet 0/0`	Moves to interface configuration mode.
`Company(config-if)#ip nat inside`	Location of private inside addresses.
`Company(config-if)#interface serial` `0/0/0`	Moves to interface configuration mode.
`Company(config-if)#ip nat outside`	Location of public outside addresses.
`Company(config-if)#`Ctrl-z	Returns to privileged mode.
`Company#copy running-config startup-` `config`	Saves the configuration to NVRAM.

CHAPTER 24

DHCP

This chapter provides information and commands concerning the following topics:

- Configuring DHCP
- Verifying and troubleshooting DHCP configuration
- Configuring a DHCP helper address
- DHCP client on a Cisco IOS Software Ethernet interface
- Configuration example: DHCP

Configuring DHCP

`Router(config)#ip dhcp pool internal`	Creates a DHCP pool called internal.
`Router(dhcp-config)#network 172.16.10.0 255.255.255.0`	Defines the range of addresses to be leased.
`Router(dhcp-config)#default-router 172.16.10.1`	Defines the address of the default router for the client.
`Router(dhcp-config)#dns-server 172.16.10.10`	Defines the address of the Domain Name System (DNS) server for the client
`Router(dhcp-config)#netbios-name-server 172.16.10.10`	Defines the address of the NetBIOS server for the client.
`Router(dhcp-config)#domain-name fakedomainname.ca`	Defines the domain name for the client.
`Router(dhcp-config)# lease 14 12 23`	Defines the lease time to be 14 days, 12 hours, 23 minutes.
`Router(dhcp-config)#lease infinite`	Sets the lease time to infinity; the default time is 1 day.
`Router(dhcp-config)#exit`	Returns to global configuration mode.
`Router(config)#ip dhcp excluded-address 172.16.10.1 172.16.10.9`	Specifies the range of addresses not to be leased out to clients.

`Router(config)#service dhcp`	Enables the DHCP service and relay features on a Cisco IOS router.
`Router(config)#no service dhcp`	Turns the DHCP service off. DHCP service is on by default in Cisco IOS Software.

Verifying and Troubleshooting DHCP Configuration

`Router#show ip dhcp binding`	Displays a list of all bindings created
`Router#show ip dhcp binding` `w.x.y.z`	Displays the bindings for a specific DHCP client with an IP address of *w.x.y.z*
`Router#clear ip dhcp binding` `a.b.c.d`	Clears an automatic address binding from the DHCP server database
`Router#clear ip dhcp binding *`	Clears all automatic DHCP bindings
`Router#show ip dhcp conflict`	Displays a list of all address conflicts recorded by the DHCP server
`Router#clear ip dhcp conflict` `a.b.c.d`	Clears address conflict from the database
`Router#clear ip dhcp conflict *`	Clears conflicts for all addresses
`Router#show ip dhcp database`	Displays recent activity on the DHCP database
`Router#show ip dhcp server` `statistics`	Displays a list of the number of messages sent and received by the DHCP server
`Router#clear ip dhcp server` `statistics`	Resets all DHCP server counters to 0
`Router#debug ip dhcp server` `{events	packets	linkage	class}`	Displays the DHCP process of addresses being leased and returned

Configuring a DHCP Helper Address

`Router(config)#interface` `fastethernet 0/0`	Moves to interface configuration mode.
`Router(config-if)#ip helper-` `address 172.16.20.2`	DHCP broadcasts will be forwarded as a unicast to this specific address rather than be dropped by the router.

NOTE: The **ip helper-address** command will forward broadcast packets as a unicast to eight different UDP ports by default:

- TFTP (port 69)
- DNS (port 53)
- Time service (port 37)
- NetBIOS name server (port 137)
- NetBIOS datagram server (port 138)
- Boot Protocol (BOOTP) client and server datagrams (ports 67 and 68)
- TACACS service (port 49)

If you want to close some of these ports, use the **no ip forward-protocol udp** *x* command at the global configuration prompt, where *x* is the port number you want to close. The following command stops the forwarding of broadcasts to port 49:

```
Router(config)#no ip forward-protocol udp 49
```

If you want to open other UDP ports, use the **ip forward-helper udp** *x* command, where *x* is the port number you want to open:

```
Router(config)#ip forward-protocol udp 517
```

DHCP Client on a Cisco IOS Software Ethernet Interface

`Router(config)#interface fastethernet 0/0`	Moves to interface configuration mode
`Router(config-if)#ip address dhcp`	Specifies that the interface acquire an IP address through DHCP

Configuration Example: DHCP

Figure 24-1 illustrates the network topology for the configuration that follows, which shows how to configure DHCP services on a Cisco IOS router using the commands covered in this chapter.

Figure 24-4   Network Topology for DHCP Configuration

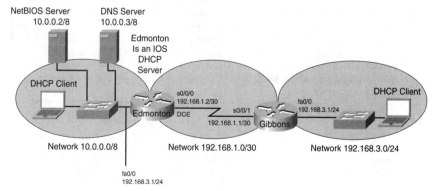

Edmonton Router

`router>`**`enable`**	Moves to privileged mode
`router#`**`configure terminal`**	Moves to global configuration mode
`router(config)#`**`host Edmonton`**	Sets the host name
`Edmonton(config)#`**`interface fastethernet 0/0`**	Moves to interface configuration mode
`Edmonton(config-if)#`**`description LAN Interface`**	Sets the local description of the interface
`Edmonton(config-if)#`**`ip address 10.0.0.1 255.0.0.0`**	Assigns an IP address and netmask
`Edmonton(config-if)#`**`no shutdown`**	Enables the interface
`Edmonton(config-if)#`**`interface serial 0/0/0`**	Moves to interface configuration mode
`Edmonton(config-if)#`**`description Link to Gibbons Router`**	Sets the local description of the interface
`Edmonton(config-if)#`**`ip address 192.168.1.2 255.255.255.252`**	Assigns an IP address and netmask
`Edmonton(config-if)#`**`clock rate 56000`**	Assigns the clock rate to the DCE cable on this side of link
`Edmonton(config-if)#`**`no shutdown`**	Enables the interface
`Edmonton(config-if)#`**`exit`**	Returns to global configuration mode
`Edmonton(config)#`**`router eigrp 10`**	Enables the EIGRP routing process for autonomous system 10
`Edmonton(config-router)#`**`network 10.0.0.0`**	Advertises the 10.0.0.0 network
`Edmonton(config-router)#`**`network 192.168.1.0`**	Advertises the 192.168.1.0 network
`Edmonton(config-router)#`**`exit`**	Returns to global configuration mode
`Edmonton(config)#`**`service dhcp`**	Verifies that the router can use DHCP services and that DHCP is enabled
`Edmonton(config)#`**`ip dhcp pool 10network`**	Creates a DHCP pool called 10network

Edmonton(dhcp-config)#**network 10.0.0.0 255.0.0.0**	Defines the range of addresses to be leased
Edmonton(dhcp-config)#**default-router 10.0.0.1**	Defines the address of the default router for clients
Edmonton(dhcp-config)#**netbios-name-server 10.0.0.2**	Defines the address of the NetBIOS server for clients
Edmonton(dhcp-config)#**dns-server 10.0.0.3**	Defines the address of the DNS server for clients
Edmonton(dhcp-config)#**domain-name fakedomainname.ca**	Defines the domain name for clients
Edmonton(dhcp-config)#**lease 12 14 30**	Sets the lease time to be 12 days, 14 hours, 30 minutes
Edmonton(dhcp-config)#**exit**	Returns to global configuration mode
Edmonton(config)#**ip dhcp excluded-address 10.0.0.1 10.0.0.5**	Specifies the range of addresses not to be leased out to clients
Edmonton(config)#**ip dhcp pool 192.168.3network**	Creates a DHCP pool called the 192.168.3network
Edmonton(dhcp-config)#**network 192.168.3.0 255.255.255.0**	Defines the range of addresses to be leased
Edmonton(dhcp-config)#**default-router 192.168.3.1**	Defines the address of the default router for clients
Edmonton(dhcp-config)#**netbios-name-server 10.0.0.2**	Defines the address of the NetBIOS server for clients
Edmonton(dhcp-config)#**dns-server 10.0.0.3**	Defines the address of the DNS server for clients
Edmonton(dhcp-config)#**domain-name fakedomainname.ca**	Defines the domain name for clients
Edmonton(dhcp-config)#**lease 12 14 30**	Sets the lease time to be 12 days, 14 hours, 30 minutes
Edmonton(dhcp-config)#**exit**	Returns to global configuration mode
Edmonton(config)#**exit**	Returns to privileged mode
Edmonton#**copy running-config startup-config**	Saves the configuration to NVRAM

Gibbons Router

router>**enable**	Moves to privileged mode.
router#**configure terminal**	Moves to global configuration mode.
router(config)#**host Gibbons**	Sets the host name.
Gibbons(config)#**interface fastethernet 0/0**	Moves to interface configuration mode.
Gibbons(config-if)#**description LAN Interface**	Sets the local description of the interface.
Gibbons(config-if)#**ip address 192.168.3.1 255.255.255.0**	Assigns an IP address and netmask.
Gibbons(config-if)#**ip helper-address 192.168.1.2**	DHCP broadcasts will be forwarded as a unicast to this address rather than be dropped.
Gibbons(config-if)#**no shutdown**	Enables the interface.
Gibbons(config-if)#**interface serial 0/0/1**	Moves to interface configuration mode.
Gibbons(config-if)#**description Link to Edmonton Router**	Sets the local description of the interface.
Gibbons(config-if)#**ip address 192.168.1.1 255.255.255.252**	Assigns an IP address and netmask.
Gibbons(config-if)#**no shutdown**	Enables the interface.
Gibbons(config-if)#**exit**	Returns to global configuration mode.
Gibbons(config)#**router eigrp 10**	Enables the EIGRP routing process for autonomous system 10.
Gibbons(config-router)#**network 192.168.3.0**	Advertises the 192.168.3.0 network.
Gibbons(config-router)#**network 192.168.1.0**	Advertises the 192.168.1.0 network.
Gibbons(config-router)#**exit**	Returns to global configuration mode.
Gibbons(config)#**exit**	Returns to privileged mode.
Gibbons#**copy running-config startup-config**	Saves the configuration to NVRAM.

This chapter provides information and commands concerning the following topics:

- Assigning IPv6 addresses to interfaces
- IPv6 and RIPng
- Configuration example: IPv6 RIP
- IPv6 tunnels: manual overlay tunnel
- Static routes in IPv6
- Floating static routes in IPv6
- Verifying and troubleshooting IPv6
- IPv6 ping

> **NOTE:** For an excellent overview of IPv6, I strongly recommend you read Jeff Doyle's book, *Routing TCP/IP Volume I*, Second Edition.

Assigning IPv6 Addresses to Interfaces

`Router(config)#ipv6 unicast-routing`	Enables the forwarding of IPV6 unicast datagrams globally on the router.
`Router(config)#interface fastethernet 0/0`	Moves to interface configuration mode.
`Router(config-if)#ipv6 enable`	Automatically configures an IPv6 link-local address on the interface and enables IPv6 processing on the interface.
	NOTE: The link-local address that the **ipv6 enable** command configures can be used only to communicate with nodes on the same link.
`Router(config-if)#ipv6 address 3000::1/64`	Configures a global IPv6 address on the interface and enables IPv6 processing on the interface.
`Router(config-if)#ipv6 address 2001:db8:0:1::/64 eui-64`	Configures a global IPv6 address with an interface identifier in the low-order 64 bits of the IPv6 address.

`Router(config-if)#ipv6 address fe80::260:3eff:fe47:1530/64 link-local`	Configures a specific link-local IPv6 address on the interface instead of the one that is automatically configured when IPv6 is enabled on the interface.
`Router(config-if)#ipv6 unnumbered type/number`	Specifies an unnumbered interface and enables IPv6 processing on the interface. The global IPv6 address of the interface specified by *type/number* will be used as the source address.

IPv6 and RIPng

`Router(config)#interface serial 0/0`	Moves to interface configuration mode.
`Router(config-if)#ipv6 rip tower enable`	Creates the RIPng process named tower and enables RIPng on the interface.
	NOTE: Unlike RIPv1 and RIPv2, where you needed to create the RIP routing process with the **router rip** command and then use the **network** command to specify the interfaces on which to run RIP, the RIPng process is created automatically when RIPng is enabled on an interface with the **ipv6 rip** *name* **enable** command.
	NOTE: Cisco IOS Software automatically creates an entry in the configuration for the RIPng routing process when it is enabled on an interface.
	NOTE: The **ipv6 router rip** *process-name* command is still needed when configuring optional features of RIPng.
`Router(config)#ipv6 router rip tower`	Creates the RIPng process named tower if it has not already been created, and moves to router configuration mode
`Router(config-router)#maximum-paths 2`	Defines the maximum number of equal-cost routes that RIPng can support.
	NOTE: The number of paths that can be used is a number from 1 to 64. The default is 4.

Configuration Example: IPv6 RIP

Figure 25-1 illustrates the network topology for the configuration that follows, which shows how to configure IPv6 and RIPng using the commands covered in this chapter.

Figure 25-1   Network Topology for IPv6/RIPng Configuration Example

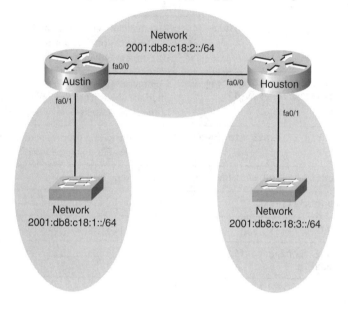

Austin Router

Router>**enable**	Moves to privileged mode
Router#**configure terminal**	Moves to global configuration mode
Router(config)#**hostname Austin**	Assigns a host name to the router
Austin(config)#**ipv6 unicast-routing**	Enables the forwarding of IPv6 unicast datagrams globally on the router
Austin(config)#**interface fastethernet 0/0**	Enters interface configuration mode
Austin(config-if)#**ipv6 enable**	Automatically configures an IPv6 link-local address on the interface and enables IPv6 processing on the interface
Austin(config-if)#**ipv6 address 2001:db8:c18:2::/64 eui-64**	Configures a global IPv6 address with an interface identifier in the low-order 64 bits of the IPv6 address

Austin(config-if)#**ipv6 rip tower enable**	Creates the RIPng process named tower and enables RIPng on the interface
Austin(config-if)#**no shutdown**	Activates the interface
Austin(config-if)#**interface fastethernet 0/1**	Enters interface configuration mode
Austin(config-if)#**ipv6 enable**	Automatically configures an IPv6 link-local address on the interface and enables IPv6 processing on the interface
Austin(config-if)#**ipv6 address 2001:db8:c18:1::/64 eui-64**	Configures a global IPv6 address with an interface identifier in the low-order 64 bits of the IPv6 address
Austin(config-if)#**ipv6 rip tower enable**	Creates the RIPng process named tower and enables RIPng on the interface
Austin(config-if)#**no shutdown**	Activates the interface
Austin(config-if)#**exit**	Moves to global configuration mode
Austin(config)#**exit**	Moves to privileged mode
Austin#**copy running-config startup-config**	Saves the configuration to NVRAM

Houston Router

Router>**enable**	Moves to privileged mode
Router#**configure terminal**	Moves to global configuration mode
Router(config)#**hostname Houston**	Assigns a host name to the router
Houston(config)#**ipv6 unicast-routing**	Enables the forwarding of IPv6 unicast datagrams globally on the router
Houston(config)#**interface fastethernet 0/0**	Enters interface configuration mode
Houston(config-if)#**ipv6 enable**	Automatically configures an IPv6 link-local address on the interface and enables IPv6 processing on the interface
Houston(config-if)#**ipv6 address 2001:db8:c18:2::/64 eui-64**	Configures a global IPv6 address with an interface identifier in the low-order 64 bits of the IPv6 address
Houston(config-if)#**ipv6 rip tower enable**	Creates the RIPng process named tower and enables RIPng on the interface

Houston(config-if)#**no shutdown**	Activates the interface
Houston(config-if)#**interface fastethernet 0/1**	Enters interface configuration mode
Houston(config-if)#**ipv6 enable**	Automatically configures an IPv6 link-local address on the interface and enables IPv6 processing on the interface
Houston(config-if)#**ipv6 address 2001:db8:c18:3::/64 eui-64**	Configures a global IPv6 address with an interface identifier in the low-order 64 bits of the IPv6 address
Houston(config-if)#**ipv6 rip tower enable**	Creates the RIPng process named tower and enables RIPng on the interface
Houston(config-if)#**no shutdown**	Activates the interface
Houston(config-if)#**exit**	Moves to global configuration mode
Houston(config)#**exit**	Moves to privileged mode
Houston#**copy running-config startup-config**	Saves the configuration to NVRAM

IPv6 Tunnels: Manual Overlay Tunnel

NOTE: Although not part of the official CCNA exam objectives, the concept of IPv6 tunnels is one that network administrators dealing with IPv6 need to be comfortable with.

Figure 25-2 illustrates the network topology for the configuration that follows, which shows how IPv6 tunnels are created.

Figure 25-2   Network Topology for IPv6 Tunnel Creation

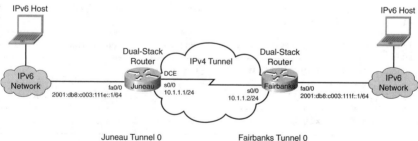

Juneau Router

`Router>enable`	Moves to privileged mode
`Router#configure terminal`	Moves to global configuration mode
`Router(config)#hostname Juneau`	Sets the host name of the router
`Juneau(config)#ipv6 unicast-routing`	Enables the forwarding of IPv6 unicast datagrams globally on the router
`Juneau(config)#interface tunnel0`	Moves to tunnel interface configuration mode
`Juneau(config-if)#ipv6 address 2001:db8:c003:1104::1/64`	Assigns an IPv6 address to this interface
`Juneau(config-if)#tunnel source serial 0/0`	Specifies the source interface type and number for the tunnel interface
`Juneau(config-if)#tunnel destination 10.1.1.2`	Specifies the destination IPv4 address for the tunnel interface
`Juneau(config-if)#tunnel mode ipv6ip`	Defines a manual IPv6 tunnel; specifically, that IPv6 is the passenger protocol and IPv4 is both the encapsulation and protocol for the IPv6 tunnel
`Juneau(config-if)#interface fastethernet 0/0`	Moves to interface configuration mode
`Juneau(config-if)#ipv6 address 2001:db8:c003:111e::1/64`	Assigns an IPv6 address to this interface
`Juneau(config-if)#no shutdown`	Activates the interface
`Juneau(config-if)#interface serial 0/0`	Moves to interface configuration mode
`Juneau(config-if)#ip address 10.1.1.1 255.255.255.252`	Assigns an IPv4 address and netmask
`Juneau(config-if)#clock rate 56000`	Sets the clock rate on interface
`Juneau(config-if)#no shutdown`	Starts the interface
`Juneau(config-if)#exit`	Moves to global configuration mode
`Juneau(config)#exit`	Moves to privileged mode
`Juneau#copy running-config startup-config`	Saves the configuration to NVRAM

Fairbanks Router

`Router>enable`	Moves to privileged mode
`Router#configure terminal`	Moves to global configuration mode
`Router(config)#hostname Fairbanks`	Sets the host name of the router
`Fairbanks(config)#interface tunnel0`	Moves to tunnel interface configuration mode
`Fairbanks(config-if)#ipv6 address 2001:db8:c003:1104::2/64`	Assigns an IPv6 address to this interface
`Fairbanks(config-if)#tunnel source serial 0/0`	Specifies the source interface type and number for the tunnel interface
`Fairbanks(config-if)#tunnel destination 10.1.1.1`	Specifies the destination IPv4 address for the tunnel interface
`Fairbanks(config-if)#tunnel mode ipv6ip`	Defines a manual IPv6 tunnel; specifically, that IPv6 is the passenger protocol and IPv4 is both the encapsulation and protocol for the IPv6 tunnel
`Fairbanks(config-if)#interface fastethernet 0/0`	Moves to interface configuration mode
`Fairbanks(config-if)#ipv6 address 2001:db8:c003:111f::1/64`	Assigns an IPv6 address to this interface
`Fairbanks(config-if)#no shutdown`	Activates the interface
`Fairbanks(config-if)#interface serial 0/0`	Moves to interface configuration mode
`Fairbanks(config-if)#ip address 10.1.1.2 255.255.255.252`	Assigns an IPv4 address and netmask
`Fairbanks(config-if)#no shutdown`	Starts the interface
`Fairbanks(config-if)#exit`	Moves to global configuration mode
`Fairbanks(config)#exit`	Moves to privileged mode
`Fairbanks#copy running-config startup-config`	Saves the configuration to NVRAM

Static Routes in IPv6

> **NOTE**:   Although not part of the CCNA exam objectives, the concept of static routes in IPv6 is one that network administrators dealing with IPv6 need to be comfortable with.

> **NOTE**:   To create a static route in IPv6, you use the same format as creating a static route in IPv4.

Figure 25-3 illustrates the network topology for the configuration that follows, which shows how to configure static routes with IPv6. Note that only the static routes on the Austin router are displayed.

Figure 25-3   Network Topology for IPv6 Static Route Configuration

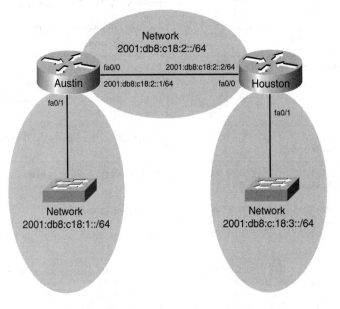

Austin(config)#`ipv6 route`
`2001:db8:c18:3::/64`
`2001:db8:c18:2::/64`
	Creates a static route configured to send all packets to a next-hop address of 2001:db8:c18:2::2

Austin(config)#`ipv6 route`
`2001:db8:c18:3::/64 fastethernet`
`0/0`
	Creates a directly attached static route configured to send packets out interface fastethernet 0/0

Austin(config)#`ipv6 route`
`2001:db8:c18:3::/64  fastethernet`
`0/0 2001:db8:c18:2::2`
	Creates a fully specified static route on a broadcast interface

Floating Static Routes in IPv6

NOTE: Although not part of the CCNA exam objectives, the concept of floating static routes in IPv6 is one that network administrators dealing with IPv6 need to be comfortable with.

To create a static route with an administrative distance (AD) set to 200, as opposed the default AD of one (1), enter the following command, for example:

`Austin(config)#` **`ipv6 route 2001:db8:c18:3::/64 fastethernet 0/0 200`**

The default ADs used in IPv4 are the same for IPv6.

Verifying and Troubleshooting IPv6

CAUTION: Using the **debug** command may severely affect router performance and might even cause the router to reboot. Always exercise caution when using the **debug** command. Do not leave **debug** on. Use it long enough to gather needed information, and then disable debugging with the **undebug all** command.

TIP: Send your **debug** output to a syslog server to ensure you have a copy of it in case your router is overloaded and needs to reboot.

`Router#`**`clear ipv6 rip`**	Deletes routes from the IPv6 RIP routing table and, if installed, routes in the IPv6 routing table
`Router#`**`clear ipv6 route *`**	Deletes all routes from the IPv6 routing table
	NOTE: Clearing all routes from the routing table will cause high CPU utilization rates as the routing table is rebuilt.
`Router#`**`clear ipv6 route 2001:db8:c18:3::/64`**	Clears this specific route from the IPv6 routing table.
`Router#`**`clear ipv6 traffic`**	Resets IPv6 traffic counters.
`Router#`**`debug ipv6 packet`**	Displays debug messages for IPv6 packets.
`Router#`**`debug ipv6 rip`**	Displays debug messages for IPv6 RIP routing transactions.

`Router#debug ipv6 routing`	Displays debug messages for IPv6 routing table updates and route cache updates.
`Router#show ipv6 interface`	Displays the status of interfaces configured for IPv6.
`Router#show ipv6 interface brief`	Displays a summarized status of interfaces configured for IPv6.
`Router#show ipv6 neighbors`	Displays IPv6 neighbor discovery cache information.
`Router#show ipv6 protocols`	Displays the parameters and current state of the active IPv6 routing protocol processes.
`Router#show ipv6 rip`	Displays information about the current IPv6 RIP process.
`Router#show ipv6 route`	Displays the current IPv6 routing table.
`Router#show ipv6 route summary`	Displays a summarized form of the current IPv6 routing table.
`Router#show ipv6 routers`	Displays IPv6 router advertisement information received from other routers.
`Router#show ipv6 static`	Displays only static IPv6 routes installed in the routing table.
`Router#show ipv6 static 2001:db8:5555:0/16`	Displays only static route information about the specific address given.
`Router#show ipv6 static interface serial 0/0`	Displays only static route information with the specified interface as the outgoing interface.
`Router#show ipv6 static detail`	Displays a more detailed entry for IPv6 static routes.
`Router#show ipv6 traffic`	Displays statistics about IPv6 traffic.
`Router#show ipv6 tunnel`	Displays IPv6 tunnel information.

IPv6 Ping

To diagnose basic network connectivity using IPv6 to the specified address, enter the following command:

```
Router#ping ipv6 2001:db8::3/64
```

The following characters can be displayed as output when using PING in IPv6.

Character	Description
!	Each exclamation point indicates receipt of a reply.
.	Each period indicates that the network server timed out while waiting for a reply.
?	Unknown error.
@	Unreachable for unknown reason.
A	Administratively unreachable. Usually means that an access control list (ACL) is blocking traffic.
B	Packet too big.
H	Host unreachable.
N	Network unreachable (beyond scope).
P	Port unreachable.
R	Parameter problem.
T	Time exceeded.
U	No route to host.

PART IX

WANs

Chapter 26   HDLC and PPP

Chapter 27   Frame Relay

HDLC and PPP

This chapter provides information and commands concerning the following topics:

- Configuring HDLC encapsulation on a serial line
- Configuring PPP on a serial line (mandatory commands)
- Configuring PPP on a serial line (optional commands), including those commands concerning the following
  - Compression
  - Link quality
  - Multilink
  - Authentication
- Verifying or troubleshooting a serial link/PPP encapsulation
- Configuration example: PPP

Configuring HDLC Encapsulation on a Serial Line

Router#`configure terminal`	Moves to global configuration mode
Router(config)#`interface serial 0/0/0`	Moves to interface configuration mode
Router(config-if)#`encapsulation hdlc`	Sets the encapsulation mode for this interface to HDLC

NOTE: HDLC is the default encapsulation for synchronous serial links on Cisco routers. You would only use the **encapsulation hdlc** command to return the link to its default state.

Configuring PPP on a Serial Line (Mandatory Commands)

Router#`configure terminal`	Moves to global configuration mode
Router(config)#`interface serial 0/0/0`	Moves to interface configuration mode
Router(config-if)#`encapsulation ppp`	Changes encapsulation from default HDLC to PPP

> **NOTE:** You must execute the **encapsulation ppp** command on both sides of the serial link for the link to become active.

Configuring PPP on a Serial Line (Optional Commands): Compression

Router(config-if)#**compress predictor**	Enables the predictor compression algorithm
Router(config-if)#**compress stac**	Enables the stac compression algorithm

Configuring PPP on a Serial Line (Optional Commands): Link Quality

Router(config-if)#**ppp quality** *x*	Ensures the link has a quality of *x* percent. Otherwise, the link will shut down.

> **NOTE:** In PPP, the Link Control Protocol allows for an optional link-quality determination phase. In this phase, the link is tested to determine whether the link quality is sufficient to bring up any Layer 3 protocols. If you use the command **ppp quality** *x*, where *x* is equal to a certain percent, you must meet that percentage of quality on the link. If the link does not meet that percentage level, the link cannot be created and will shut down.

Configuring PPP on a Serial Line (Optional Commands): Multilink

Router(config-if)#**ppp multilink**	Enables load balancing across multiple links

Configuring PPP on a Serial Line (Optional Commands): Authentication

Router(config)#**username routerb password cisco**	Sets a username of routerb and a password of **cisco** for authentication from the other side of the PPP serial link. This is used by the local router to authenticate the PPP peer.
Router(config)#**interface serial 0/0/0**	Moves to interface configuration mode.

`Router(config-if)#ppp` `authentication pap`	Turns on Password Authentication Protocol (PAP) authentication only.
`Router(config-if)#ppp` `authentication chap`	Turns on Challenge Handshake Authentication Protocol (CHAP) authentication only.
`Router(config-if)#ppp` `authentication pap chap`	Defines that the link will use PAP authentication, but will try CHAP if PAP fails or is rejected by other side.
`Router(config-if)#ppp` `authentication chap pap`	Defines that the link will use CHAP authentication, but will try PAP if CHAP fails or is rejected by other side.
`Router(config-if)#ppp pap sent-` `username routerb password cisco`	This command must be set if using PAP in Cisco IOS Software Release 11.1 or later.

TIP: When setting authentication, make sure that your usernames match the name of the router on the other side of the link, and that the passwords on each router match the other. Usernames and passwords are case sensitive. Consider the following example:

`Edmonton(config)#username Calgary` `password cisco`	`Calgary(config)#username Edmonton` `password cisco`
`Edmonton(config)#interface serial` `0/0/0`	`Calgary(config)#interface serial` `0/0/0`
`Edmonton(config-if)#encapsulation` `ppp`	`Calgary(config-if)#encapsulation` `ppp`
`Edmonton(config-if)#ppp` `authentication chap`	`Calgary(config-if)#ppp` `authentication chap`

NOTE: Because PAP does not encrypt its password as it is sent across the link, recommended practice is that you use CHAP as your authentication method.

Verifying or Troubleshooting a Serial Link/PPP Encapsulation

`Router#show interfaces serial` *x*	Lists information for serial interface *x*
`Router#show controllers serial` *x*	Tells you what type of cable (DCE/DTE) is plugged into your interface and whether a clock rate has been set

`Router#debug serial interface`	Displays whether serial keepalive counters are incrementing
`Router#debug ppp`	Displays any traffic related to PPP
`Router#debug ppp packet`	Displays PPP packets that are being sent and received
`Router#debug ppp negotiation`	Displays PPP packets related to the negotiation of the PPP link
`Router#debug ppp error`	Displays PPP error packets
`Router#debug ppp authentication`	Displays PPP packets related to the authentication of the PPP link
`Router#debug ppp compression`	Displays PPP packets related to the compression of packets across the link

TIP: With frequent lab use, serial cable pins often get bent, which might prevent the router from seeing the cable. The output from the command **show controllers interface serial** *x* shows no cable even though a cable is physically present.

Configuration Example: PPP

Figure 26-1 illustrates the network topology for the configuration that follows, which shows how to configure PPP using the commands covered in this chapter.

Figure 26-1   Network Topology for PPP Configuration

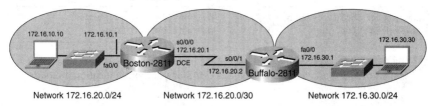

Network 172.16.20.0/24   Network 172.16.20.0/30   Network 172.16.30.0/24

NOTE: The host name, password, and interfaces have all been configured as per the configuration example in Chapter 6, "Configuring a Single Cisco Router."

Boston Router

`Boston>enable`	Moves to privileged mode
`Boston#configure terminal`	Moves to global configuration mode

`Boston(config)#username Buffalo password academy`	Sets the local username and password for PPP authentication of the PPP peer
`Boston(config-if)#interface serial 0/0/0`	Moves to interface configuration mode
`Boston(config-if)#description Link to Buffalo Router`	Defines the locally significant link description
`Boston(config-if)#ip address 172.16.20.1 255.255.255.252`	Assigns an IP address and netmask
`Boston(config-if)#clock rate 56000`	Sets the clock rate to the data communications equipment (DCE) side of link
`Boston(config-if) #encapsulation ppp`	Turns on PPP encapsulation
`Boston(config-if)#ppp authentication chap`	Turns on CHAP authentication
`Boston(config-if)#no shutdown`	Turns on the interface
`Boston(config-if)#exit`	Returns to global configuration mode
`Boston(config)#exit`	Returns to privileged mode
`Boston#copy running-config startup-config`	Saves the configuration to NVRAM

Buffalo Router

`Buffalo>enable`	Moves to privileged mode
`Buffalo#configure terminal`	Moves to global configuration mode
`Buffalo(config)#username Boston password academy`	Sets the username and password for PPP authentication
`Buffalo(config-if)#interface serial 0/0/1`	Moves to interface configuration mode
`Buffalo(config-if)#description Link to Boston Router`	Defines the locally significant link description
`Buffalo(config-if)#ip address 172.16.20.2 255.255.255.252`	Assigns an IP address and netmask
`Buffalo(config-if) #encapsulation ppp`	Turns on PPP encapsulation

Buffalo(config-if)#**ppp authentication chap**	Turns on CHAP authentication
Buffalo(config-if)#**no shutdown**	Turns on the interface
Buffalo(config-if)#**Ctrl-Z**	Exits back to privileged mode
Buffalo#**copy running-config startup-config**	Saves the configuration to NVRAM

CHAPTER 27

Frame Relay

This chapter provides information and commands concerning the following topics:

- Configuring Frame Relay
  - Setting the Frame Relay encapsulation type
  - Setting the Frame Relay encapsulation LMI type
  - Setting the Frame Relay DLCI number
  - Configuring a Frame Relay **map** statement
  - Configuring a description of the interface (optional)
  - Configuring Frame Relay using subinterfaces
- Verifying Frame Relay
- Troubleshooting Frame Relay
- Configuration examples: Frame Relay

Configuring Frame Relay

Setting the Frame Relay Encapsulation Type

`Router(config)#interface serial 0/0/0`	
`Router(config-if)#encapsulation frame-relay`	Turns on Frame Relay encapsulation with the default encapsulation type of cisco.
Or	
`Router(config-if)#encapsulation frame-relay ietf`	Turns on Frame Relay encapsulation with the encapsulation type of ietf (RFC 1490). Use the ietf encapsulation method if connecting to a non-Cisco router.

Setting the Frame Relay Encapsulation LMI Type

`Router(config-if)#frame-relay lmi-type {ansi │ cisco │ q933a}`	Depending on the option you select, this command sets the LMI type to the ANSI standard, the Cisco standard, or the ITU-T Q.933 Annex A standard.

NOTE: As of Cisco IOS Software Release 11.2, the LMI type is auto-sensed, making this command optional.

Setting the Frame Relay DLCI Number

`Router(config-if)#frame-relay interface-dlci 110`	Sets the DLCI number of 110 on the local interface and enters Frame Relay DLCI configuration mode
`Router(config-fr-dlci)#exit`	Returns to interface configuration mode
`Router(config-if)#exit`	Returns to global configuration mode
`Router(config)#`	

Configuring a Frame Relay map Statement

`Router(config-if)#frame-relay map ip 192.168.100.1 110 broadcast`	Maps the remote IP address (192.168.100.1) to the local DLCI number (110). The optional **broadcast** keyword specifies that broadcasts across IP should be forwarded to this address. This is necessary when using dynamic routing protocols.
`Router(config-if)#no frame-relay inverse arp`	Turns off Inverse ARP.

NOTE: Cisco routers have Inverse Address Resolution Protocol (IARP) turned on by default. This means that the router will go out and create the mapping for you. If the remote router does not support IARP, or you want to control broadcast traffic over the permanent virtual circuit (PVC), you must statically set the DLCI/IP mappings and turn off IARP.

You need to issue the **no frame-relay inverse-arp** command before you issue the **no shutdown** command; otherwise, the interface performs IARP before you can turn it off.

Configuring a Description of the Interface (Optional)

`Router(config-if)#description` `Connection to the Branch office`	Optional command to allow you to enter in additional information such as contact name, PVC description, and so on

Configuring Frame Relay Using Subinterfaces

Subinterfaces enable you to solve split-horizon problems and to create multiple PVCs on a single physical connection to the Frame Relay cloud.

`Router(config)#interface serial 0/0/0`	
`Router(config-if)#encapsulation frame-relay ietf`	Sets the Frame Relay encapsulation type for all subinterfaces on this interface
`Router(config-if)#frame-relay lmi-type ansi`	Sets the LMI type for all subinterfaces on this interface
`Router(config-if)#no ip address`	Ensures there is no IP address set to this interface
`Router(config-if)#no shutdown`	Enables the interface
`Router(config-if)#interface serial 0/0/0.102 point-to-point`	Creates a point-to-point subinterface numbered 102
`Router(config-subif)#ip address 192.168.10.1 255.255.255.0`	Assigns an IP address and netmask to the subinterface
`Router(config-subif)#frame-relay interface-dlci 102`	Assigns a DLCI to the subinterface
`Router(config-subif)#interface serial 0/0/0.103 point-to-point`	Creates a point-to-point subinterface numbered 103
`Router(config-subif)#ip address 192.168.20.1 255.255.255.0`	Assigns an IP address and netmask to the subinterface
`Router(config-subif)#frame-relay interface-dlci 103`	Assigns a DLCI to the subinterface
`Router(config-subif)#exit`	Returns to interface configuration mode
`Router(config-if)#exit`	Returns to global configuration mode
`Router(config)#`	

NOTE: There are two types of subinterfaces:

- **Point-to-point**, where a single PVC connects one router to another and each subinterface is in its own IP subnet.

- **Multipoint**, where the router is the middle point of a group of routers. All other routers connect to each other through this router, and all routers are in the same subnet.

NOTE: Use the **no ip split-horizon** command to turn off split-horizon commands on multipoint interfaces so that remote sites can see each other.

Verifying Frame Relay

Router#**show frame-relay map**	Displays IP/DLCI map entries
Router#**show frame-relay pvc**	Displays the status of all PVCs configured
Router#**show frame-relay lmi**	Displays LMI statistics
Router#**clear frame-relay counters**	Clears and resets all Frame Relay counters
Router#**clear frame-relay inarp**	Clears all Inverse ARP entries from the map table

TIP: If the **clear frame-relay inarp** command does not clear Frame Relay maps, you might need to reload the router.

Troubleshooting Frame Relay

Router#**debug frame-relay lmi**	Used to help determine whether a router and Frame Relay switch are exchanging LMI packets properly

Configuration Examples: Frame Relay

Figure 27-1 shows the network topology for the Frame Relay configuration that follows using the commands covered in this chapter.

Figure 27-1   *Frame Relay Network*

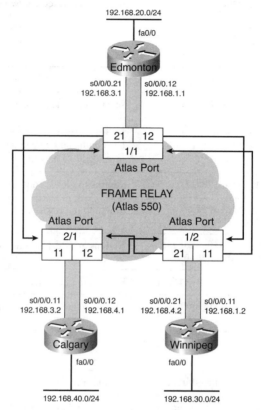

192.168.20.0/24

NOTE: This diagram assumes the use of an Adtran Atlas 550 device to simulate the Frame Relay cloud. Three physical ports (1/1, 2/1, and 2/2) are used to interconnect the three cities.

Edmonton Router

`router>`**`enable`**	Moves to privileged mode.
`router#`**`configure terminal`**	Moves to global configuration mode.
`router(config)#`**`host Edmonton`**	Sets the host name.
`Edmonton(config)#`**`no ip domain-lookup`**	Turns off DNS queries so that spelling mistakes do not slow you down.

`Edmonton(config)#enable secret cisco`	Sets the encrypted password to **cisco**.
`Edmonton(config)#line console 0`	Moves to line console configuration mode.
`Edmonton(config-line)#login`	The user will be prompted for a password.
`Edmonton(config-line)#password class`	Sets the console line password to **class**.
`Edmonton(config-line)#logging synchronous`	The command being entered will be appended to a new line.
`Edmonton(config-line)#exit`	Returns to global configuration mode.
`Edmonton(config)#interface fastethernet 0/0`	Moves to interface configuration mode.
`Edmonton(config-if)#ip address 192.168.20.1 255.255.255.0`	Assigns an IP address and netmask.
`Edmonton(config-if)#no shutdown`	Enables the interface.
`Edmonton(config-if)#interface serial 0/0/0`	Moves to interface configuration mode.
`Edmonton(config-if)#encapsulation frame-relay`	Turns on Frame Relay encapsulation.
`Edmonton(config-if)#no shutdown`	Enables the interface.
`Edmonton(config-if)#interface serial 0/0/0.12 point-to-point`	Creates subinterface 12.
`Edmonton(config-subif)#description link to Winnipeg router DLCI 12`	Creates a locally significant description of the interface.
`Edmonton(config-subif)#ip address 192.168.1.1 255.255.255.0`	Assigns an IP address and netmask.
`Edmonton(config-subif)#frame-relay interface-dlci 12 point-to-point`	Assigns a DLCI number.
`Edmonton(config-subif)#interface serial 0/0/0.21`	Creates subinterface 21.
`Edmonton(config-subif)#description link to Calgary router DLCI 21`	Creates a locally significant description of the interface.

`Edmonton(config-subif)#`**`ip address`** **`192.168.3.1 255.255.255.0`**	Assigns an IP address and netmask.
`Edmonton(config-subif)#`**`frame-`** **`relay interface dlci 21`**	Assigns a DLCI number.
`Edmonton(config-subif)#`**`exit`**	Returns to interface configuration mode.
`Edmonton(config-if)#`**`exit`**	Returns to global configuration mode.
`Edmonton(config)#`**`router eigrp 100`**	Turns on the EIGRP routing process 100.
`Edmonton(config-router)#`**`network`** **`192.168.1.0`**	Advertises network 192.168.1.0, which connects to Winnipeg.
`Edmonton(config-router)#`**`network`** **`192.168.3.0`**	Advertises network 192.168.3.0, which connects to Calgary.
`Edmonton(config-router)#`**`network`** **`192.168.20.0`**	Advertises network 192.168.20.0, which is directly connected to the local fastethernet 0/0 interface.
`Edmonton(config-router)#`Ctrl z	Returns to privileged mode.
`Edmonton#`**`copy running-config`** **`startup-config`**	Saves the configuration to NVRAM.

Winnipeg Router

`router>`**`enable`**	Moves to privileged mode.
`router#`**`configure terminal`**	Moves to global configuration mode.
`router(config)#`**`host Winnipeg`**	Sets the host name.
`Winnipeg(config)#`**`no ip domain-`** **`lookup`**	Turns off DNS queries so that spelling mistakes do not slow you down.
`Winnipeg(config)#`**`enable secret`** **`cisco`**	Sets the encrypted password to **cisco**.
`Winnipeg(config)#`**`line console 0`**	Moves to line console configuration mode.
`Winnipeg(config-line)#`**`login`**	The user will be prompted for a password to access the console port.
`Winnipeg(config-line)#`**`password`** **`class`**	Sets the console line password to **class**.

`Winnipeg(config-line)#logging synchronous`	The command being entered will be appended to a new line.
`Winnipeg(config-line)#exit`	Returns to global configuration mode.
`Winnipeg(config)#interface fastethernet 0/0`	Moves to interface configuration mode.
`Winnipeg(config-if)#ip address 192.168.30.1 255.255.255.0`	Assigns an IP address and netmask.
`Winnipeg(config-if)#no shutdown`	Enables the interface.
`Winnipeg(config-if)#interface serial 0/0/0`	Moves to interface configuration mode.
`Winnipeg(config-if)#encapsulation frame-relay`	Turns on Frame Relay encapsulation.
`Winnipeg(config-if)#no shutdown`	Enables the interface.
`Winnipeg(config-if)#interface serial 0/0/0.11 point-to-point`	Creates subinterface 11.
`Winnipeg(config-subif)#description link to Edmonton router DLCI 11`	Creates a locally significant description of the interface.
`Winnipeg(config-subif)#ip address 192.168.1.2 255.255.255.0`	Assigns an IP address and netmask.
`Winnipeg(config-subif)#frame-relay interface-dlci 11`	Assigns a DLCI number.
`Winnipeg(config-subif)#interface s 0/0.21 point-to-point`	Creates subinterface 21.
`Winnipeg(config-subif)#description link to Calgary router DLCI 21`	Creates a locally significant description of the interface.
`Winnipeg(config-subif)#ip address 192.168.4.2 255.255.255.0`	Assigns an IP address and netmask.
`Winnipeg(config-subif)#frame-relay interface-dlci 21`	Assigns a DLCI number.
`Winnipeg(config-subif)#exit`	Returns to interface configuration mode.
`Winnipeg(config-if)#exit`	Returns to global configuration mode.
`Winnipeg(config)#router eigrp 100`	Turns on EIGRP routing process 100.

`Winnipeg(config-router)#`**`network`** `192.168.1.0`	Advertises network 192.168.1.0 to Edmonton.
`Winnipeg(config-router)#`**`network`** `192.168.4.0`	Advertises network 192.168.4.0 to Calgary.
`Winnipeg(config-router)#`**`network`** `192.168.30.0`	Advertises network 192.168.30.0 directly connected to fastethernet 0/0.
`Winnipeg(config-router)#`Ctrl z	Returns directly to privileged mode.
`Winnipeg#`**`copy running-config startup-config`**	Saves the configuration to NVRAM.

Calgary Router

`router>`**`enable`**	Moves to privileged mode.
`router#`**`configure terminal`**	Moves to global configuration mode.
`router(config)#`**`host Calgary`**	Sets the host name.
`Calgary(config)#`**`no ip domain-lookup`**	Turns off DNS queries so that spelling mistakes do not slow you down.
`Calgary(config)#`**`enable secret cisco`**	Sets the encrypted password to **cisco**.
`Calgary(config)#`**`line console 0`**	Moves to line console configuration mode.
`Calgary(config-line)#`**`login`**	The user will be prompted for a password to use the console port.
`Calgary(config-line)#`**`password class`**	Sets the console line password to **class**.
`Calgary(config-line)#`**`logging synchronous`**	The command being entered will be appended to a new line.
`Calgary(config-line)#`**`exit`**	Returns to global configuration mode.
`Calgary(config)#`**`interface fastethernet 0/0`**	Moves to interface configuration mode.
`Calgary(config-if)#`**`ip address 192.168.40.1 255.255.255.0`**	Assigns an IP address and netmask.
`Calgary(config-if)#`**`no shutdown`**	Enables the interface.

`Calgary(config-if)#interface serial 0/0/0`	Moves to interface configuration mode.
`Calgary(config-if)#encapsulation frame-relay`	Turns on Frame Relay encapsulation.
`Calgary(config-if)#no shutdown`	Enables the interface.
`Calgary(config-if)#int s0/0/0.11 point-to-point`	Creates subinterface 11.
`Calgary(config-subif)#description link to Edmonton router DLCI 11`	Creates a locally significant description of the interface.
`Calgary(config-subif)#ip address 192.168.3.2 255.255.255.0`	Assigns an IP address and netmask.
`Calgary(config-subif)#frame-relay interface-dlci 11 point-to-point`	Assigns a DLCI number.
`Calgary(config-subif)#interface serial 0/0/0.12`	Creates subinterface 12.
`Calgary(config-subif)#description link to Winnipeg router DLCI 12`	Creates a locally significant description of the interface.
`Calgary(config-subif)#ip address 192.168.4.1 255.255.255.0`	Assigns an IP address and netmask.
`Calgary(config-subif)#frame-relay interface-dlci 12`	Assigns a DLCI number.
`Calgary(config-subif)#exit`	Returns to interface configuration mode.
`Calgary(config-if)#exit`	Returns to global configuration mode.
`Calgary(config)#router eigrp 100`	Turns on EIGRP routing process 100.
`Calgary(config-router)#network 192.168.3.0`	Advertises the network to Edmonton.
`Calgary(config-router)#network 192.168.4.0`	Advertises the network to Calgary.
`Calgary(config-router)#network 192.168.40.0`	Advertises the local fastethernet 0/0 network.
`Calgary(config-router)#`Ctrl-Z	Returns directly to privileged mode.
`Calgary#copy running-config startup-config`	Saves the configuration to NVRAM.

Network Security

Chapter 28   IP Access Control List Security

Chapter 29   Security Device Manager

IP Access Control List Security

This chapter provides information and commands concerning the following topics:

- Access list numbers
- Using wildcard masks
- ACL keywords
- Creating standard ACLs
- Applying standard ACLs to an interface
- Verifying ACLs
- Removing ACLs
- Creating extended ACLs
- Applying extended ACLs to an interface
- The **established** keyword (optional)
- Creating named ACLs
- Using sequence numbers in named ACLs
- Removing specific lines in named ACLs using sequence numbers
- Sequence number tips
- Including comments about entries in ACLs
- Restricting virtual terminal access
- Configuration examples: ACLs

Access List Numbers

1–99 or 1300–1999	Standard IP
100–199 or 2000–2699	Extended IP
600–699	AppleTalk
800–899	IPX
900–999	Extended IPX
1000–1099	IPX Service Advertising Protocol

Using Wildcard Masks

When compared to an IP address, a wildcard mask identifies which addresses get matched to be applied to the **permit** or **deny** argument in an access control list (ACL) statement:

- A 0 (zero) in a wildcard mask means to check the corresponding bit in the address for an exact match.
- A 1 (one) in a wildcard mask means to ignore the corresponding bit in the address—can be either 1 or 0.

Example 1: 172.16.0.0 0.0.255.255

> 172.16.0.0 = 10101100.00010000.00000000.00000000
> 0.0.255.255 = 00000000.00000000.11111111.11111111
> result =   10101100.00010000.*xxxxxxxx.xxxxxxxx*
> 172.16.*x.x* (Anything between 172.16.0.0 and 172.16.255.255 will match the example statement.)

> **TIP:** An octet of all 0s means that the octet has to match exactly to the address. An octet of all 1s means that the octet can be ignored.

Example 2: 172.16.8.0 0.0.7.255

> 172.168.8.0 = 10101100.00010000.00001000.00000000
> 0.0.0.7.255 = 00000000.00000000.00000111.11111111
> result =   10101100.00010000.00001*xxx.xxxxxxxx*
> 00001*xxx* =   00001*000* to 00001*111* = 8–15
> *xxxxxxxx* =   00000000 to 11111111 = 0–255
> Anything between 172.16.8.0 and 172.16.15.255 will match the example statement.

ACL Keywords

any	Used in place of 0.0.0.0 255.255.255.255, will match any address that it is compared against
host	Used in place of 0.0.0.0 in the wildcard mask, will match only one specific address

Creating Standard ACLs

`Router(config)#`**`access-list 10 permit`** `172.16.0.0 0.0.255.255`	Read this line to say, "All packets with a source IP address of 172.16.$x.x$ will be permitted to continue through the internetwork."
`access-list`	ACL command.
`10`	Arbitrary number between 1 and 99, or 1300 and 1999, designating this as a standard IP ACL.
`permit`	Packets that match this statement will be allowed to continue.
`172.16.0.0`	Source IP address to be compared to.
`0.0.255.255`	Wildcard mask.
`Router(config)#`**`access-list 10 deny host`** `172.17.0.1`	Read this line to say, "All packets with a source IP address of 172.17.0.1 will be dropped and discarded."
`access-list`	ACL command.
`10`	Number between 1 and 99, or 1300 and 1999, designating this as a standard IP ACL.
`deny`	Packets that match this statement will be dropped and discarded.
`host`	Keyword.
`172.17.0.1`	Specific host address.

`Router(config)#access-list 10 permit any`	Read this line to say, "All packets with any source IP address will be permitted to continue through the internetwork."
`access-list`	ACL command.
`10`	Number between 1 and 99, or 1300 and 1999, designating this as a standard IP ACL.
`permit`	Packets that match this statement will be allowed to continue.
`any`	Keyword to mean all IP addresses.

TIP: An implicit **deny** statement is hard-coded into every ACL. You cannot see it, but it states "deny everything not already permitted." This is always the last line of any ACL. If you want to defeat this implicit **deny**, put a **permit any** statement in your standard ACLs or **permit ip any any** in your extended ACLs as the last line.

Applying Standard ACLs to an Interface

`Router(config)#interface fastethernet 0/0`	Moves to interface configuration mode.
`Router(config-if)#ip access-group 10 in`	Takes all access list lines that are defined as being part of group 10 and applies them in an inbound manner. Packets going into the router from fastethernet 0/0 will be checked.

TIP: Access lists can be applied in either an inbound direction (keyword **in**) or in an outbound direction (keyword **out**).

TIP: Apply a standard ACL as close as possible to the destination network or device.

Verifying ACLs

`Router#show ip interface`	Displays any ACLs applied to that interface
`Router#show access-lists`	Displays the contents of all ACLs on the router
`Router#show access-list` *access-list-number*	Displays the contents of the ACL by the number specified
`Router#show access-list` *name*	Displays the contents of the ACL by the *name* specified
`Router#show run`	Displays all ACLs and interface assignments

Removing ACLs

`Router(config)#no access-list 10`	Removes *all* ACLs numbered 10

Creating Extended ACLs

`Router(config)#access-list 110 permit tcp 172.16.0.0 0.0.0.255 192.168.100.0 0.0.0.255 eq 80`	Read this line to say, "HTTP packets with a source IP address of 172.16.0.*x* will be permitted to travel to the destination address 192.168.100.*x*."
`access-list`	ACL command.
`110`	Number is between 100 and 199, or 2000 and 2699, designating this as an extended IP ACL.
`permit`	Packets that match this statement will be allowed to continue.
`tcp`	Protocol must be TCP.

`172.16.0.0`	Source IP address to be compared to.
`0.0.0.255`	Wildcard mask for the source IP address.
`192.168.100.0`	Destination IP address to be compared to.
`0.0.0.255`	Wildcard mask for the destination IP address.
`eq`	Operand, means "equal to."
`80`	Port 80, indicating HTTP traffic.
`Router(config)#access-list 110 deny tcp any` `192.168.100.7 0.0.0.0 eq 23`	Read this line to say, "Telnet packets with any source IP address will be dropped if they are addressed to specific host 192.168.100.7."
`access-list`	ACL command.
`110`	Number is between 100 and 199, or 2000 and 2699, designating this as an extended IP ACL.
`deny`	Packets that match this statement will be dropped and discarded.
`tcp`	Protocol must be TCP protocol.
`any`	Any source IP address.
`192.168.100.7`	Destination IP address to be compared to.
`0.0.0.0`	Wildcard mask; address must match exactly.
`eq`	Operand, means "equal to."
`23`	Port 23, indicating Telnet traffic.

Applying Extended ACLs to an Interface

Router(config)#**interface fastethernet 0/0** Router(config-if)#**ip access-group 110 out**	Moves to interface configuration mode and takes all access list lines that are defined as being part of group 110 and applies them in an outbound manner. Packets going out fastethernet 0/0 will be checked.

TIP: Access lists can be applied in either an inbound direction (keyword **in**) or in an outbound direction (keyword **out**).

TIP: Only one access list can be applied per interface, per direction.

TIP: Apply an extended ACL as close as possible to the source network or device.

The established Keyword (Optional)

Router(config)#**access-list 110 permit tcp 172.16.0.0 0.0.0.255 192.168.100.0 0.0.0.255 eq 80 established**	Indicates an established connection

NOTE: A match will now occur only if the TCP datagram has the ACK or the RST bit set.

TIP: The **established** keyword will work only for TCP, not UDP.

TIP: Consider the following situation: You do not want hackers exploiting port 80 to access your network. Because you do not host a web server, it is possible to block incoming traffic on port 80 ... except that your internal users need web access. When they request a web page, return traffic on port 80 must be allowed. The solution to this problem is to use the **established** command. The ACL will allow the response to enter your network, because it will have the ACK bit set as a result of the initial request from inside your network. Requests from the outside world will still be blocked because the ACK bit will not be set, but responses will be allowed through.

Creating Named ACLs

`Router(config)#ip access-list extended serveraccess`	Creates an extended named ACL called serveraccess and moves to named ACL configuration mode.
`Router(config-ext-nacl)#permit tcp any host 131.108.101.99 eq smtp`	Permits mail packets from any source to reach host 131.108.101.99.
`Router(config-ext-nacl)#permit udp any host 131.108.101.99 eq domain`	Permits Domain Name System (DNS) packets from any source to reach host 131.108.101.99.
`Router(config-ext-nacl)#deny ip any any log`	Denies all other packets from going anywhere. If any packets do get denied, this logs the results for you to look at later.
`Router(config-ext-nacl)#exit`	Returns to global configuration mode.
`Router(config)#interface fastethernet 0/0` `Router(config-if)#ip access-group serveraccess out`	Moves to interface configuration mode and applies this ACL to the fastethernet interface 0/0 in an outbound direction.

Using Sequence Numbers in Named ACLs

`Router(config)#ip access-list extended serveraccess2`	Creates an extended named ACL called serveraccess2.
`Router(config-ext-nacl)#10 permit tcp any host 131.108.101.99 eq smtp`	Uses a sequence number 10 for this line.
`Router(config-ext-nacl)#20 permit udp any host 131.108.101.99 eq domain`	Sequence number 20 will be applied after line 10.
`Router(config-ext-nacl)#30 deny ip any any log`	Sequence number 30 will be applied after line 20.

`Router(config-ext-nacl)#exit`	Returns to global configuration mode.
`Router(config)#interface fastethernet 0/0`	Moves to interface configuration mode.
`Router(config-if)#ip access-group serveraccess2 out`	Applies this ACL in an outbound direction.
`Router(config-if)#exit`	Returns to global configuration mode.
`Router(config)#ip access-list extended serveraccess2`	Moves to named ACL configuration mode for the ACL serveraccess2.
`Router(config-ext-nacl)#25 permit tcp any host 131.108.101.99 eq ftp`	Sequence number 25 places this line after line 20 and before line 30.
`Router(config-ext-nacl)#exit`	Returns to global configuration mode.

TIP: Sequence numbers are used to allow for easier editing of your ACLs. The preceding example used numbers 10, 20, and 30 in the ACL lines. If you had needed to add another line to this ACL, it would have previously been added after the last line—line 30. If you had needed a line to go closer to the top, you would have had to remove the entire ACL and then reapply it with the lines in the correct order. Now you can enter in a new line with a sequence number, placing it in the correct location.

NOTE: The *sequence-number* argument was added in Cisco IOS Software Release 12.2(14)S. It was integrated into Cisco IOS Software Release 12.2(15)T.

Removing Specific Lines in Named ACLs Using Sequence Numbers

`Router(config)#ip access-list extended serveraccess2`	Moves to named ACL configuration mode for the ACL serveraccess2
`Router(config-ext-nacl)#no 20`	Removes line 20 from the list
`Router(config-ext-nacl)#exit`	Returns to global configuration mode

Sequence Number Tips

- Sequence numbers start at 10 and increment by 10 for each line.
- If you forget to add a sequence number, the line is added to the end of the list.
- Sequence numbers are changed on a router reload to reflect the increment by 10 policy (tip 1). If your ACL has numbers 10, 20, 30, 32, 40, 50, and 60 in it, on reload these numbers become 10, 20, 30, 40, 50, 60, 70.
- Sequence numbers cannot be seen when using the Router#**show running-config** or Router#**show startup-config** command. To see sequence numbers, use one of the following commands:

    ```
    Router#show access-lists
    Router#show access-lists list name
    Router#show ip access-list
    Router#show ip access-list list name
    ```

Including Comments About Entries in ACLs

Router(config)#**access-list 10 remark only Jones has access**	The **remark** command allows you to include a comment (limited to 100 characters).
Router(config)#**access-list 10 permit 172.16.100.119**	Read this line to say, "Host 172.16.100.119 will be permitted through the internetwork."
Router(config)#**ip access-list extended telnetaccess**	Creates a named ACL called telnetaccess and moves to named ACL configuration mode.
Router(config-ext-nacl)#**remark do not let Smith have telnet**	The **remark** command allows you to include a comment (limited to 100 characters).
Router(config-ext-nacl)#**deny tcp host 172.16.100.153 any eq telnet**	Read this line to say, "Deny this specific host Telnet access to anywhere in the internetwork."

TIP: You can use the **remark** command in any of the IP numbered standard, IP numbered extended, or named IP ACLs.

TIP: You can use the **remark** command either before or after a **permit** or **deny** statement. Therefore, be consistent in your placement to avoid any confusion as to which line the **remark** statement is referring.

Restricting Virtual Terminal Access

Router(config)#**access-list 2 permit host 172.16.10.2**	Permits host 172.16.10.2 to Telnet into this router based on where this ACL is applied.
Router(config)#**access-list 2 permit 172.16.20.0 0.0.0.255**	Permits anyone from the 172.16.20.*x* address range to Telnet into this router based on where this ACL is applied.
	The implicit **deny** statement restricts anyone else from being permitted to Telnet.
Router(config)#**line vty 0 4**	Moves to vty line configuration mode.
Router(config-line)**access-class 2 in**	Applies this ACL to all 5 vty virtual interfaces in an inbound direction.

TIP: When restricting access through Telnet, use the **access-class** command rather than the **access-group** command, which is used when applying an ACL to a physical interface.

Configuration Examples: ACLs

Figure 28-1 illustrates the network topology for the configuration that follows, which shows five ACL examples using the commands covered in this chapter.

Figure 28-1   Network Topology for ACL Configuration

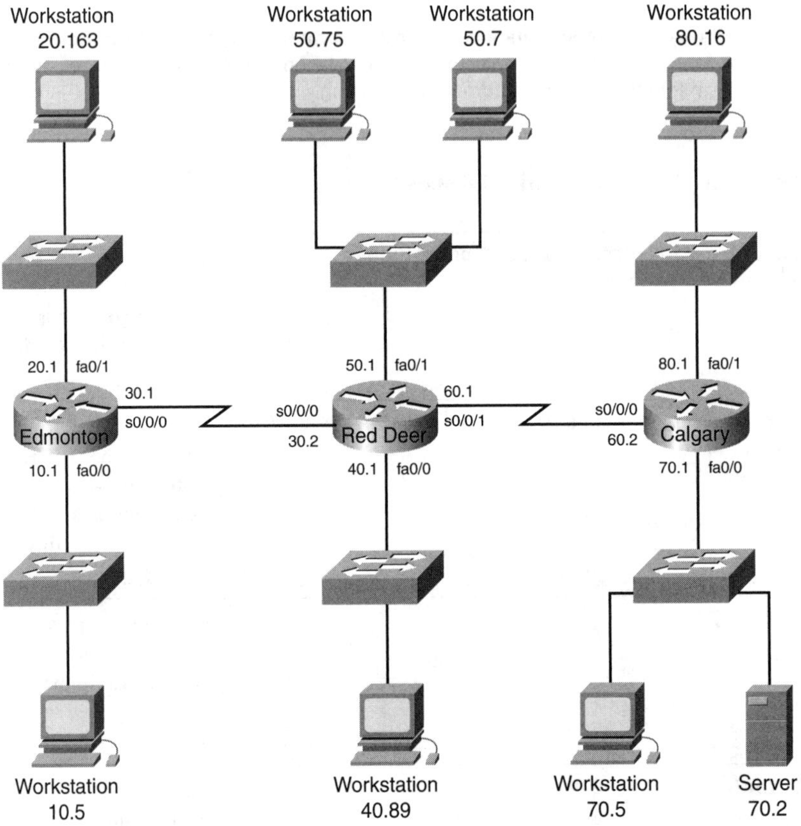

Example 1: Write an ACL that prevents the 10.0 network from accessing the 40.0 network but allows everyone else to.

RedDeer(config)#**access-list 10 deny 172.16.10.0 0.0.0.255**	The standard ACL denies complete network for complete TCP/IP suite of protocols.
RedDeer(config)#**access-list 10 permit any**	Defeats the implicit **deny**.
RedDeer(config)#**interface fastethernet 0/0**	Moves to interface configuration mode.
RedDeer(config)#**ip access-group 10 out**	Applies ACL in an outbound direction.

Example 2: Write an ACL that states that 10.5 cannot access 50.7. Everyone else can.

Edmonton(config)#`access list 115 deny ip host` `172.16.10.5 host 172.16.50.7`	The extended ACL denies specific host for entire TCP/IP suite.
Edmonton(config)#`access list 115 permit ip any any`	All others are permitted through.
Edmonton(config)#`interface fastethernet 0/0`	Moves to interface configuration mode.
Edmonton(config)#`ip access-group 115 in`	Applies the ACL in an inbound direction.

Example 3: Write an ACL that states that 10.5 can Telnet to the Red Deer router. No one else can.

RedDeer(config)#`access-list 20 permit host` `172.16.10.5`	The standard ACL allows a specific host access. The implicit **deny** statement filters everyone else out.
RedDeer(config)#`line vty 0 4`	Moves to virtual terminal lines configuration mode.
RedDeer(config-line)#`access-class 20 in`	Applies ACL 20 in an inbound direction. Remember to use **access-class**, not **access-group**.

Example 4: Write a named ACL that states that 20.163 can Telnet to 70.2. No one else from 20.0 can Telnet to 70.2. Any other host from any other subnet can connect to 70.2 using anything that is available.

Calgary(config)#`ip access-list extended` `serveraccess`	Creates a named ACL and moves to named ACL configuration mode.
Calgary(config-ext-nacl)#`10 permit tcp host` `172.16.20.163 host 172.16.70.2 eq telnet`	The specific host is permitted Telnet access to a specific destination.

`Calgary(config-ext-nacl)#20 deny tcp 172.16.20.0 0.0.0.255 host 172.16.70.2 eq telnet`	No other hosts are allowed to Telnet to the server.
`Calgary(config-ext-nacl)#30 permit ip any any`	Defeats the implicit **deny** statement and allows all other traffic to pass through.
`Calgary(config-ext-nacl)#exit`	Returns to global configuration mode.
`Calgary(config)#interface fastethernet 0/0`	Moves to interface configuration mode.
`Calgary(config)#ip access-group serveraccess out`	Sets the ACL named serveraccess in an outbound direction on the interface.

Example 5: Write an ACL that states that hosts 50.1–50.63 are not allowed web access to 80.16. Hosts 50.64–50.254 are. Everyone can do everything else.

`RedDeer(config)#access-list 101 deny tcp 172.16.50.0 0.0.0.63 host 172.16.80.16 eq 80`	Creates an ACL that denies HTTP traffic from a range of hosts to a specific destination
`RedDeer(config)#access-list 101 permit ip any any`	Defeats the implicit **deny** statement and allows all other traffic to pass through
`RedDeer(config)#interface fastethernet 0/0`	Moves to interface configuration mode
`RedDeer(config)#ip access-group 101 in`	Applies the ACL in an inbound direction

CHAPTER 29

Security Device Manager

This chapter provides information and commands concerning the following topics:

- Security Device Manager: Connecting with CLI
- Security Device Manager: Connecting with GUI
- SDM Express Wizard with no CLI preconfiguration
- Resetting the router to factory defaults using SDM
- SDM user interfaces
  - Configuring interfaces using SDM
  - Configuring routing using SDM
- SDM monitor mode
- Using SDM to configure a router to act as a DHCP server
- Using SDM to configure an interface as a DHCP client
- Using SDM to configure NAT/PAT
- What to do if you lose SDM connectivity because of an **erase startup-config** command

Security Device Manager: Connecting with CLI

> **NOTE:** Cisco recommends that you use the Cisco Router and Security Device Manager (SDM) to configure your router. However, Cisco also realizes that most implementations of a router with SDM will be to use the command-line interface (CLI) for initial configuration; then, after the routers have been added to the network, all future configuration will take place using SDM.

If you have a router that has the SDM files already installed on it, console into the router and power the router on. If there is no configuration on the router, the Startup Wizard will appear.

Cisco Router and Security Device Manager (SDM) is installed on this device. This feature requires the one-time use of the username "cisco" With the password "cisco". The default username and password have a privilege level of 15 Please change the publicly known initial credentials using SDM or the CLI. Here are the cisco IOS commands Username <myuser> privilege 15 secret 0 <mypassword> No username cisco Replace <myuser> and <mypassword> with the username and password you want to use. For more information about SDM please follow the instructions in the QUICK START GUIDE for your router or go to http://www.cisco.com/go/sdm -	
User Access Verification	
Username:**cisco**	Enter username **cisco**.
Password:**xxxxx**	Enter password **cisco**.
yourname#	Now at CLI prompt.
yourname#**configure terminal**	Moves to global configuration mode.
yourname(config)#**username scott privilege 15 secret 0 tower**	Sets the local username and password for working with SDM. This takes effect after you save the configuration to NVRAM and reload the router.

yourname(config)#**no username cisco**	Removes the default username of cisco from the configuration.
yourname(config)#**hostname 2821**	Sets the host name of the router.
2821(config)#**no ip http access-class 23**	Removes ACL 23 from the configuration.

NOTE: Access list 23 is an access control list (ACL) that permits only addresses from the 10.10.10.0/29 subnet to access the router through the GUI. This ACL was part of the default configuration of the router when it was shipped from Cisco. If you are going to change the IP address of the LAN interface and then use the GUI to configure the rest of the router, you need to remove this ACL so that using the GUI will work.

2821(config)#**interface gigabitethernet 0/0**	Moves to interface configuration mode
2821(config-if)#**ip address 192.168.100.1 255.255.255.0**	Sets the IP address and netmask
2821(config-if)#**no shutdown**	Enables the interface
2821(config-if)#**exit**	Returns to global configuration mode
2821(config)#**exit**	Returns to privileged mode
2821#**copy running-config startup-config**	Saves the configuration to NVRAM

From here, you can either continue configuring the router with the CLI or you can connect to the router using the GUI and continue the configuration using SDM, which is explained in the next section.

Security Device Manager: Connecting with GUI

SDM has, by default, a one-time username and password set on a router. This one-time username/password combination is cisco/cisco. Plug your router's first Fast Ethernet (or Gigabit Ethernet) port into a switch. Plug your PC into the same switch. Configure your PC's IP address to be 10.10.10.2/29 (10.10.10.2 with a subnet mask of 255.255.255.248). Open your PC's Internet browser and enter the following command in the browser's address bar:

http://10.10.10.1

You will see a screen similar to the one shown in Figure 29-1. This is where you will use the username/password combination of cisco/cisco.

NOTE: If you have begun your configuration through the CLI, as shown in the previous section, you need to set your PC's address to 192.168.100.2/24 or something else in the 192.168.100.0/24 network. You cannot use 192.168.100.1/24 because that was the address you set on your router's Fast Ethernet or Gigabit Ethernet interface. You also use the username and password credentials that you have previously configured from the CLI, and not the default credentials of cisco/cisco.

Figure 29-1   Connect to Router Challenge Window

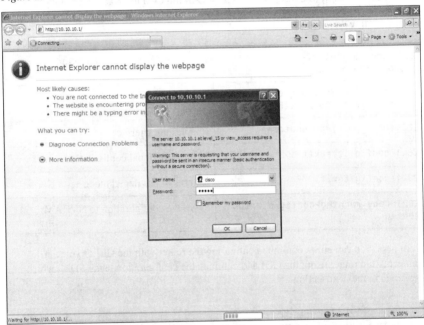

From here, you will see a pop-up asking you whether you want to use HTTP or HTTPS, as shown in Figure 29-2. Click **OK** to use HTTPS, or click **Cancel** to use HTTP. This example uses HTTPS.

Figure 29-2   HTTP or HTTPS

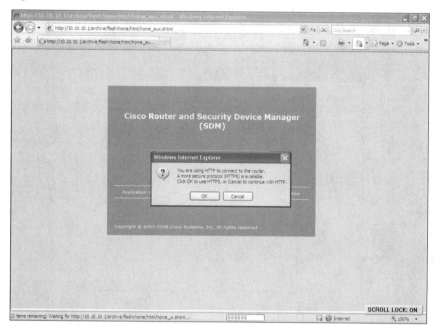

You might be asked to enter your username/password combination again or to accept a digital signature from Cisco IOS Software. If you are challenged, go ahead and enter **cisco/ cisco** or the username/password configured in CLI. If you are asked to verify a digital signature, click **OK**.

> **NOTE:**   If you have already started your configuration from the CLI, you do not need to go through the next section.

SDM Express Wizard with No CLI Preconfiguration

If you are connecting to the router through the GUI and there is no configuration on the router, you are taken to the first screen of the Cisco SDM Express Wizard, shown in Figure 29-3. Click **Next** to continue, or click **Cancel** to exit the wizard.

Figure 29-3   Welcome to the Cisco SDM Express Wizard

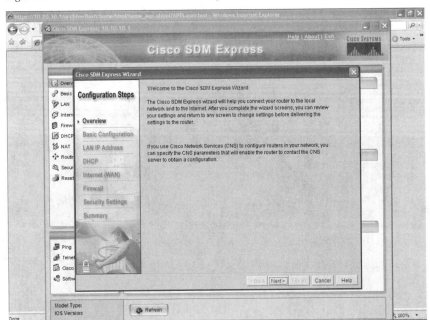

Figure 29-4 shows the first screen of the SDM Express Wizard—the basic configuration. Here, you enter such information as your router's name, the domain to which the router belongs, the username and password of the device, and the enable secret password.

Figure 29-4   Basic Configuration

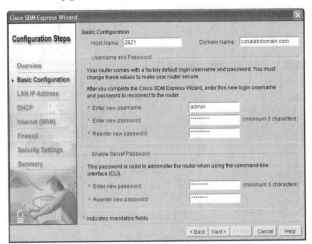

Figure 29-5 shows the next screen—Router Provisioning. Here, you provision (set up) this router using one of two choices—SDM Express or a CNS Server. Continue using SDM Express by leaving that radio button checked and clicking **Next** to continue.

Figure 29-5   Router Provisioning

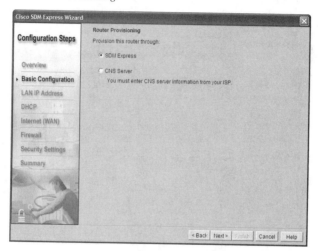

The screen in Figure 29-6 asks you to configure the LAN interface on the router. The router in this example is a 2821, so you have Gigabit Ethernet LAN interfaces, along with VLAN 1 to choose from. If you are using a 2811, you have Fast Ethernet interfaces to choose from. Change the IP address on the LAN from the default 10.10.10.1 to **192.168.100.1/24**, and then click **Next**.

Figure 29-6   LAN Interface Configuration

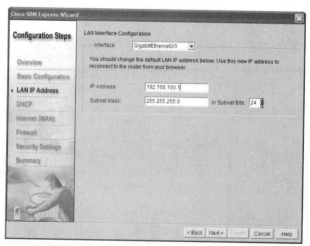

Figure 29-7 shows the DHCP Server Configuration screen, where you can configure the router to act as a DHCP server for other hosts on the LAN. For the purposes of this example, you are not going to configure the DHCP server, so click **Next**.

Figure 29-7   DHCP Server Configuration

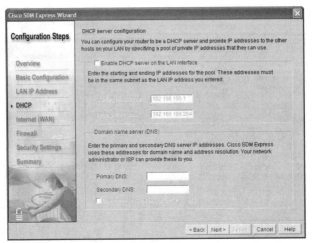

The next item to set up on the router is the WAN interface. Although you have three possible WAN interfaces, as shown in Figure 29-8, you are allowed to configure only one interface through the SDM Express Wizard. For the interface you want to configure, highlight that interface and click **Add Connection**. From here, you are taken to another window asking you to configure each interface—IP address, encapsulation type, subnet mask, and so on. Figure 29-9 and Figure 29-10 show the screens where you enter this information. Enter all the appropriate information in each screen, click **OK**, and then click **Next** when done.

Figure 29-8   WAN Configuration

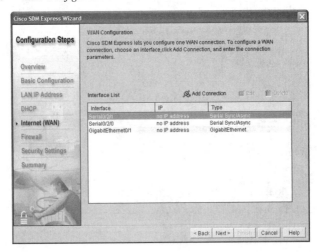

Figure 29-9   *Add Serial Connection*

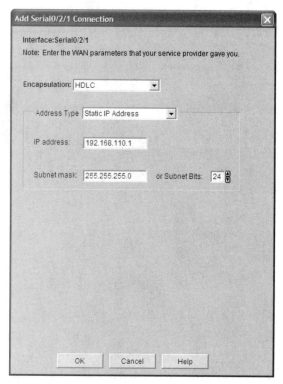

Figure 29-11 shows the Advanced Options for the Internet (WAN) interface, where you are asked to set up a default route for your router. Enter the appropriate information, if needed, or uncheck the Create Default Route box if you do not want a default route set; then click **Next**.

Figure 29-10   Add Gigabit Ethernet Connection

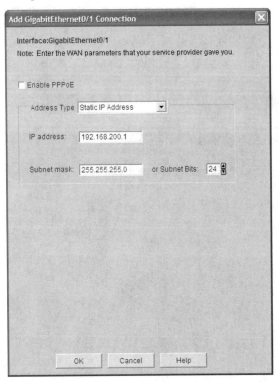

Figure 29-11   Internet (WAN)—Advanced Options

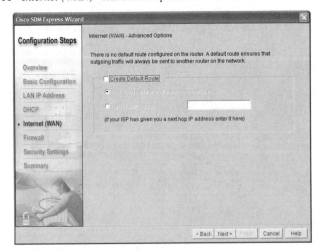

The next screen of the SDM Express Wizard asks whether you want to enable Network Address Translation (NAT) on this router. Figure 29-12 shows the main screen, and Figure 29-13 shows the pop-up window that appears when you want to add an address translation rule. When you have finished entering your NAT information, click **Next**.

Figure 29-12   Internet (WAN)—Private IP Addresses

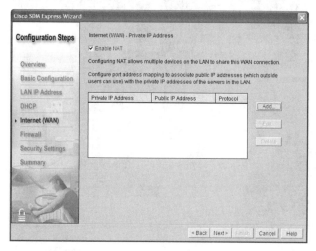

Figure 29-13   Add Address Translation Rule

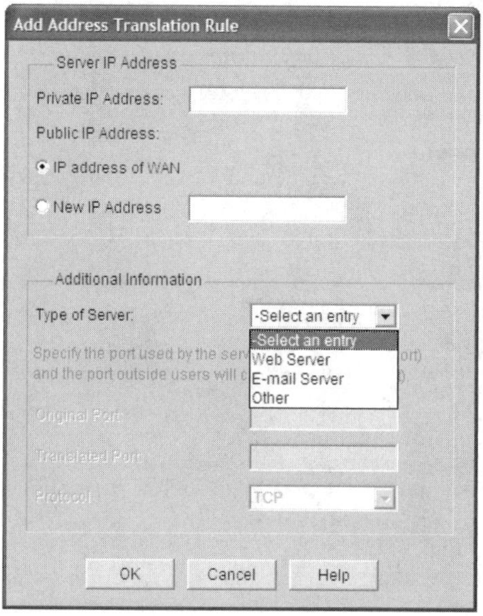

Figure 29-14 shows the Security Configuration Screen, where you can select different security settings for the router. If you are unsure about what to select, leave the default settings of everything checked, and then click **Next**.

Figure 29-14 Security Configuration

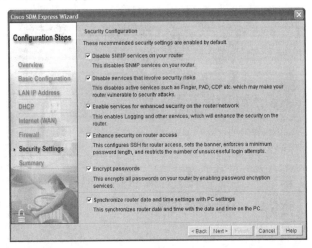

Figure 29-15 shows a summary for the SDM Express configuration. Here, you can scroll up and down to see the summary of changes that you made to the router. If you are satisfied with the changes, click **Finish**. If not, click **Back** and make your changes.

Figure 29-15 Cisco SDM Express Configuration

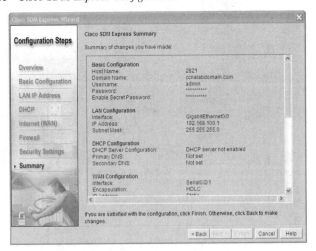

Cisco SDM Express provides final instructions on how to reconnect to the router if you made changes to the LAN interface, as shown in Figure 29-16.

Figure 29-16   Reconnection Instructions

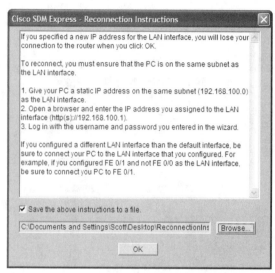

After resetting your PC's address to one in the same subnet as the router's LAN interface, restart your Internet browser and enter the router's LAN interface address in the address bar. You might be asked to select either HTTP or HTTPS, as shown in Figure 29-2. Depending on your browser setup, you might be asked for your username/password again, or be asked to disable pop-ups. SDM needs pop-ups enabled to function.

Figure 29-17 shows the screen that appears when SDM is loading up into the browser. You might be asked to enter your username/password combination again, or to accept a digital signature from Cisco IOS Software. If you are challenged, go ahead and enter your new username and password. If you are asked to verify a digital signature, click **OK**.

Figure 29-18 shows the home screen of the SDM. From here, you can go to other screens to configure and monitor the status of the router.

Figure 29-17 Loading Cisco SDM

Figure 29-18 Cisco SDM Home Page

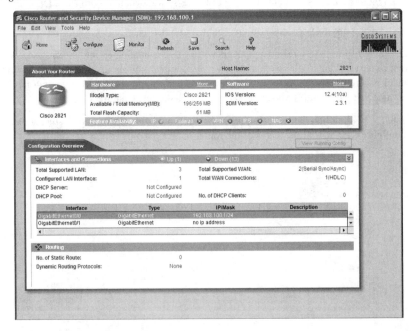

Resetting the Router to Factory Defaults Using SDM

Starting at the SDM home page, to reset the router back to factory defaults, first click the **Configure** button at the top of the SDM screen, and then click **Additional Tasks** on the left side of the screen under the Tasks column. Depending on the resolution of your desktop, you might have to scroll down on the left side of the screen to see the Additional Tasks button.

The Additional Tasks screen contains a section called Configuration Management, as shown in Figure 29-19. One of the options here is Reset to Factory Defaults. This screen shows you how to reconnect to the router after resetting it. Click the **Reset Router** button to start the process. A pop-up will appear asking you to confirm your desire to reset the router. Clicking Yes resets the router. Another pop-up will appear asking you to relaunch SDM to continue, as shown in Figure 29-20.

Figure 29-19   Resetting the Router

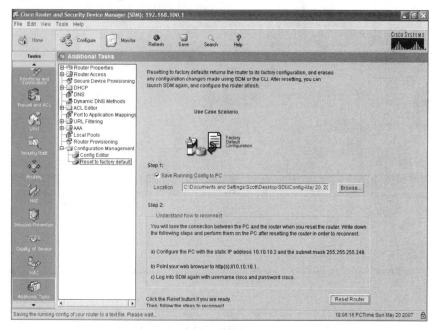

Figure 29-20   Relaunch SDM to Continue

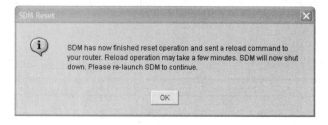

SDM User Interfaces

Many screens within SDM allow you to perform different tasks, as described in the sections that follow.

Configuring Interfaces Using SDM

Starting from the home page, click **Configure** from the top line and then **Interfaces and Connections** on the category bar on the left side of the screen under the Tasks column. Here you will be shown a screen link, as displayed in Figure 29-21.

Figure 29-21 Interfaces and Connections

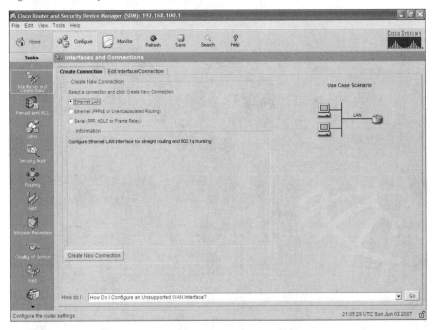

To configure an interface that has not been previously configured, select the connection you want to make and click the **Create New Connection** button. You are taken to a wizard screen that looks like Figure 29-22. For this example, you want to configure the other LAN interface on this router, GigabitEthernet 0/1. Choose the interface you want to configure, and then click **Next**.

Figure 29-22   LAN Wizard

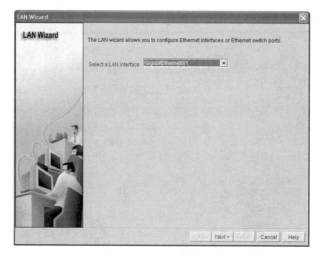

Figure 29-23 shows the first screen of the wizard, which provides information about what the wizard will be able to accomplish. Click **Next** to continue to the next screen.

Figure 29-23   LAN Wizard

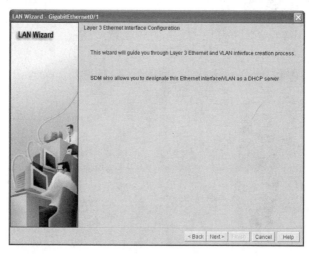

Figure 29-24 shows the next screen of the wizard. If you want this interface to be a gateway for a LAN, with no trunking involved, select the **Configure this interface for straight routing** option, and then click the **Next** button to continue.

Figure 29-24 LAN Wizard

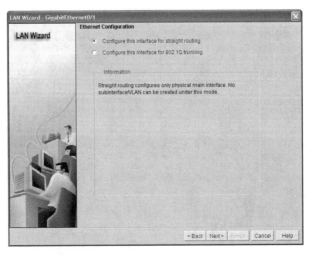

In the next screen, shown in Figure 29-25, you can assign an IP address and subnet mask to the interface. Click **Next** to continue.

Figure 29-25 LAN Wizard: IP Address and Subnet Mask

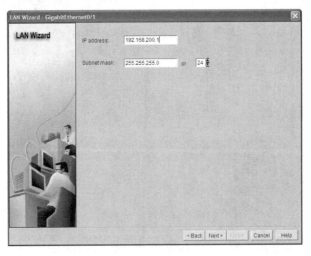

After assigning the IP address and subnet mask, you are taken to the next screen of the wizard (shown in Figure 29-26), which asks whether you want to enable a DHCP server on this interface. The default answer is No. Click **Next** to continue.

Figure 29-26   LAN Wizard: DHCP Server

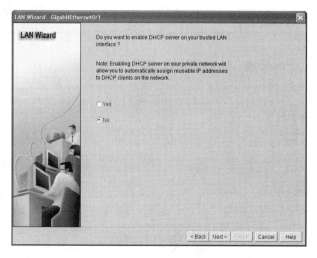

Figure 29-27 shows the final screen of the wizard, where you see a summary of what you have configured. If you want to test the connectivity of the interface, check the box at the bottom of the screen, **Test the connectivity after configuring**, and click **Finish**, or just click **Finish** to send your changes to the router for implementation.

Figure 29-27   LAN Wizard: Summary

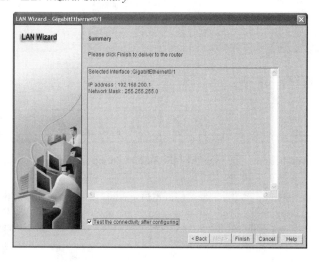

After the configuration is sent to the router, you are taken back to the Interfaces and Connections screen. If you want to make changes to your interfaces, choose the **Edit Interface/Connection** tab, highlight the interface you want to edit, and click the

Edit button. Here you can makes changes to the address or subnet mask; you can also associate ACL or inspection rules to the interface. NAT and quality of service (QoS) options can also be edited from here.

Configuring Routing Using SDM

Starting from the SDM home page, Figure 29-28 shows the screen that appears when you click **Configure** from the top line and then **Routing** on the category bar on the left side of the screen under the Tasks column.

Figure 29-28   Routing

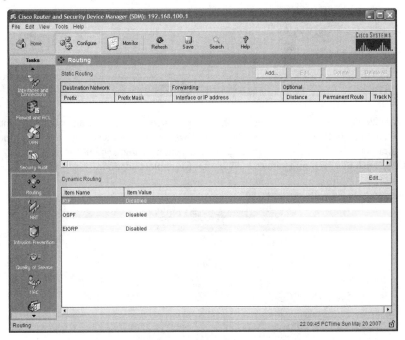

Clicking the **Add** button in the middle of the Static Routing section allows you to create a static route, as shown in Figure 29-29.

Clicking the **Edit** button on the right side of the Dynamic Routing section of this screen allows you to configure the dynamic routing protocols of RIP, Open Shortest Path First Protocol (OSPF), and Enhanced Interior Gateway Routing Protocol (EIGRP), as shown in Figure 29-30.

Figure 29-29   Add IP Static Route

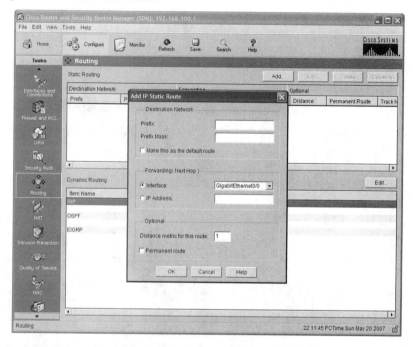

Figure 29-30   Edit IP Dynamic Routing

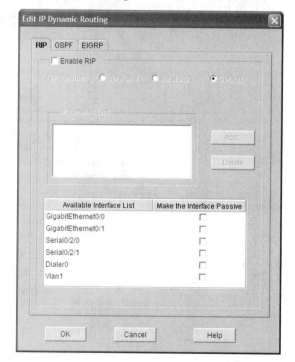

SDM Monitor Mode

Figure 29-31 shows the monitor mode of the SDM. Monitor mode lets you view current information about the router, its interfaces, its firewall status, active VPN connections, and any messages in the router event log.

Figure 29-31   SDM Monitor Mode

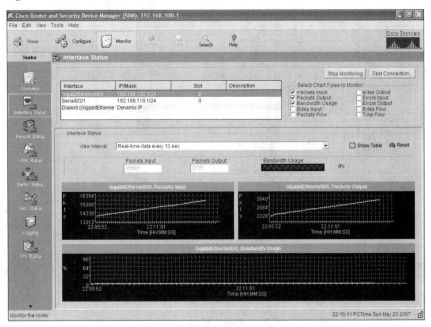

The following table describes how to navigate through the SDM monitor mode to accomplish some key tasks.

Task	SDM Navigation
View information about router interfaces	From the toolbar, click **Monitor Mode**, and then in the left frame, click **Interface Status**. From the Select Interface field on the upper-left side of the Interface Status window, select the interface for which you want to view information, and then in the Available Items group, select the information you want to view.
View graphs of CPU or memory usage	From the toolbar, click **Monitor Mode**, and then click the Overview page.

View information about the firewall	From the toolbar, click **Monitor Mode**, and then in the left frame, click **Firewall Status**.
View information about VPN Connections	From the toolbar, click **Monitor Mode**, and then in the left frame, click **VPN Status**. From the Select a Category field, select whether to view information about Internet Key Exchange security associations (IKE SA), IPsec Tunnels, or Dynamic Multipoint VPN (DMVPN) Tunnels.
View messages in the router event log	From the toolbar, click **Monitor Mode**, and then in the left frame, click **Logging**.

Using SDM to Configure a Router to Act as a DHCP Server

From the home page of the SDM, click **Configure**, and then click **Additional Tasks** from the category bar on the left side under Tasks. From there, you should see the section titled DHCP on the left side of the Configure window (see Figure 29-32).

Figure 29-32   Additional Tasks: DHCP

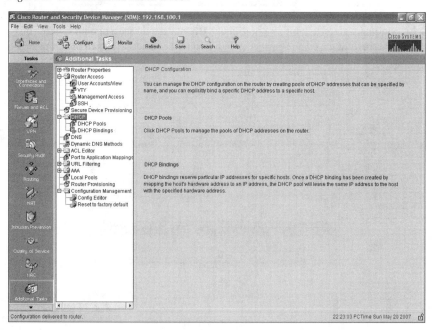

Click **DHCP Pools** to bring up a screen showing you which DHCP pools have already been created. Click the **Add** button to create a new DHCP pool from the screen in Figure 29-33.

Figure 29-33 Add DHCP Pool

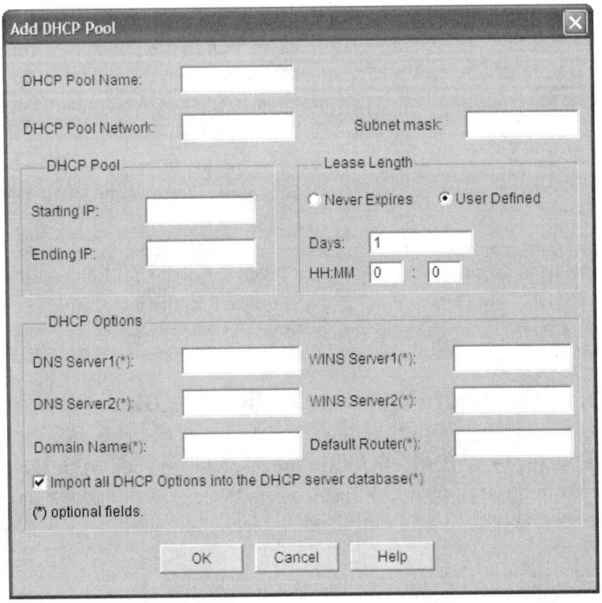

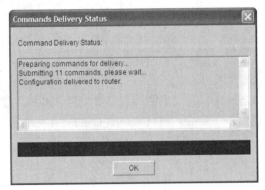

After entering your DHCP Information, click **OK**. You should see a pop-up window that shows the status of the commands being delivered to the router, as shown in Figure 29-34.

Figure 29-34 Command Delivery Status

As shown in Figure 29-35, clicking the **DHCP Pool Status** button will show you which IP addresses have been leased out in this DHCP pool.

Figure 29-35   DHCP Pool Status

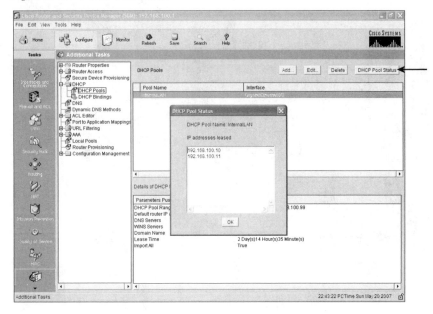

Using SDM to Configure an Interface as a DHCP Client

Having a router interface get an IP address from a DHCP server is often used when you are connecting your router to a Digital Subscriber Line (DSL) or cable modem for access to the Internet. The IP address for the interface needs to come from your provider. As shown in Figure 29-36, start in the Configure screen of SDM, and click the **Interfaces and Connections** button on the category bar. Select the connection named **Ethernet (PPPoE or Unencapsulated Routing)**, and then click the **Create New Connection** button at the bottom of the screen. The Ethernet WAN Configuration Wizard will pop up, as shown in Figure 29-37. Click the **Next** button to begin.

Figure 29-36 Interfaces and Connections

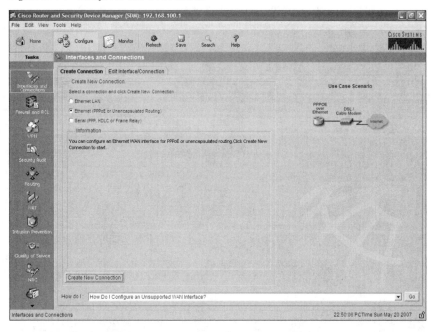

Figure 29-37 Welcome to the Ethernet WAN Configuration Wizard

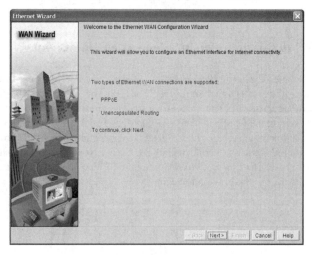

The next screen of the wizard, shown in Figure 29-38, asks whether you need to configure the router as a Point-to-Point Protocol over Ethernet (PPPoE) client. Check with your Internet service provider (ISP) to determine whether you need this.

Figure 29-38   Encapsulation

Figure 29-39 shows the next screen of the wizard. Because you want this interface to be assigned an IP address from the ISP, choose the radio button named **Dynamic (DHCP Client)**. If the ISP has provided you with a host name, enter it in the Hostname box. Click **Next** when finished.

Figure 29-39   IP Address

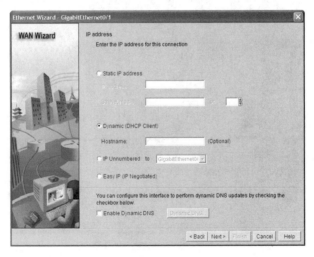

Figure 29-40 shows the next screen of the wizard: Authentication. Enter the appropriate information as provided by your ISP. Click **Next** when you have finished.

Figure 29-40 Authentication

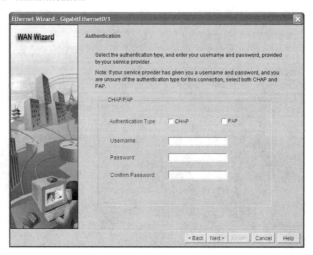

Figure 29-41 is the final screen of the Ethernet WAN Configuration Wizard, which provides a summary of what you have entered and what will be delivered to the router. If you need to make changes, click **Back**, or click **Finish** to send your configuration to the router.

Figure 29-41 Summary

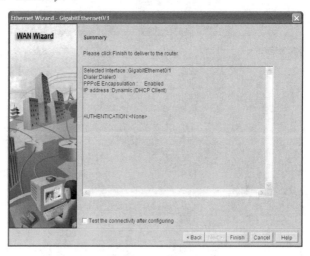

The Interfaces and Connections screen has a tab named Edit Interface Connection. By clicking on this, you will see all interfaces on your router. Select the interface that you chose to make a DHCP client (assume it is GigabitEthernet 0/1 for this example), and then click the **Test Connection** button, as shown in Figure 29-42. Clicking the **Start**

button begins a series of tests to determine whether the interface is working, as shown in Figure 29-43.

Figure 29-42   Connectivity Testing and Troubleshooting

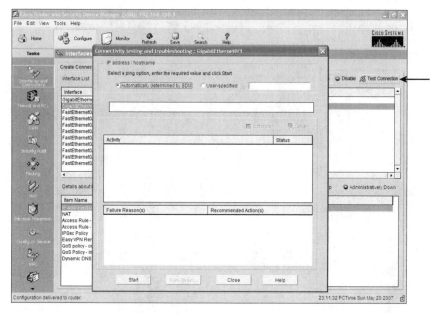

Figure 29-43   Test Connection Successful

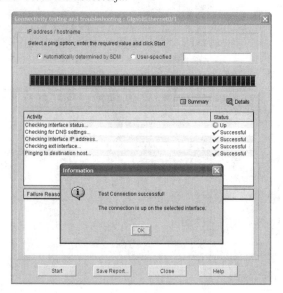

Using SDM to Configure NAT/PAT

From the Configure screen of SDM, click the **NAT** button on the category bar, as shown in Figure 29-44. You have two options: Basic or Advanced NAT. Make your selection, and then click the **Launch the selected task** button to begin configuration. The NAT Wizard then appears on the screen, as shown in Figure 29-45. Click **Next** to begin the wizard.

Figure 29-44   NAT

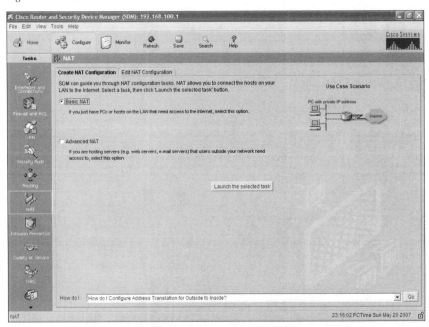

Figure 29-45   NAT Wizard

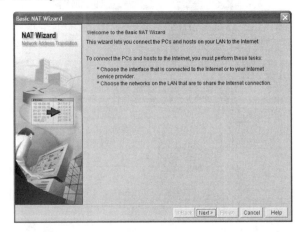

The next screen in the wizard, shown in Figure 29-46, allows you to choose the interface that connects to the Internet—the outside interface. For this example, the GigabitEthernet 0/1 interface is connected to the Internet. You also choose your range of IP addresses that will be translated—your inside interfaces. For this example, choose the addresses that are connected to the Internal LAN—GigabitEthernet 0/0 for this example. Click **Next** when finished.

Figure 29-46   Sharing the Internet Connection

Figure 29-47 shows the summary of the configuration that you will deliver to the router. If this is correct, click **Finish**; otherwise, click **Back** to return to the previous screen and make your corrections.

Figure 29-47   Summary of the Configuration

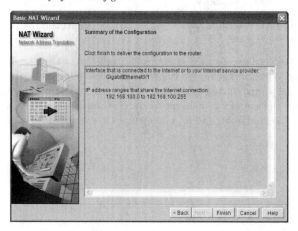

What to Do If You Lose SDM Connectivity Because of an erase startup-config Command

If you enter the **erase startup-config** command and you reboot the router, you will find the router wanting to enter into setup mode, without asking for the SDM username and password challenge. If this happens and you want to use SDM again, do the following.

`Router>enable`	Moves to privileged mode
`Router#configure terminal`	Moves to global configuration mode
`Router(config)#ip http server`	Enables the HTTP server on the router
`Router(config)#ip http secure-server`	Enables the HTTP secure server on the router
`Router(config)#ip http authentication local`	Allows local authentication methods to be used
`Router(config)#ip http timeout-policy idle 600 life 86400 requests 10000`	Creates a policy for dealing with inactivity on the router
`Router(config)#username scott privilege 15 secret 0 tower`	Creates a local entry for use with authentication
`Router(config)#interface gigabitethernet 0/0`	Moves to interface configuration mode
`Router(config-if)#ip address 192.168.100.1 255.255.255.0`	Assigns an IP address and netmask
`Router(config-if)#no shutdown`	Enables the interface

At this point, you need to connect your PC and the router to a switch, set the IP address of the PC to an address that is local to 192.168.100.1/24 — for example, the address 192.168.100.2/24 — and connect using a browser. You use the username and password that you just created on the router with the **username** command. You might want to reset the router to factory defaults to restore any other settings to the router.

PART XI

Appendixes

Appendix A   Binary/Hex/Decimal Conversion Chart

Appendix B   Create Your Own Journal Here

Binary/Hex/Decimal Conversion Chart

The following chart lists the three most common number systems used in networking: decimal, hexadecimal, and binary. Some numbers you will remember quite easily, as you use them a lot in your day-to-day activities. For those other numbers, refer to this chart.

Decimal Value	Hexadecimal Value	Binary Value
0	00	0000 0000
1	01	0000 0001
2	02	0000 0010
3	03	0000 0011
4	04	0000 0100
5	05	0000 0101
6	06	0000 0110
7	07	0000 0111
8	08	0000 1000
9	09	0000 1001
10	0A	0000 1010
11	0B	0000 1011
12	0C	0000 1100
13	0D	0000 1101
14	0E	0000 1110
15	0F	0000 1111
16	10	0001 0000
17	11	0001 0001
18	12	0001 0010
19	13	0001 0011

Decimal Value	Hexadecimal Value	Binary Value
20	14	0001 0100
21	15	0001 0101
22	16	0001 0110
23	17	0001 0111
24	18	0001 1000
25	19	0001 1001
26	1A	0001 1010
27	1B	0001 1011
28	1C	0001 1100
29	1D	0001 1101
30	1E	0001 1110
31	1F	0001 1111
32	20	0010 0000
33	21	0010 0001
34	22	0010 0010
35	23	0010 0011
36	24	0010 0100
37	25	0010 0101
38	26	0010 0110
39	27	0010 0111
40	28	0010 1000
41	29	0010 1001
42	2A	0010 1010
43	2B	0010 1011
44	2C	0010 1100

Decimal Value	Hexadecimal Value	Binary Value
45	2D	0010 1101
46	2E	0010 1110
47	2F	0010 1111
48	30	0011 0000
49	31	0011 0001
50	32	0011 0010
51	33	0011 0011
52	34	0011 0100
53	35	0011 0101
54	36	0011 0110
55	37	0011 0111
56	38	0011 1000
57	39	0011 1001
58	3A	0011 1010
59	3B	0011 1011
60	3C	0011 1100
61	3D	0011 1101
62	3E	0011 1110
63	3F	0011 1111
64	40	0100 0000
65	41	0100 0001
66	42	0100 0010
67	43	0100 0011
68	44	0100 0100
69	45	0100 0101

Decimal Value	Hexadecimal Value	Binary Value
70	46	0100 0110
71	47	0100 0111
72	48	0100 1000
73	49	0100 1001
74	4A	0100 1010
75	4B	0100 1011
76	4C	0100 1100
77	4D	0100 1101
78	4E	0100 1110
79	4F	0100 1111
80	50	0101 0000
81	51	0101 0001
82	52	0101 0010
83	53	0101 0011
84	54	0101 0100
85	55	0101 0101
86	56	0101 0110
87	57	0101 0111
88	58	0101 1000
89	59	0101 1001
90	5A	0101 1010
91	5B	0101 1011
92	5C	0101 1100
93	5D	0101 1101
94	5E	0101 1110

Decimal Value	Hexadecimal Value	Binary Value
95	5F	0101 1111
96	60	0110 0000
97	61	0110 0001
98	62	0110 0010
99	63	0110 0011
100	64	0110 0100
101	65	0110 0101
102	66	0110 0110
103	67	0110 0111
104	68	0110 1000
105	69	0110 1001
106	6A	0110 1010
107	6B	0110 1011
108	6C	0110 1100
109	6D	0110 1101
110	6E	0110 1110
111	6F	0110 1111
112	70	0111 0000
113	71	0111 0001
114	72	0111 0010
115	73	0111 0011
116	74	0111 0100
117	75	0111 0101
118	76	0111 0110
119	77	0111 0111

Decimal Value	Hexadecimal Value	Binary Value
120	78	0111 1000
121	79	0111 1001
122	7A	0111 1010
123	7B	0111 1011
124	7C	0111 1100
125	7D	0111 1101
126	7E	0111 1110
127	7F	0111 1111
128	80	1000 0000
129	81	1000 0001
130	82	1000 0010
131	83	1000 0011
132	84	1000 0100
133	85	1000 0101
134	86	1000 0110
135	87	1000 0111
136	88	1000 1000
137	89	1000 1001
138	8A	1000 1010
139	8B	1000 1011
140	8C	1000 1100
141	8D	1000 1101
142	8E	1000 1110
143	8F	1000 1111
144	90	1001 0000

Decimal Value	Hexadecimal Value	Binary Value
145	91	1001 0001
146	92	1001 0010
147	93	1001 0011
148	94	1001 0100
149	95	1001 0101
150	96	1001 0110
151	97	1001 0111
152	98	1001 1000
153	99	1001 1001
154	9A	1001 1010
155	9B	1001 1011
156	9C	1001 1100
157	9D	1001 1101
158	9E	1001 1110
159	9F	1001 1111
160	A0	1010 0000
161	A1	1010 0001
162	A2	1010 0010
163	A3	1010 0011
164	A4	1010 0100
165	A5	1010 0101
166	A6	1010 0110
167	A7	1010 0111
168	A8	1010 1000
169	A9	1010 1001

Decimal Value	Hexadecimal Value	Binary Value
170	AA	1010 1010
171	AB	1010 1011
172	AC	1010 1100
173	AD	1010 1101
174	AE	1010 1110
175	AF	1010 1111
176	B0	1011 0000
177	B1	1011 0001
178	B2	1011 0010
179	B3	1011 0011
180	B4	1011 0100
181	B5	1011 0101
182	B6	1011 0110
183	B7	1011 0111
184	B8	1011 1000
185	B9	1011 1001
186	BA	1011 1010
187	BB	1011 1011
188	BC	1011 1100
189	BD	1011 1101
190	BE	1011 1110
191	BF	1011 1111
192	C0	1100 0000
193	C1	1100 0001
194	C2	1100 0010

Decimal Value	Hexadecimal Value	Binary Value
195	C3	1100 0011
196	C4	1100 0100
197	C5	1100 0101
198	C6	1100 0110
199	C7	1100 0111
200	C8	1100 1000
201	C9	1100 1001
202	CA	1100 1010
203	CB	1100 1011
204	CC	1100 1100
205	CD	1100 1101
206	CE	1100 1110
207	CF	1100 1111
208	D0	1101 0000
209	D1	1101 0001
210	D2	1101 0010
211	D3	1101 0011
212	D4	1101 0100
213	D5	1101 0101
214	D6	1101 0110
215	D7	1101 0111
216	D8	1101 1000
217	D9	1101 1001
218	DA	1101 1010
219	DB	1101 1011

Decimal Value	Hexadecimal Value	Binary Value
220	DC	1101 1100
221	DD	1101 1101
222	DE	1101 1110
223	DF	1101 1111
224	E0	1110 0000
225	E1	1110 0001
226	E2	1110 0010
227	E3	1110 0011
228	E4	1110 0100
229	E5	1110 0101
230	E6	1110 0110
231	E7	1110 0111
232	E8	1110 1000
233	E9	1110 1001
234	EA	1110 1010
235	EB	1110 1011
236	EC	1110 1100
237	ED	1110 1101
238	EE	1110 1110
239	EF	1110 1111
240	F0	1111 0000
241	F1	1111 0001
242	F2	1111 0010
243	F3	1111 0011
244	F4	1111 0100
245	F5	1111 0101

Decimal Value	Hexadecimal Value	Binary Value
246	F6	1111 0110
247	F7	1111 0111
248	F8	1111 1000
249	F9	1111 1001
250	FA	1111 1010
251	FB	1111 1011
252	FC	1111 1100
253	FD	1111 1101
254	FE	1111 1110
255	FF	1111 1111

_____

_____

_____

_____

_____

_____

_____

_____

_____

_____

_____

_____

_____

_____

_____

_____

_____

_____

_____

BOOKS ONLINE

ENABLED

THIS BOOK IS SAFARI ENABLED

INCLUDES FREE 45-DAY ACCESS TO THE ONLINE EDITION

The Safari® Enabled icon on the cover of your favorite technology book means the book is available through Safari Bookshelf. When you buy this book, you get free access to the online edition for 45 days.

Safari Bookshelf is an electronic reference library that lets you easily search thousands of technical books, find code samples, download chapters, and access technical information whenever and wherever you need it.

TO GAIN 45-DAY SAFARI ENABLED ACCESS TO THIS BOOK:

- Go to **http://www.ciscopress.com/safarienabled**

- Complete the brief registration form

- Enter the coupon code found in the front of this book before the "Contents at a Glance" page

If you have difficulty registering on Safari Bookshelf or accessing the online edition, please e-mail customer-service@safaribooksonline.com.

What Do You Want to Do?

I want to:	Chapter	Page
Assign an IPv4 address on my interface	6	59
Assign an IPv6 address on my interface	25	237
Change the name of my router	6	54
Check the settings for HyperTerminal	4	37
Check to see whether my serial cable is DCE or DTE without walking over to my router	22	216
Configure a switch	11	105
Configure a wireless access point to connect to my LAN	15	161
Configure a wireless client to connect to my WLAN	15	174
Configure an Interface as a DHCP client using SDM	29	307
Configure and troubleshoot EIGRP	9	81
Configure and troubleshoot OSPF	10	91
Configure and troubleshoot RIPng with IPv6	25	238
Configure and troubleshoot RIPv2 in IPv4	8	75
Convert a number in binary to hexidecimal or decimal, or vice versa	A	317
Copy IOS to a TFTP server	16	188
Create a host table so that I can Telnet or ping using names rather than IP addresses	6	61
Create a MOTD or login banner	6	60
Create a static route	7	69
Create and apply a named access control list (ACL)	28	276
Create and apply a standard access control list (ACL)	28	271
Create and apply an extended access control list (ACL)	28	273
Create VLANs on my switch	12	117
Delete all VLANs on my switch	12	120
Know the difference between 568A and 568B cables	4	42
Perform a password recovery on my router	17	196
Perform a password recovery on my switch	17	198
Reset my router to factory defaults	6	62
Reset my switch to factory defaults	11	107
Review subnetting	1	3
Review VLSM	2	21
Save my running-configuration locally	6	62
Save my running-configuration to a TFTP server	16	186